W9-ABQ-497

The Queen's Orders
of
CHIVALRY

The Queen's Orders

of

CHIVALRY

Brigadier Sir *IVAN DE LA BERE*

K.C.V.O., C.B., C.B.E.

Secretary of the Central Chancery of Knighthood, St. James's Palace

1945-1960

Spring Books • London

This revised edition published in 1964 by
Spring Books
Westbook House · Fulham Broadway · London
by arrangement with William Kimber & Co. Ltd.
© Copyright William Kimber & Co. Ltd. 1961
Printed in Czechoslovakia by Tisk, Brno

Contents

List of Illustrations

Part One

The Queen's Orders of Chivalry

CHAPTER I

Honours from Ancient Times to the Present Day

Even in very remote times, particularly amongst those engaged in the profession of arms, the ambition existed to possess some sort of title, rank or mark of merit which would distinguish the holder and raise his standing in the eyes of his fellows.

Throughout history, monarchs, princes and governments have realised the value, and in fact necessity, of giving rewards of some kind as incentives to loyal and devoted service and gallantry in battle.

On a change of dynasty or government the new holders of power in a country frequently abolish and annul the honours given by their predecessors after condemning such awards as unnecessary and worthless. Usually, however, no great time elapses before the new rulers find it advisable either to revive the former honours or to introduce some new but similar rewards for outstanding service. Consider, for example, the revolutionary party which succeeded the Czarist régime in Russia. This party, in addition to instituting the new Orders of Lenin and Suvorov, continued to make appointments to the Order of Alexander Nevsky which had been founded in the reign of the Empress Catherine.

In earlier times honours were often given in the form of gold chains, badges or medallions worn on the habit or the hat, while accoutrements and weapons were frequently presented as awards for gallantry.

Since the Middle Ages, knighthood and the insignia of orders of chivalry have gradually replaced the gifts of land, money or weapons which were bestowed in those days as rewards for meritorious service and help in battle.

As was the case in later days in Christian countries, there were strict laws of selection for dignities and honours amongst the peoples of ancient China, Egypt, Persia, Greece and Italy. In the annals of all these countries proofs are to be found that personal ornaments, weapons and other 'triumphal gifts' were frequently presented as rewards for victory in battle.

Tacitus, when describing the Germanic tribes, wrote:

It is not the custom that any man shall receive his arms (*arma sumere*) until the State has proved him and found him worthy of such reward. Then in full Council the youth is equipped with shield and spear by one of the Chiefs.

Though in England in early days decorative 'cognizances' were sometimes given as distinguishing marks and as rewards for loyal service, it would appear that it was not until the reigns of King Richard the Second and King Henry the Fourth that the giving of chains to be worn round the neck was introduced on any considerable scale. These chains were usually made of gold and were fashioned in a variety of designs. Some represented cods of the broom-plant, or *Planta Genesta* (in connection with the royal surname), while others were made of links in the shapes of flowers, animals or religious figures. They frequently had attached to them an appendant badge in the form of some portion of the donor's crest or escutcheon. Similar badges were often given to the personal servants and retainers of the great nobles and other persons of consequence. Silver or gold 'chains of honour' were introduced about the same time for wear by certain officers of the crown on whom the Sovereign wished to confer a special mark of distinction. These chains of honour were usually composed in the form of the letter 'S' repeated throughout the whole length of the chain. Many historians accept that the 'S's' stood for the words *sanctus spiritus*, but some suggest that they represented the word *souvenez* to act as a reminder to the wearer of his allegiance to the royal donor. These chains were known as 'collars of the King's Livery'. They were not given as symbols of a knightly fraternity but as tokens of royal favour which were to be worn as pledges of loyalty. According to some antiquarians, collars of 'S's' were at one time worn by knights bachelor, but this is doubtful. It would appear more likely that the wearing of them was confined to such dignitaries as chief justices, and the Sovereign's heralds and sergeants-at-arms—in fact the holders of much the same offices in connection with which collars of 'S's' are worn at the present day.

Until the beginning of the nineteenth century appointment to the orders of chivalry in England was restricted to the members of noble families and persons of high rank in the armed services. These appointments were greatly sought after and valued. Naturally the more rare the award the greater its fame and value in the general estimation. Examples of such highly prized distinctions in European countries are the Portuguese Order of Christ, the Dannebrog of Denmark, the Golden Fleece of the Spanish Grandee and Austrian noble, the Annunziata of Italy and—probably the most coveted of all—the Garter of the English knight.

In continental countries the award of insignia on a somewhat lavish scale started much earlier than it did in England. In some European countries there were, long before the eighteenth century, numerous orders and decorations, comprising several classes or grades, appointment to which was by no means confined to those of high rank or noble birth.

In France, for instance, there appears to have been a great variety of orders and decorations—so much so that there is a story that General Moreau, a famous Napoleonic general and a great gourmet, having been particularly delighted by the gastronomic skill of the chef on a certain occasion, sent for him and told him of his appreci-ation. He said that, as there were so many existing French orders and so great a number of holders of them, he intended to invest him with the insignia of a new order of his own invention, to be called the 'Order of the Excellent Saucepan.' Up till quite recently in France a man was considered rather a failure if he had not been appointed to the Legion of Honour by the time he was forty years of age, and even now there are about 300,000 members of this Order which was founded in 1802. The present French Government aims at reducing the present official quota by about two thirds. None the less about one Frenchman in six has an order or decoration of one sort or another.

In the year 1834 Sir Robert Peel, speaking in the House of Commons, said that while he supported the granting of honours to naval and military officers, as rewards for their service in the defence of their country, he hoped that no order of chivalry would be instituted for the purpose of rewarding such persons as eminent scientists who had distinguished themselves in civil life. He said:

> 'I cannot think that it would raise the character of science in this country to establish a new system of reward and I deprecate the institution of a new Order for them.
>
> In my opinion, it really would have conferred little additional credit on Sir Isaac Newton if that eminent man had appeared with a blue riband, a red riband or a Star upon his chest. The practice would not be correspondent with the simplicity of the English character. I see a clear distinction between military services and scientific merit.'

It is amusing to note that a somewhat similar remark was made a good many years later by the famous Lord Cromer who rendered such magnificent service in Egypt, namely 'It is immaterial to me whether I have a red or blue riband on my tummy.'

A hundred years ago Ulster King of Arms wrote in his *Book of Orders* that, 'while in continental courts honourable decorations are very numerous, in our own country, Orders, Decorations and Medals are very few and very sparingly distributed and are only bestowed by the Sovereign for eminent services'. Though this statement may well have been true a hundred years ago, it is certainly not so today. Prior to 1814 it was almost unknown for a person other than a royal prince to hold the insignia of more than one British order of chivalry, as the insignia of the junior order had to be returned on appointment to a senior order. It will be described later, in Chapter V, how even the great Duke of Wellington on appointment to the Garter was required to return the insignia of the Bath.

In the opinion of the author there is in this country now a far greater variety of orders, decorations and medals—official, semi-official and unofficial—than is either necessary or desirable. There is also a pronounced tendency to give too many knighthoods and appointments in the senior classes of orders to persons who have not deserved such high awards and who would have been amply rewarded by an honour of a considerably lower grade.

The first large increases in the number of honours given in this country date back to the various enlargements of the Order of the

Bath in the nineteenth century, the institution of the Order of Saint Michael and Saint George in 1818, and the foundation by King Edward the Seventh of the Imperial Service Order in 1904.

The next and far larger increase came when the Order of the British Empire was instituted by King George the Fifth in 1917. Full details of the institution and history of this order are to be found in Chapter VIII.

Though nowadays in this country comparatively few people have a very keen interest in the subject, the majority of the population would agree that on the whole it is right for the honours not to be cast very widely. They would agree, too, that in these days of democracy—used here in the best sense of that much-abused word—if honours are to be given at all they should be distributed in such a way that persons in all classes of the community and in every walk of life are able to qualify for appropriate recognition by their Sovereign of some particularly brave action or some meritorious achievement in the service of the country. In these days it would not be sufficient or advisable merely to reward the leaders of the nation and a limited number of persons of high rank and position in the Armed and Civil Services.

It is not suggested, therefore, that though it is now very large the total number of honours awarded should be greatly reduced, but rather that a stricter scrutiny should be made in the selection of those who receive so high an honour as knighthood or the appointment to the comparatively high third class of an order of chivalry such as Commandership of the Order of the British Empire—namely the C.B.E. In the opinion of most people far too many honours of a high grade are given for purely political services.

Moreover, honours of so high a grade or class should not be given to those who have really not done anything out of the ordinary for the good of their country but have perhaps merely made themselves well known, and usually highly paid, public figures by their ability to excel in the worlds of entertainment and sport. A distinction ought to be drawn between the awards given to such persons and to those who have rendered service of real value to their country and to mankind generally, such as the production of an invention of great benefit to the community, the conducting of valuable life-saving medical research or the rendering of long and devoted service to charitable institutions or welfare organisations.

Knighthood has been given in recent years to a number of persons for whom many unbiased observers think a much junior award such as an O.B.E. would have been adequate. Again, it is obviously illogical to give to some person who has excelled in some sporting activity the same grade of award in an order of chivalry (namely that carrying the right to use the same postnominal letters—for example, a C.B.E.) as that given to a civilian who has performed distinguished service of national importance or to a senior officer who, without corresponding financial reward, has rendered 'gallant and distinguished service' in time of war involving responsibility for the command, safety and general welfare of several thousand servicemen.

Some think that it would be a good plan to institute a new decoration which could be given to those who have excelled in the world of sport and who have rendered valuable administrative service to some particular sport.

Thus, while it is not the intention to suggest that the present total number of honours given should be greatly reduced, it is essential that this total should not be steadily increased, but the names of those to be honoured should receive the strictest scrutiny. Otherwise these honours will be cheapened and will no longer be sought and prized highly as rewards for outstanding service and effort.

Examination of the following facts will prove how the total of honours given in this country has increased since the beginning of this century. Whereas until towards the end of the nineteenth century there was only one quite small honours list each year, containing about a hundred names,there are now each year two extremely large main honours lists. The New Year and Birthday Honours Lists for 1963, for instance, each contained over two thousand names of recipients of an order, a decoration or a medal. Moreover, even as recently as 1938, after allowing for the considerable number of awards made at that time in the comparatively new Order of the British Empire (instituted in 1917), it was only necessary for the sovereign to hold four comparatively small investitures annually (two 'state-dress' investitures at Buckingham Palace and two 'morning dress' ceremonies at Saint James's Palace), whereas in recent years it has been necessary to hold not less than thirteen of these ceremonies in each year, even though several of the former Commonwealth countries and colonies no longer accept British honours for their nationals.

Another point which requires consideration is that it is not infrequent for military leaders of high rank to receive so many honours that sometimes most of the letters of the alphabet are placed after their names as indications of these honours. It seems excessive and must sometimes be embarrassing to the person concerned when he can have as many as twenty letters placed after his name. Moreover, it often becomes impossible—and in fact contrary to regulations—for such a person to wear all his insignia at one time, and there would seem to be little point in possessing insignia which cannot be worn because there is not sufficient space on the recipient's uniform for this to be done. Examples are Admiral of the Fleet the Rt. Hon. Earl Mountbatten of Burma, K.G., G.C.B., G.C.S.I., G.C.I.E., G.C.V.O., D.S.O., and Field Marshal the Rt. Hon. Viscount Slim, K.G., G.C.B., G.C.M.G., G.C.V.O., G.B.E., D.S.O., M.C.

Again, it has become the custom in evening dress for some distinguished persons holding numerous high honours to wear only one or at the most two of the highest of these so that an impression is given that it is not thought worthwhile to wear certain junior orders. It seems sensible to suggest, therefore, that, while treating as quite separate and leaving entirely out of consideration such awards as are given by the personal choice of the Sovereign (namely the Garter, the Thistle, the Order of Merit and the Royal Victorian Order), when a person receives an appointment in an order of chivalry senior to that in which he already holds an appointment he should surrender the appointment in the junior order. It is suggested, for example, that a person who is appointed to be a Knight Commander of the Order of the Bath, if he is already a Knight Commander of Saint Michael and Saint George or a Knight Commander of the Order of the British Empire, should resign from both of these junior orders and discontinue the wearing of their insignia and the use of the postnominal letters connected therewith.

This, after all, was the procedure in this country until the nineteenth century when honours were far less widely bestowed than they are nowadays. In those days, when a person was appointed to the Order of the Garter it was looked upon as a promotion, and if he was already a Knight of the Thistle or the Bath he had to resign from the junior order and hand back the insignia belonging to it.

In the same way it is suggested that the number of different awards for gallantry in the three armed services might usefully be co-ordinated and reduced.

The Victoria Cross and the Distinguished Service Order are common to all three services. It would appear to be sensible, therefore, that the lesser gallantry awards should also be made common to all. For instance, each of the armed services has its own separate gallantry cross for officers and warrant officers: the Distinguished Service Cross for the Navy, the Military Cross for the Army, and the Distinguished Flying Cross for the Royal Air Force. Surely it would be quite adequate and suitable if, as is the case in most other countries, there were one gallantry cross which would be an officer's and warrant officer's award common to all three services.

Similarly, each of the armed services has its own brands of gallantry medals. The Royal Navy has the Conspicuous Gallantry Medal and the Distinguished Service Medal, the Army has the Distinguished Conduct Medal and the Military Medal, while the Royal Air Force has its own Conspicuous Gallantry Medal and the Distinguished Flying Medal. Surely it would be sufficient and more suitable if there were two gallantry medals common to all three services—perhaps one medal for 'Conspicuous Gallantry' and another medal for 'Brave Conduct'.

It is of interest to note that at one time when the Victoria Cross was awarded to personnel of the Royal Navy it was suspended from a blue ribbon, while personnel of the Army wore it from a crimson ribbon, thus making two divisions of the award. In 1918 it was realised that this difference was confusing and pointless, and now in all three armed services holders of the Victoria Cross wear it suspended from a riband of the same colour, namely crimson, thus making this very high award common to all of them and exactly similar in design.

If the suggestions made above for an officer's cross and two gallantry medals for other ranks to be made common to all three armed services were to be adopted, there would then be five gallantry awards common to all three services instead of the present eleven. They would comprise one for all ranks (the Victoria Cross), one for senior officers (the Distinguished Service Order), one for junior officers or warrant officers (the Gallantry Cross), and two for other ranks (a Conspicuous Gallantry Medal and a Brave Conduct Medal).

It should be noted that, in addition to the various gallantry awards to which reference has been made, all ranks of the armed services—and civilians—are now eligible to receive distinctively marked awards for gallantry in the Order of the British Empire, while for gallantry in 'non-operational' action—that is, not in the presence of the enemy—either in war or peacetime, all ranks are eligible to receive awards of the George Cross or the George Medal. The proposal made above should surely provide a sufficiency of gallantry awards.

At the same time, it is suggested that no real necessity exists for special awards for distinguished 'non-operational' service in the Royal Air Force, namely the Air Force Cross and the Air Force Medal. There are no corresponding awards for the Royal Navy and the Army, and now that provision has been made, as explained above, for a special class of awards for gallantry within the Order of the British Empire, for which the ribands are marked distinctively by the attachment of a special emblem, it would seem that awards in this new section of the Order of the British Empire would be just as suitable for rewarding distinguished flying service in hazardous conditions as they are for distinguished and hazardous service on and under the sea or on land. Therefore awards of the Air Force Cross and Air Force Medal, in the opinion of the author, might well be discontinued.

A move in the right direction has been made in the case of civil gallantry awards. The George Cross, George Medal, awards in the Gallantry Class of the Order of the British Empire, and Commendations for Bravery are now the customary rewards for brave action by civilians or other persons who are not members of the armed services. The Albert Medal and the Police and Fire Services Medals for Gallantry and the Edward Medal are now only awarded posthumously, and even this practice might well be ended by substituting for them posthumous awards of the George Cross and George Medal.

Similarly the Ministry of Transport medal for saving life at sea (the Sea Gallantry Medal) is now given extremely rarely, and it could easily be dispensed with, particularly as the general public know little or nothing about this medal, nor precisely for what services it is given. The author desires again to emphasise that it is not intended to advocate a great reduction in the total number of awards given for gallantry, but merely a reduction in the number of different awards which exist at present. None the less, as stated earlier, a constant watch must be kept on the total number of awards given for gallantry in order to prevent diminution of their value.

Regrettably the great majority of the appointments made in the junior classes of the orders of chivalry now fail to rouse much public interest, and if honours were to be made still more easily attainable the honours list might well become a matter for ridicule.

As Sir Winston Churchill stated in the House of Commons in March 1944, 'the object of presenting medals, stars and ribbons is to give pride and pleasure to those who have deserved them.' It follows that if awards of this nature are given too lavishly there is little pleasure in gaining them and little pride in holding them.

Another point which should be considered and remedied is the steady reduction during this century in the quality of much of the British insignia.

In former days British insignia compared extremely favourably with those of foreign countries. Not only were they valued especially highly because they could not be obtained by a mere financial contribution, but also because they were well made and of high quality.

From the time of introduction of stars made of metal until about the middle of the nineteenth century almost all insignia of orders were made of high carat gold and pure silver, but about the beginning of the twentieth century the quality began to decrease steadily. For instance, until about 1860 the badges of all three classes of the Order of the Bath (G.C.B., K.C.B., C.B.) were made of gold, and not only the gold collars of the Knights Grand Cross (G.C.B.) but the badges and stars of G.C.B.s and K.C.B.s and the badges of C.B.s were all due to be returned on the death of the holders, though for various reasons some were in fact not returned. Now the collars of G.C.B.s are no longer made of gold but of silver-gilt and the quality of the insignia for the badges and stars has been reduced similarly. At the present day the quality and appearance of the badges in the Civil Division of the Order of the Bath is very poor, and should certainly be improved.

Nowadays the only insignia which are returnable on death are those of the three great orders (Garter, Thistle and Patrick), the Royal Victorian Chain, and the collars of all the other orders. Until 1962 the badges and stars of the higher classes of the Indian Orders— the Star of India and the Indian Empire—had to be returned on the death of the holders but this rule no longer exists.

A great deal of the insignia of deceased holders of other orders now finds its way into the hands of collectors—mainly those residing abroad. Few people nowadays have sufficient space for displaying the insignia of their ancestors, and, in any case, the majority of those who possess such space are usually not greatly interested in these honourable mementoes.

A number of legatees into whose possession such insignia eventually come voluntarily return them so that they may be renovated and given to new recipients of those particular awards. They usually do so gladly, because, though they do not wish to sell these insignia themselves, they dislike the idea of their being sold by others to collectors in years to come.

It is suggested, therefore, that it would be far better if all insignia from companionship or commandership upwards, namely all insignia not worn on a brooch with medals on the breast, were to be returned on the death of the former holders. Not only would such a rule effect considerable economy in the provision of new insignia but it would also become practicable to restore the quality of all insignia to the former high standard as far fewer new ones would have to be purchased.

It should be noted that until the 1914–1918 War all British war medals were not only of particularly handsome design but were also made of pure silver and of such generally high quality that they were held in admiration throughout the world. Now campaign stars and medals are of a very low quality. In 1918, for instance, the star issued to those who fought in France in the autumn of 1914 (the Mons Star) cost only 2½d., while the campaign stars given for service in the war of 1939—1945 were no better in appearance or quality. The quality of the O.B.E. and M.B.E. badges should also be improved. It is very low compared with the corresponding classes of the Sovereign's personal order, namely, those of the M.V.O. (IV) and M.V.O. (V), and is also inferior to that of the badge of the Imperial Service Order (I.S.O). Another point to be considered is that it does considerable damage to the prestige of this country to present insignia of poor quality to foreigners who have rendered valuable service, and the financial saving by so doing is trifling.

The preparation of an honours list on a sound and equitable system is a very difficult matter. It is a subject on which it is easy to make critical comment, but it is not possible to produce an honours list which would please everybody. If too large a number of honours is given, the critics say that they have been given too cheaply—as they certainly are in some foreign countries, where meritorious service is by no means a prerequisite and where they can often be obtained by a generous financial contribution in the right quarter. On the other hand, if too few honours are given there is equal criticism, and accusations are made of favouritism towards some sections of the community. For instance, if a well-known cricketer receives an honour the followers of football complain that their heroes have been overlooked and slighted. Similar criticism is made by those not interested in that particular form of sport or entertainment when honours are given to individuals concerned with racing, athletics, boxing, cycling, tennis, golf or any of the forms of public entertainment in the theatre, cinema and elsewhere.

At least, however, it can be stated without fear of contradiction that official honours cannot be obtained in a bare-faced way in this country, as was possible soon after the war of 1914–1918 by donations to the political funds controlled by the Prime Minister, David Lloyd George, and which eventually amounted to some three million pounds. For instance we read in a political history of the time that an applicant for a baronetcy who at the most critical moment of the war had been fined £1,000 for hoarding huge quantities of food, though at first unsuccessful, in due course received this honour on payment of £5,000. Many others paid more, for this or higher honours.

It is right and laudable to endeavour to obtain some suitable recognition for a person who has served his country well or has performed some brave or particularly meritorious action deserving of an award of honour from the Sovereign.

Enquiries are often made as to how such recommendations should be submitted. The answer is that recommendation of a civilian domiciled in this country who is not in government service should be submitted for consideration either to the Prime Minister or to the Lord Lieutenant of the County in which the individual recommended is domiciled. The Secretaries of State at the Foreign Office, Commonwealth Relations Office and Colonial Office are also authorised to submit an agreed number of recommendations for those who are working under their respective controls and administrations. Similarly the First Lord of the Admiralty and the Secretaries of State for War and Air submit direct to the Sovereign recommendations for appointment in the military divisions of the Orders of the Bath and British Empire for those who are working under them.

The Ministers of Her Majesty in other Commonwealth countries overseas are also authorised, if they so desire, to submit recommendations for honours direct to the Sovereign.

The Sovereign is the 'Fount of all Official Honours' and therefore every award of an official nature must receive the approval of the Sovereign before publication of it is made in the *London Gazette*. Actually, as stated previously, the only honours for which the Sovereign personally selects recipients are the following:

The Order of the Garter.

The Order of the Thistle.

The Order of Merit.

The Royal Victorian Order and the Victorian Chain.

Royal Medals of Honour and Medals for Long Service.

The Sovereign formerly selected also recipients of the Order of Saint Patrick and the Crown of India, but, as both of these orders are now obsolescent, they need not be considered here, though brief notes thereon are to be found in Chapter X.

Though there is nothing to prevent a person from formally submitting his own name for an honour, and though this was sometimes done in former days, such action would be, to say the least, unusual nowadays, and even if it were taken it would be unlikely to succeed. As stated above, such self-recommendation, however, has occurred sometimes in the past even though it may perhaps have been made in an indirect manner.

The story is well known of the General in the 1914–1918 War who wrote to the following effect when recommending one of his staff-officers for a decoration:

This officer is highly deserving of an award for gallantry for the fearless way in which he has visited dangerous front-line areas. I know this to be so as he has invariably accompanied me on such visits.

In his book *Old Diplomacy* Lord Hardinge of Penshurst (himself a K.G., P.C., G.C.B., G.C.S.I., G.C.M.G., G.C.I.E., G.C.V.O.) wrote, 'Though I have more than once refused the offer of a British

Order for reasons which I regarded as sufficient, I have never asked for one, and it is difficult to imagine how anybody could have the brass to do so, though I knew such to be frequently the case.'

The following letter from the Duke of Wellington to a very senior officer who had written to express dissatisfaction at not having been honoured with appointment to the Order of the Bath provides an incomparable example of a suitable reply to self-recommendation for an honour:

LESACA,
10th September, 1813.

My dear Sir,

I received last night your letters of 22nd July and 9th September and I acknowledge that I wish you had followed the advice of—— and had omitted to send me either, and I will detain both till I shall have received your answer on what I am about to state to you. I have never interfered directly to procure for any officer those marks of His Majesty's Favour by which many have been honoured. Nor do I believe that any have ever applied for them or have hinted through any other quarter their desire to obtain them.

They have been conferred, as far as I have any knowledge, spontaneously, in the only mode, in my opinion, in which honours or distinctions can be received with satisfaction. The only share that I have had in these transactions has been by bringing the merits and services of the several officers of the Army distinctly under the view of The Sovereign and the Public, in my reports to the Secretary of State; and I am happy to state that no General in this Army has more frequently than yourself deserved and obtained this favourable report of your services and conduct. It is impossible for me even to guess what are the shades of distinction by which those are guided who advise the Prince Regent in the bestowing of those honourable marks of distinction and you will not expect that I should enter upon such a discussion. What I would recommend to you is to express neither disappointment nor wishes upon the subject, even to an intimate friend, much less to the Government. Continue, as you have done hitherto, to deserve the honourable Distinction to which you aspire and you may be certain that, if the Government is wise, you will obtain it.

If you should not obtain it, you may depend upon it that there is no person in whose good opinion you would be solicitous who will think the worse of you on that account. The comparison between myself, who have been the most favoured of His Majesty's subjects, and you will not be deemed quite correct and I advert to my own situation only to tell you that I recommend to you conduct which I have always followed. Notwithstanding the numerous favours that I have received from the Crown, I have never solicited one; and I have never hinted nor would any one of my friends or relations venture to hint to me a desire to receive even one; and much as I have been favoured, the consciousness that it has been done spontaneously by The King and Regent gives me more satisfaction than anything else. I recommend to you the same conduct and patience; and above all, resignation if, after all, you should not succeed in acquiring what you wish; and I beg you to recall your letters which you may be certain will be no use to you.

Believe me, etc.,
WELLINGTON.

The names of those who have been awarded honours are announced in the *London Gazette*. There are at the present day two main honours lists annually—one published on New Year's Day and the other on whatever Saturday in June may be selected as the most suitable date for celebrating the 'official birthday' of the Sovereign.

There are also frequent comparatively small intermediate honours lists announcing awards made in connection with military or 'policing' operations overseas or for immediate awards for brave peacetime actions either at home or overseas.

All persons who are awarded orders, decorations or medals are entitled to place the appropriate letters after their names immediately after the announcement of the award has been published in the *London Gazette*. For example, it would be correct immediately to describe a recipient of the award indicated by the following post-nominal letters: V.C., or G.C.B., or K.B.E., or C.M.G., or D.S.O., or M.B.E., or G.M., or B.E.M., or similar awards, as might be appropriate. But when it is announced in the *London Gazette* that the Queen has given directions for certain persons who had not previously received the accolade to be appointed Knights Grand Cross or Knights Commanders in an order of chivalry or has signified her intention of conferring the honour of knighthood on certain persons, it is not correct for those concerned to use the prefix 'Sir' immediately. This prefix should not be used until the person concerned has actually received the accolade—that is to say, has been actually 'dubbed with the sword' by the Sovereign or by some other person who has been authorised to perform this ceremony on the Sovereign's behalf.

Exceptions to this rule are made in the cases of those who are unable to present themselves to receive the accolade either owing to prolonged illness or absence abroad. In such cases a knight bachelor designate can be given letters patent in lieu of any future attendance at an investiture ceremony for the purpose of being dubbed.* These letters patent are of a permanent nature and authorise him to style himself with the distinctive appellation of a knight—namely, to use the prefix 'Sir'—in exactly the same way as would be permissible if he had been dubbed by the Sovereign. The procedure is somewhat different in the cases of those who have been appointed to be Knights Grand Cross or Knights Commanders of an order of chivalry, e.g. the Orders of the Bath, Saint Michael and Saint George, etc. When necessary these persons can be given a Dispensation Warrant, which is a document of a temporary nature and which authorises them to style themselves as a knight until such time as they are able to present themselves to receive the accolade from the Sovereign or from some other person appointed to perform the ceremony of conferring knighthood on the Sovereign's behalf.

Similarly, when an announcement is made in the *London Gazette* that the Queen has been pleased to signify her intention to confer a peerage or a baronetcy on a person, that person should not adopt the style of a peer or a baronet or be addressed in that manner until a second announcement has been published by the Home Office in the *London Gazette*. This is usually published a few weeks later and gives full details of the place and county in connection with which the peerage or baronetcy is to be connected. These later announcements are made in the following manner:

For a Peerage.
The Queen has been pleased by Letters Patent under the Great Seal of the Realm to confer the dignity of a Barony of the United Kingdom upon . . . ., and the heirs male of his body lawfully

---

*The wording of the letters patent is as follows: *The Queen has been pleased by Letters Patent under the Great Seal of the Realm to confer the honour of Knighthood upon——.*

begotten, by the name, style and title of Baron ...... of ....
(town) in the County of ....

For a Life Peerage.
The Queen has been pleased by Letters Patent under the Great
Seal of the Realm to confer the dignity of a Barony of the United
Kingdom for life upon .... by the name, style and title of
Baron .... of .... (town) in the County of ....

For a Baronetcy.
The Queen has been pleased by Letters Patent under the Great Seal
of the Realm to confer the dignity of a Baronet of the United
Kingdom upon .... of .... in the County of ......
and the heirs male of his body lawfully begotten.

With ladies who are appointed Dames the situation is somewhat different, as they are not dubbed with the sword. Thus immediately after an announcement has been published in the *London
Gazette* that a lady has been appointed a Dame Grand Cross or a
Dame Commander of an order of chivalry it is correct for her to
assume her new title and description and to be addressed as 'dame'
in addition to placing the appropriate letters after her name, namely
G.C.V.O or D.C.V.O., G.B.E. or D.B.E.

No one in this country other than the Sovereign is permitted to
confer knighthood upon a person or to invest him with the insignia
connected therewith unless letters patent and the appropriate warrants
have been signed by the Sovereign, delegating the necessary authority
to some other member of the Royal Family. Overseas the only
persons authorised to confer knighthood on the Sovereign's behalf
are the Governors-General of certain Commonwealth countries,
and in rare circumstances such other persons as may be authorised
to do so by a special warrant signed by the Queen.

The Queen's ministers in New Zealand and Australia, as they
have always done in the past, continue to submit a considerable
number of names for honours of all classes. Recommendations are
also submitted from Her Majesty's ministers in Nigeria, Sierra
Leone, Jamaica, Trinidad, Uganda and Rhodesia. For some years
after Canada became a self-governing Dominion, on the recommendation of the Sovereign's ministers there, a limited number of
hereditary titles and some knighthoods were conferred together with
appointments in the various orders of chivalry. This policy continued

throughout the period of the war of 1914–1918. On 22nd May 1919 the Prime Minister of Canada requested King George the Fifth to discontinue the granting to Canadian citizens of titular honours. This policy was reversed in 1933 when the Prime Minister of Canada submitted recommendations for a number of awards in the New Year Honours List of 1934. He also submitted recommendations for the two honours lists immediately following that. In 1935, however, when a new government came into power, the award of titular honours in Canada was again discontinued.

The conferring of honours which did not involve the use of titles continued in Canada until 1st July 1946, but since that date no appointments to the orders of chivalry have been made though recommendations for the award of decorations or medals for acts of exceptional bravery such as the George Cross and George Medal are still submitted to the Queen for approval from time to time.

The Government of South Africa discontinued the submission of recommendations for honours at the end of the 1939–1945 war, and the Governments of India, Pakistan, Ceylon and Ghana no longer submit recommendations for awards to nationals of their respective countries.

CHAPTER II

Knighthood

Unfortunately, the chroniclers of early days were not always reliable and accurate, and they often differed from one another so widely in their relation of events and incidents that it is impossible now to do more than guess at the true origins of knighthood, and of how this institution developed into the great fraternities of the orders of chivalry. In fact, these ancient writers varied so extremely in their statements that there is scarcely any point of time between the establishment of the ancient Egyptian monarchy and the twelfth century of the Christian era which has not been selected by one or other of them for the commencement of chivalry. In 1870 Joseph Edmondson in his writings suggested that the ceremonies of knighthood originated with the ancient Germans, who apparently had an *ordo equestris* similar to that of ancient Rome, to which reference is made later in this chapter. However, most antiquaries agree that the golden age of knighthood was during the twelfth, thirteenth and fourteenth centuries, when chivalry attained its greatest splendours and thereafter began to decline and lose its prestige.

Knighthood has been described rather aptly as a medieval institution which distinguished the nobility from the common people, and there is no doubt that in medieval times, except in the case of those who had made the Church their profession, knighthood was eagerly sought by those of gentle birth. It was certainly the distinguishing mark of the majority of the upper class, to which only two professions were acceptable, namely the Church and chivalry.

In those times it was difficult, if not impossible, for a man to rise from the lower to the upper class, not only because of social considerations, but also because of the professional training required by the code of chivalry.

A boy belonging to a noble family received a strict military training. First of all, when about ten years of age, he was given a post as a page, either in the house of an important relative, or in the castle of some great noble. His duties included waiting upon his lord and lady; and in addition to a general education, which was sometimes rather limited, he was taught obedience to discipline, equestrianism, the manners of a gentleman and certain strict rules of etiquette. When he reached the age of fifteen or so, many hours were spent in learning the use of weapons, especially the spear and sword, and in due course, at the age of about sixteen or seventeen, he was promoted to the rank of esquire.

He became, in fact, the personal assistant or aide-de-camp to the noble or knight, with whom he rode to war, assisting him in the donning of his armour and in other preparations for battle. The word 'Esquire' was probably derived from the Latin *scutifer*, the shield-bearer. Nowadays, of course, the word has become meaningless, and it is placed quite indiscriminately and with no regard to social position after the name of anyone of the male sex who has attained school-leaving age.

Formerly, as an esquire grew to manhood he took an increasing part in the actual fighting; and eventually, when he had proved himself worthy by his loyalty, bravery and skill at arms, unless he declined it because he was financially unable to support that honour, he was promoted to knighthood.

Though the birth and growth of knighthood in Europe is a subject on which great obscurity prevails, it is at least certain that it is the most ancient dignity of Christendom. It should be realised, therefore, that, though nowadays a knight bachelor occupies a comparatively low position in the official order of precedence, the rank of knight is most ancient and was in early days the most illustrious title to be obtained. It may be said that in the past knighthood was the first of all military dignities and the foundation of all subsequent honours. As Edmondson wrote in his *Complete Body of Heraldry* (published in 1780):

Knighthood is a degree of honour of very high antiquity and the practice of it was in use among the Old Franks, from whom the Saxons, who had the same common descent, learnt it, bringing it with them on their settlement in England.

Lawrence Archer, in his *Orders of Chivalry* wrote that though amongst the nations of antiquity there may have been no regular orders of chivalry as we now understand the term, certain rules of chivalrous behaviour existed and these rules were in many ways similar to those in force in the Middle Ages. It is certain, for instance, that the importance of bravery and loyalty occupied a prominent place in these rules.

The chiefs of the ancient Teutonic peoples were each attended by a 'train' of martial youths of noble birth, and similar customs prevailed in France and Britain. Later on these trains of youths became bands or brotherhoods of knights, bound together by oaths of fidelity. Amongst the Barbarians, too, the idea of knighthood, though it was wholly military in purpose, seems to have included elaborate ceremonial rites.

Apart from fanciful fables such as that ascribing the origin of knighthood to the Archangel Gabriel, while the exact time of its introduction is debatable, it is certain that there was in ancient Rome a separate class or knightly order—the *Ordo Equestris*. Some suggest that Julius Caesar was the originator of this order, but it may well have existed before his time. The Roman knights were *Equites*, or 'mounted nobles', and we know that this *Ordo Equestris* had a high place in the order of precedence and ranked next after senators. Similar comparisons may be drawn with the French *Chevaliers*, the Spanish *Cavalleroes* and the German *Reiters*. Knighthood was directly concerned with the horse, and all members of noble families fought on horseback. Perhaps one of the most ancient orders of chivalry was the 'Order of the Golden Angel', or, as it was afterwards called, the 'Order of Saint George', which is said to have been instituted by Constantine the Great in the year A.D. 312. We read in some ancient histories that the badge of the order portrayed Saint George killing a dragon and that the knights wore a long cloak of sky blue colour. According to some, the 'Order of Saint Lazarus' was instituted in the fourth or fifth century, while in the course of the next few hundred years a great many orders, such as the Knights Templars and the Knights of the Holy Sepulchre of Jerusalem, were founded.

At all events, it is now generally agreed that the medieval form of knighthood flourished during the days of Charlemagne's Empire and that the highly ceremonial rites in use then were derived from a mixture of the ideas and institutions of the decaying Roman Empire and the elaborate procedures of the Teutonic knights.

Tacitus tells us, when describing the solemn and ceremonial form of knighthood which existed in the Frankish Empire from the end of the ninth to the beginning of the eleventh century, how this included the fastening of spurs on a knightly aspirant, the striking of a blow on his shoulder or cheek and the girding on him of a belt and sword. He described this as *Primus juventae honos*.

Nicolas, in his *History of the Orders*, wrote:

Knighthood is one of the most ancient dignities of Christendom and was originally both of a religious and military character and was conferred upon Sovereigns, Princes, Peers and others of exalted birth and condition, except Ecclesiastics.

The rule for the exclusion of ecclesiastics from knighthood has always existed, and still exists today, the reason being presumably that as priests, being 'Men of God', should not be attacked with the sword, they should not themselves use a sword in battle. As the prime purpose of knighthood was the use of arms in combat, priests, being unarmed, were clearly ineligible for the accolade. It is for this reason that, though a number of high ecclesiastical dignitaries—archbishops, bishops and other senior clerics—have during comparatively recent times received appointments in senior classes of certain orders of chivalry, except for two cases none has been actually dubbed with the sword.

Of these two exceptions one, with his archbishop's approval, surrendered Holy Orders so that he might receive the accolade; the other was knighted in error as it was not realised that many years prior to the time of the conferment of knighthood he had become a clerk in holy orders, and he did not himself draw attention to this fact.

In ancient times no person could be *born* a knight, and the records show that both in England and France monarchs were sometimes knighted after their accession to the throne. We know, for instance, that in England both Edward the Third (1327) and Henry the Seventh (1485) were knighted, after coming to the throne, by one of their own subjects. Similarly the boy king Edward the Sixth was knighted in 1547, nine days after his accession, by his uncle, the Duke of Somerset. This was in accordance with the laws of chivalry, which ordained that even a king could only obtain knighthood at the hand of some other knight and that no one, however exalted his rank, could confer knighthood on another unless he had previously had this honour conferred correctly upon himself.

Knighthood was an established military guild; and however nobly born a man might be, the conferring of knighthood upon him added to his dignity—just as at the present day in England a duke of ancient lineage feels, and rightly so, that he is being greatly honoured when he is dubbed a Knight of the Garter. Similarly, when he attains a suitable age, the Prince of Wales receives knighthood and is invested with the insignia of the Garter, though in fact from the date on which the Sovereign gives orders that he is to be styled with that title he becomes *ex officio* a Companion of the Order of the Garter.

In medieval days knighthood became a brotherhood throughout Christendom, and included therein were the great majority of 'gentlemen of blood who practised the profession of arms'.

Some trace the use of the term 'knight' in England to the Anglo-Saxon word *cnyht* (or *cniht* or *cnite*) of which the original meaning was a 'youth' or 'military follower' and which afterwards came to mean a 'trusted servant', and later still, as the dignity of the term increased, the 'military tenant of an earl or bishop'.

By the time of the twelfth and thirteenth centuries the word 'knight' conveyed a definite dignity attached to a certain rank in the profession of arms. There are some who maintain that knighthood was introduced into Britain at the time of the Norman Conquest (1066). The eminent historian Stubbs did not agree with this. He considered that intelligent kings such as Canute (1017) and Edward the Confessor (1042) could hardly have failed to introduce to their country an institution which was flourishing in many other countries of Europe with which they were closely acquainted. We read, too, that in earlier days King Alfred made his grandson Athelstan a knight and that at this ceremony he invested him with a scarlet mantle set with precious gems and bound round his body a belt, with a sword in a golden scabbard. The Saxon form of knighting appears to have included some form of 'bathing', and both in England and in other countries of Europe 'knighthood by the bath' was combined with religious rites such as confession, absolution and elaborate ritual.

The subject of bathing when knighthood was conferred is discussed more fully in Chapter V, which deals with the Order of the Bath.

In the Middle Ages the act of bathing had come to be regarded more as a symbolic than a sanitary act, and we are told by one historian that Queen Isabella of Spain only had one bath during her lifetime, namely, on the night before her wedding. However, another historian wrote: 'The origins of the ceremony of bathing before the gift of knighthood were utilitarian. At some time in the Middle Ages a certain Sovereign could not bring himself within knighting distance of a candidate for knighthood who was blissfully unaware that he stank abominably. With great tact this Sovereign said to those about him "Peradventure this brave fellow requires rest and refreshment after his great and prolonged heroism. Therefore take him away, and give him a bath and fresh raiment and sustenance and then bring him before me again to be knighted."'

Ingulfus, writing in the tenth century, describes how at the investiture of a knight, the bishop, after accepting his sword, placed it on the knight's neck, with a benediction. It would seem from perusal of various ancient documents in the British Museum and elsewhere that in Saxon times bishops may well have been empowered to confer knighthood; and in fact this practice seems to have been authorised until as late as the year 1102, when it was forbidden by a synod, held at Westminster. Religious rites appear to have been included, too, in the ceremony of the knighting of William the Conqueror (1066), when he became King of England, though it seems certain that he must actually have been dubbed previously in Normandy. A possible explanation is that he took part in a second ceremony in order to become a knight on the soil of England, in the same way as the leader of the English forces, according to report, received knighthood from William the Conqueror in token of his acceptance of the latter's lordship over him.

We read elsewhere that later on Lanfranc, Archbishop of Canterbury, knighted the Conqueror's son, William Rufus; while in the Anglo-Saxon Chronicle of the year 1085 it is recorded that William the Conqueror '*dubadde his sunn Henric to ridere*'.

It seems reasonable to assume that, when it was practicable, the normal procedure was for the king to perform the actual dubbing, while, in times of peace at least, the prelate laid the knight's sword upon the altar and blessed it. If so, this would agree with the procedure now in use at installation services of Knights Grand Cross of the Order of the Bath, which are described in detail in Chapter V.

The *Chronicles* of Peter of Blois, when describing the ceremony of knighthood about the year 1150, refer to the 'offering by the knight of his sword on the altar', while other accounts of knighting ceremonies from the year 1250 onwards frequently included the phrase *'cingulo militiae decorare'*, implying the girding on of a sword as part of the proceedings.

With knighthood was associated every honourable, generous and high sentiment, including the undertaking to see justice done and freedom maintained. The ideal attributes of a 'true knight' were modesty and self-denial, and Chaucer wrote of the *'veray parfit gentil knighte'* who loved *'chivalrie, trouthe, honour and curtesie'*. The ideal character of a knight was described in the following acrostic by Cardinal Capucius in the year 1247:

M agnanimus	*in adversitate*
I ngenuus	*in consanguinitate*
L argifluus	*in honestate*
E gregius	*in curialitate*
S trenuus	*in virile probitate*

Chivalry was the formulation of certain rules and regulations which aimed at rendering the upper classes worthy of their exceptional privileges, and in its golden age none could be dubbed a knight who was not of gentle birth. The laws of knighthood insisted, with the greatest force, on the necessity for a knight 'inviolably to keep his word'. They inspired a horror of lying, falsehood and deceit and emphasised the necessity always to help and defend widows and orphans. We read that the Knights of the Round Table swore 'never to act outrageously or to commit treason or murder and by no means to be cruel but to give money unto him that asketh it and always to succour Ladies and Orphans'. In fact, the aim of a true knight was to do unto others as he hoped they would do unto him in similar circumstances. To express it succinctly in modern terms, it might be said that the motto of the ideal knight in the great days of chivalry was the absolute antithesis of that obtaining nowadays in some sections of the world of commerce—'I'm all right, Jack'.

'As I am a true knight' was the most solemn assurance that could be given of fidelity and truth, and that he was 'a true and valiant knight' was the highest compliment that the Commons of England* could pay to Edward, Duke of York, grandson of Edward the Third.

The high ecclesiastics were continually emphasising the necessity of protecting the Church, and for this reason they encouraged the combination of knighthood with strict religious rites. The philosopher John of Salisbury wrote that the functions of knighthood are 'to protect the Church, to fight against treachery and to prevent injustice'. The Church taught that the ideals of a chivalrous knight were 'faithfulness to his Saviour and his Sovereign'. But the knights themselves in reality usually laid greater stress on the ideals of loyalty to their Sovereign lord: courage, fighting ability and generosity. The knights' oath was: 'I do swear before God that I will not fight against the King and that I will defend against oppression all gentlewomen, widows and orphans.'

From the monarch's point of view the primary obligations of a knight were to provide himself with arms and armour, with as many armed followers as might be practicable, and the rendering to his Sovereign of a certain minimum period of service in each year when called upon for this.

Though in the early days of chivalry there were in the countries of Europe several ways of conferring knighthood and a considerable variety of rites and ceremonies, two main methods prevailed in the Middle Ages. The first and simpler method was that used on the battlefields when the candidate knelt before the royal commander of the army and was 'stricken with the sword upon his back and shoulder' while some such words as '*Avancez Chevalier au nom de Dieu*' or '*Soyez preux, hardi et loyal*' were pronounced.

It has been suggested that the significance of striking the back and shoulder of the new knight in this manner was that it was intended to mark the final occasion on which it would be permissible for the candidate to tolerate such an affront.

* *Rotuli Parliamentorum*, Vol. III.

With the second method of knighting there was associated far greater ceremony, which in some countries included the presentation of robes, arms and spurs, and entailed numerous solemnities of a religious nature. We read, for instance, of Charlemagne girding his son, Louis the Pious, when he knighted him, with a belt and sword. Again, we read in his dissertation on knighthood, written by Elias Ashmole, then Windsor herald, in 1672, that 'the principal ensigns of Knighthood are a horse, shield and lance, belt and sword, gilt spurs, a gold ring and a gold Chain or Collar'. It has been shown how some historians considered that in early days certain high ecclesiastics were authorised to confer knighthood, while others went so far as to suggest that at one period anyone who was himself a knight was entitled to perform this ceremony. But the latter suggestion is extremely doubtful, and it was probably only certain very senior knights who were given this authority. At all events, European monarchs and princes gradually arrogated to themselves alone the power to confer knighthood, while reserving the right to delegate this duty to others in special circumstances.

Thus, in due course, in England, the Sovereign began drastically to limit the power to confer knighthood, and it was ordained eventually that knights could only be made by the monarch himself, or by his 'lieutenants in the wars', namely, the commanders of the royal armies, and a few others of exalted birth and station who were 'possessed of special royal authority'. We read, for instance, that at the Battle of Wakefield (1460) four gentlemen were knighted by the Duke of Somerset, eight by the Earl of Northumberland and four by the Earl of Devonshire. Elsewhere we read of Simon de Montfort knighting Gilbert de Clare, and it would be possible to quote many similar examples. This delegation of authority was greatly reduced in the reign of King Henry the Eighth, though it was still vested in the commanders of the royal armies. Even Queen Elizabeth the First, who was one of the most tenacious of all sovereigns of the royal prerogatives, permitted several of her subjects to confer knighthood on her behalf—notably the Earls of Leicester and Essex—though we read that 'the profuse manner in which the Earl of Essex, as Commander of the Expedition to Cadiz in 1596, bestowed this honour gave Her Majesty great offence'. Thus it gradually became the custom for monarchs to confer all knighthoods personally, unless this was quite impracticable. Sometimes the accolade of knighthood was bestowed by a foreign monarch, but we read that 'Queen Elizabeth preferred her sheep not to be branded by a foreign shepherd', while elsewhere she is reported to have said 'My dogs shall wear only my Collars'. None the less, until the end of the eighteenth century knighthood conferred on an English subject by a foreign monarch appears to have been recognised as authority for that person to style himself in the same way as he would have done if he had been knighted by his own Sovereign in England.

But it is now well over a hundred years since an ordinance was published forbidding British subjects to accept foreign knighthoods unless special permission had been granted by their Sovereign for such a reward to be given. At the present day no British subject may accept a foreign title of nobility, but further details connected with the acceptance of foreign honours are to be found in Chapter XV.

Similarly, foreigners who receive what are called honorary appointments in the British knightly classes of chivalry now receive only the appropriate insignia and are not dubbed with the sword or authorised to style themselves with the prefix 'Sir'.

There have been, however, one or two accidental infringements of this rule owing to the fact that it was not realised at the time of the dubbing that the recipient was not of British nationality.

One interesting example was the late Sir Percival Phillips, a famous war correspondent for the *Daily Express* during the 1914–1918 war, who at the end of that war, though he was a citizen of the United States of America, received the insignia of a Knight Commander of the Order of the British Empire and was knighted in company with Sir Philip Gibbs and three other well-known British war correspondents. Amongst other foreigners who received knighthood in comparatively recent days were Basil Zaharoff who was made a G.C.B. by King Edward VII, and Slatin Pasha who received a K.C.V.O. from George V, while George Frankenstein, G.C.V.O. (an Austrian) and Matthew Izycki de Notto, K.C.B. (a Polish Air Marshal) were knighted by George VI when they took British nationality.

We have seen how, over the ages, the Church attempted frequently to temper the ferocity of the knights and to include in the code of chivalry certain Christian ideals—service to God and observance

of the virtues of faith, charity and humility. Similarly, from time
to time ecclesiastical rites were included in the ceremonies of knighthood in an endeavour to give them religious sanctity. The two
elements of war and religion were brought together at the time of
the Crusades, which was certainly a part of the golden age of chivalry.
The Crusades collected numerous knights from many countries
to fight for the Christian faith, to defend churches and ecclesiastics
and to protect women and children, and thereby they contributed
to the idealization of chivalry and were naturally greatly encouraged
by the Church. Many of the crusading knights were members of
religious or monastic fraternities, as opposed to princely orders
of chivalry. Examples of these monastic orders were the Knights
Templars, who were founded in Burgundy, and the Knights
Hospitallers of the Order of Saint John of Jerusalem, later known
as the Knights of Rhodes and later still as the Knights of Malta.
The latter was a crusading order largely designed for the care of
the poor and for the nursing of sick pilgrims, and it flourished
greatly in Malta, where all important European countries had separate
headquarters or *Auberges*, as they were then described. In Malta,
too, existed large and well-equipped hospitals which were maintained
by the knights. It may be of interest to note that the headquarters
of the Sovereign Order of the Knights of Malta is now in Rome,
while there is an off-shoot of the original order, the Order of Saint
John, with its chancery at Saint John's Gate at Clerkenwell, in London.
This order now has the Queen as its Sovereign though it is not
one of the official orders of Chivalry.

The professional life of a knight, apart from fighting in wars,
consisted very largely of participation in jousts and tournaments,
but a knight was also a courtier fully cognizant of the rules of
etiquette and privilege. It must be realised, however, that many
of the knightly virtues were rather more preached than practised.
Few knights lived up to their lofty ideals completely, but at least
the Rules of knighthood helped to ameliorate many of the merciless
and brutal manners of the times, which would otherwise have
received no check or discouragement. As explained, in theory a knight
was a defender of widows and orphans, but in practice wardships and
marriages were bought and sold in much the same way as transactions are carried out in the stock-exchanges and money-markets
of the present day. There are innumerable records of the marriages

of very young girls and of the knighthoods of very young boys—
sometimes children of seven or eight years of age—so that they
might be kept safe from the evils of wardship and the consequent
theft of their estates and fortunes.

The attitude of men towards women and children in the Middle
Ages was curiously mixed and, in spite of the much-advertised
courtesy and gallantry, wife-beating and cruelty to children were
frequent and accepted as reasonable behaviour amongst all classes.
Moreover, more often than not the object of a knight's chivalrous
love was the wife of another knight.

It must be realised, too, that war was sometimes an extremely
profitable profession for a knight in that, if he was fortunate, he
often obtained a large sum for the ransom of an enemy nobleman
whom he had overthrown in battle and whose life he had spared.
The value of the loot obtained after a successful campaign was also
often considerable. It should be noted that the merciful treatment
usually given to those of high rank and large possessions was
seldom offered to those in the lower ranks. Even the Black Prince,
who was particularly famous for his chivalrous and generous nature,
on some occasions showed great harshness and lack of mercy in
his treatment of prisoners—notably at the capture of the town
of Limoges in France. In 1160 Peter of Blois criticised very adversely
the behaviour of some knights and he stated: 'The so-called Order
of Knighthood is now Dis-order.'

Professor Hearnshaw, in his *Essay on Chivalry*, asked: 'What is
the meaning of Chivalry? Is it not the gloss put by fine manners
on vice and selfishness and contempt for the rights of man?'
However, he went on to state that 'taking it all in all, Chivalry
marked a distinct social advance and it inculcated an ideal of social
service: service to the weak by the strong: service to the poor by
the wealthy.' Dr. William Shaw, in his book *The Knights of England*,
suggested that from the year 880 to about 1250 the only form of
real knighthood in England was the highly ceremonial investiture
which subsequently developed into the ritual of 'The Bath' and
that the number of 'Full Knights' was small. He considered that
the majority of those described loosely as knights were really only
'Tenants of the Crown' and were in fact 'Batteliers' or helpers of
the Sovereign in battle. He considered that it was not until about
the middle of the thirteenth century that the dignity of knighting

by dubbing with the sword was introduced on a wide scale, and that it was not till then that the whole body of military tenants of the crown, or batteliers, became entitled to knighthood, whereupon they became 'knights batteliers'. It would seem that, though all these tenants of the crown were theoretically entitled to be knighted, many were anxious to avoid this honour which compelled them, at great expense and inconvenience to themselves, to come forward when called upon to strengthen the king's armies. We read of monarchs periodically ordering these military tenants to present themselves to be knighted and to assume the obligations of this 'honour' or, alternatively, to pay a considerable fine in lieu of military service. The collection of these fines proved a most profitable source of income for the crown and continued until the reign of Charles the First. For instance, in the reign of Edward the Second (1307) it was ordained that every man who held landed property of the crown amounting in value to twenty pounds per annum, upon becoming of age, had to 'take the Order of Knighthood' or pay a substantial fine for exemption.

Later on, soon after his accession, King James the First (1603) summoned all persons possessed of crown lands worth forty pounds per annum to present themselves for knighting or in lieu pay a heavy fine.

Thus, this type of knighthood came to be avoided by 'poor gentlemen' and coveted by 'rich citizens', sometimes described as 'carpet knights' to distinguish them from those dubbed on the battle-field. It was not until the reign of Charles the Second that this usage, which had been made an illegal source of profit to the monarch and a grievous oppression to the subject, was finally abolished. Dr. Shaw wrote:

> From the days of the Restoration, there began the sole and simple conception of knighthood as a personal dignity conferred by the ceremony of dubbing by the Sovereign or his deputy and, when this change had been effected, it became a recognised custom to confer upon civilians also what had originated as a purely military dignity.

As stated in the previous chapter, the only person now entitled to confer knighthood in this country is the Queen, and no other person is permitted to dub a knight unless letters patent and whatever authorising warrants may be necessary have been signed by the Queen, delegating to that person the power to confer the accolade and to invest with the appropriate insignia on the Queen's behalf. Examples of such delegations in recent years have been those made to Queen Elizabeth the Queen Mother, Prince Philip, Duke of Edinburgh, and the Duke of Gloucester. Such delegations of authority are not of a permanent nature but refer only to certain specific occasions. Overseas the Governors-General of Australia and New Zealand are authorised to confer knighthood on the Sovereign's behalf; and from time to time members of the Royal Family, when making official visits to Commonwealth countries overseas, may be authorised to act similarly. Formerly the Governors-General of Canada, South Africa and India were also authorised to confer knighthood.

As explained in the previous chapter, if a person on whom a knighthood is to be conferred cannot, owing to illness or prolonged absence abroad, present himself to be knighted, he can in lieu of this ceremony be given letters patent under the Great Seal, authorising him to style himself as a knight bachelor. The first-known occasion of the granting of letters patent of this nature was in 1777 when Robert Chambers, who was then resident as a judge in Bengal, was given authority to style himself as a knight, as he was unable to attend an investiture in London to be dubbed there.

The granting of letters patent completes entirely the procedure in so far as a knight bachelor is concerned. There has, however, been at least one comparatively recent exception to this rule, and that was in the case of the late Sir Aubrey Smith, the well-known actor, who was then residing in America. In ignorance of the regulations on this subject, though he had received letters patent authorising him to style himself as a knight, he made a special journey to London in order that he might be dubbed by his Sovereign. In the special circumstances of the case, King George the Sixth permitted him to attend an investiture for this purpose. There was a somewhat similar incident during the reign of Queen Victoria when a person who had already been knighted was received and dubbed a second time owing to a mistake by the office concerned. In the opinion of the author it is a great pity that a knight bachelor is not allowed to receive a dispensation warrant instead of letters patent, so that, while he will not have to wait an unduly long time until he can style himself as a knight, he can postpone his attendance at an investiture in order that he may be dubbed—the arrangement for those who receive appointments as knights commanders in an order of chivalry. Great disappointment is caused to those knights bachelor who return to England a year or so after they have been appointed to knighthood by letters patent, in that they are not allowed to present themselves before their Sovereign to be dubbed because they have received a document dispensing with this ceremony.

It was not until the middle of the fourteenth century that an official and reasonably accurate list of knights was published.

Like most things connected with knighthood, the origin of the term 'knight bachelor' has been a matter for discussion among antiquaries for several centuries. Once again we have to guess at the original meaning of this term. As explained previously, Dr. William Shaw, in his *Knights of England*, suggested that the Norman-French word *battalere* or *battelier* (one who fought on the battle-field) became confused with the base Latin word *baccalaurius*, which in its anglicised form became 'knight bachelor'. This may well be the correct solution. Some maintain, however, that knights bachelor were not originally 'full knights' but were of a middle degree between knights and esquires or, as the historian Camden described them, *'Bas Chevaliers'*. Some historians disagree with Camden's interpretation of the term, but at least it seems to be an intelligent suggestion and one that cannot be too lightly dismissed.

Other antiquaries contend that the term 'bachelor' meant that the title did not pass to the eldest son on the death of a knight, just as if the latter were unmarried and without an heir. Another writer describes a knight bachelor as 'a sort of unmarried apprentice-knight who was given the particularly dangerous assignments'. It was his belief that when on the battle-field some hazardous attack or dangerous enterprise had to be carried out the call was 'Bachelors to the front'. Some suggest that knights bachelor were the equivalent of the Roman *Milites Baccalaurii*, who were quite distinct from and considerably junior in rank to the *Equites Aurati*. That these two subdivisions did exist in the seventeenth century seems to be proved by the wording of a warrant of that time which ordained that 'Baronets shall have precedence over *Equites Aurati* and *Milites Baccalaurii*'.

It has been stated by some historians that King Henry the Eighth decreed that knights bachelor should wear a 'collar of S's' with a badge in the form of a Tudor rose pendant from a blue and white riband, but the author has been unable to discover any documentary proof of this statement.

It would appear that later on an attempt was made to obtain permission from King Charles the First for knights bachelor to wear a distinctive riband and badge, but the application was unsuccessful. Nowadays knights bachelor are not presented with any insignia by the Sovereign, but are permitted to purchase a plaque or badge which ranks in seniority next below the star of the most junior order of chivalry, namely that of a Knight Commander of the Order of the British Empire. This badge is worn on the left breast, like the star of an order. It is about three inches long and two inches wide and consists of an 'oval medallion of vermilion colour, enclosed by a scroll bearing a cross-hilted sword, belted and sheathed, between two spurs, the whole set about the sword belt—all gilt'. Authority to purchase this badge can be obtained from the Secretary of State at the Home Office. While certain records of appointments of knights bachelor are maintained at the Home Office, the official registry of the Imperial Society of Knights Bachelor is at the College of Arms (in Queen Victoria Street, London).

Finally, it must be explained that every person who is appointed to be a Knight Companion of the Orders of the Garter or Thistle, or a Knight Grand Cross or Knight Commander of any of the other orders of chivalry, must be dubbed as a knight bachelor before he is invested with the appropriate insignia of the order to which he has been appointed.

The class of knights known formerly as knights bannerets, and now non-existent, has sometimes, though quite inaccurately, been confused with those who were baronets or knights bachelor. A knight banneret was a knight who, being possessed of considerable estates and having distinguished himself by some outstanding act of bravery in time of war, was elected to that rank. Thereupon he became entitled to 'carry in the field a Square Banner [actually three feet square] containing his Arms and to command such Knights, Esquires and soldiers as he had himself furnished for the King's Army and who were serving under his personal banner'. Though Joseph Edmondson wrote that knights banneret were first created in the eighth century, most historians consider that the dignity was not given earlier than the middle of the thirteenth century.

This class of knight was recognised in England and Scotland as an established order of society. According to documents of the thirteenth century the wife of a knight banneret was described and addressed as 'banneress'. A similar dignity existed in France, and the holders were described as *Chevaliers à Banière*. The following procedure, which only occurred in times of war, was observed when a knight banneret was created. The knight was conducted by two senior knights to the Royal Commander of the Army, bearing his pennon or guidon of arms. The heralds then announced that he had shown himself valiant in the field and deserved to be advanced into the degree of knight banneret. Then the Commander of the Army, in the presence of all the nobility and captains, caused the points of his pennon to be 'rent off'.

Turning to the title of baronet, though a baronet is not nowadays automatically a knight bachelor also, he is styled with the prefix 'Sir' and the suffix 'Bt.', but when baronetcies were first conferred a part of the honour was that the newly-made baronet was at the same time dubbed as a knight. Moreover, for a considerable period the eldest son of a baronet appears to have been described as a knight baronet, and on attaining the age of twenty-one to have been authorised to style himself as a knight bachelor, with the prefix 'Sir', while on the death of his father he succeeded to his baronetcy. The theoretical origin of the baronetage was that, as King James the First considered that 'the ancient honour of Knighthood had fallen into disrepute owing to the lavish manner in which it had been conferred', he decided in the year 1611 to institute the new honour of baronetcy. It appears to be more in accordance with the facts, however, that he invented this new honour as a means of raising a considerable amount of money and valuable reinforcements for his army in Ireland, and that those on whom a baronetcy was conferred really purchased this honour. Candidates for baronetcy had to be 'men of quality and good reputation' and they not only had to pay a thousand pounds for this new title, but had also to undertake to maintain thirty footsoldiers in Ireland for a period of three years.

It was promised originally that not more than two hundred baronets would be created, but eventually that number was far exceeded. Though, as explained above, King James the First agreed that a person who was created a baronet should also be knighted and that his eldest son should become a knight bachelor on attaining the age of twenty-one, there was considerable ambiguity in the wording of the royal warrant. It has been suggested that what the King really intended was that the eldest son of a baronet should succeed to the baronetcy on the death of his father and then have the right also to style himself as a knight.

In 1827 the former arrangement was clearly revoked by King George the Fourth in so far as it affected the future right of the eldest son of a baronet to style himself as a knight during his father's lifetime. This revocation, however, was not made retrospective.

Under the royal warrant of 1827 it was made clear that in future the eldest son would be permitted on his father's death to succeed to the baronetcy, and only then to use the title of Sir, though he would not in fact be dubbed as a knight. This rule still holds good.

In 1625, fourteen years after the rank of baronet had been instituted, King Charles the First created a number of 'Baronets of Nova Scotia' for the 'advancement of that colony'. In 1629 he instituted a badge for the Baronets of Scotland. This badge was worn round the neck from an 'orange-tawny riband' and was 'an escutcheon argent, a saltire azure, with an Imperial Crown above the escutcheon, and enclosed with the motto *Fax mentis honestae gloria*'.

After the 'Union' of 1707, the arms of the Baronets of Scotland were charged with the Badge of Ulster, the 'Red Hand', and they became Baronets of the United Kingdom. No Baronets of Scotland were created after the year 1707, and no Baronets of Ireland after 1801.

The baronet's badge of the present day is worn round the neck, in a manner similar to that for wearing the neck-badge of an order of chivalry. It is suspended from an orange riband, with narrow edges of blue, one and threequarter inches in width. The badge consists of a shield of the Arms of Ulster, namely a red hand on a silver field, and it is surmounted by an imperial crown, the whole being enclosed by an oval border embossed with gilt scroll-work, having a design of roses, thistles and shamrocks.

Nowadays a newly made baronet does not attend an investiture and does not receive the accolade. Nor is any badge presented to him by the Sovereign, but he is permitted, if he so desires, to purchase one.

The Baronet's badge in the present order of precedence of honours is placed immediately after the badge of the Order of Merit. It

GARTER PROCESSION AT WINDSOR *circa* 1672
Under the canopy is King Charles II wearing the Sovereign's robes, and escorted by Gentlemen of the Body Guard. He is preceded by the Chancellor, Prelate and officers of the order. In front of them walk the Garter Knights preceded by the Heralds. Behind the canopy follow the Bodyguard of the Yeomen of the Guard.
Radio Times Hulton Picture Library

GARTER PROCESSION AT WINDSOR IN 1950
King George VI and Queen Elizabeth are preceded by the Chancellor (Lord Halifax, K.G.), the Prelate and other officers of the order. The pages, officers in attendance and the Yeomen of the Guard follow the Sovereign.
Picture Service

INSIGNIA OF THE ORDER OF THE GARTER

The collar with the 'George' badge appendant; the riband and the 'Lesser George' badge which should be worn when the collar is not being worn; the garter as it should be tied round the leg; and a star of Stuart pattern.

British Combine Photo

cannot be worn in miniature, and the riband is not worn with non-ceremonial uniform.

The Registry of the Baronetage is at the Home Office, where the official Roll of Baronets is maintained.

As a knight was, and still is, created by formal investiture, he could and still can only be deprived of this honour by formal degradation. In the old days knighthood in certain respects resembled the priesthood. Just as a priest who had committed some serious crime or dishonourable act was deprived of his Holy Orders by the ceremony of 'un-frocking', so a knight had his accoutrements of honour taken off him. Even in very early days there was considerable doubt as to whether or not knighthood was forfeitable for any crime other than treason or cowardice, and in fact there were very few occasions when degradation was carried out on conviction of felony. The most recent occasion on which a person was degraded from his honours for treason occurred during the 1914–1918 war, when Sir Roger Casement, an Irishman who, in addition to having his appointment as a K.C.M.G. cancelled, was executed.

We read that, after an installation of knights in Westminster Abbey, when the procession returned to the Chapter House, the Sovereign's Master-Cook, who was waiting outside the door of the Abbey, 'having a large chopping-knife in his hand', severally said to each Knight Companion:

'Sir, you know what great oath you have taken, which, if you keep it, will be of great honour to you but, if you break it, I shall be compelled by my office to hack your spurs from off your heels'.

These ceremonies of degradation were performed publicly and the unfortunate knight, after having his spurs hacked off and broken in pieces, and after being stripped of his armour, shoes, gloves and coat of arms, had his sword broken over his head by the heralds and was then beheaded and quartered. Comparatively few reports of such degradation exist. Nicolas wrote in his *History* that the earliest account of a degradation of a knight was that of Sir Andrew Harcla, Earl of Carlisle, who in the reign of King Edward the Second was convicted of high treason and received the following sentence: '*Que vous soietz degrade : que vous perditz noun de count, pur vous et pur vos heirs, a touts jours : que vous soietz deceynt del Espée*'. According to some chroniclers he was also 'divested of his shoes and gloves and immediately afterwards beheaded'.

Another instance of degradation—also for treason—is that of Sir Ralph Grey in 1468. He was taken to Doncaster, where his 'gold spurs were hewn from his heels while his sword and all his armour were broken'.

Again in 1621 we read that Sir Francis Mitchell, having been found guilty of 'grievous exactions', was degraded publicly in Westminster Hall by the heralds in the presence of the Earl Marshal. After his spurs had been broken and thrown away, his belt was cut and his sword was broken over his head, and finally he was pronounced to be 'no longer a Knight but to be a Knave'.

This would appear to be the last-known case of public degradation. An account of the degradation of certain knights of the Order of the Bath and the story of one case of subsequent restoration are included in Chapter V, which deals with that order.

It is a popular mistake to think that after the Sovereign has dubbed a person nowadays the words 'Rise, Sir ——' are pronounced. This is not the case.

In fact, when a knight-elect attends a public investiture in order that he may be knighted his name and the honour he is to receive are announced by either the Lord Chamberlain, if he is to receive a knighthood in one of the orders of chivalry, or by the Home Secretary if he is to be dubbed a knight bachelor. After his name has been announced, the knight-elect moves forward until he is immediately in front of the Sovereign and kneels on the knighting-stool. The Sovereign then lays the blade of the sword first on his right and then on his left shoulder but no words are spoken during this operation. After he has been dubbed, the new knight stands up, steps to the side of the knighting-stool and the Sovereign then shakes hands with him and addresses appropriate words of congratulation to him.

When a knight-elect attends for a private investiture, as he enters the room in which the Sovereign is receiving him his name is announced by the Equerry-in-Waiting or other member of the Household in attendance, and the procedure followed is similar to that described above.

Some of those on whom knighthood is to be conferred either do not like the sound of their first Christian name or else prefer to use one of their other Christian names. Some have been in the habit of using instead of their real first Christian name another form of it or even what is really a 'nickname'—for example, Fred instead of Frederick, Harry instead of Henry, Jack instead of John, Rex instead of Reginald, etc. Though it is permissible for a person to describe himself by whatever name or nickname he prefers *after* he has been knighted, he can only be dubbed under his proper Christian name, and accordingly, when his name is announced at an investiture, prior to his being dubbed, his first Christian name is always read out together with his surname.

Leaving out of account, as they are now obsolescent,* the Order of Saint Patrick (to which no appointment other than for Royal Princes, viz. Duke of Windsor in 1927 and Duke of Gloucester in 1934, has been made since 1922) and the orders which were given formerly for services in India (to which no appointments have been made since 1947), there are now six official British Orders of Chivalry:

The Most Noble Order of the Garter.
The Most Ancient and Most Noble Order of the Thistle.
The Most Honourable Order of the Bath.
The Most Distinguished Order of Saint Michael and Saint George.
The Royal Victorian Order.
The Most Excellent Order of the British Empire.

* Brief descriptions of these orders are to be found in Chapter X.

CHAPTER III

The Most Noble Order of the Garter

Several centuries ago Selden, the historian, wrote: 'The Order of the Garter exceeds in majesty, honor and fame all Chivalrous Orders of the World'; while it is nearly three hundred years since Ashmole declared: 'The garter excels and out-vies all other institutions of Honour in the whole world.'

Though the story of the foundation and origin of the Order and its ensigns has been discussed and disputed by innumerable antiquaries during the past four hundred years, it still remains obscure. In fact it is not possible to state with certainty either the exact date of the foundation of the order or the precise cause of its institution because all the annals of the order for the first two hundred years of its existence are both imperfect and unreliable. The original Statutes ordained for the governance of the order by its founder, King Edward the Third, have long since perished and there is no real proof of the authenticity of the supposed copies which still exist. There is reason to believe that these copies were compiled long after the originals had disappeared and they certainly seem to contain a number of errors and inaccuracies. In 1672 Ashmole, in his *Institutions*, published what he thought might be accepted as a reasonably accurate reproduction of the earliest-known form of the Statutes. It was not until the reign of Henry the Eighth, when completely revised statutes were compiled, that the annals of the order began to be maintained with any real accuracy and regularity.

The earliest collection of records and facts relating to the order is the *Register*, compiled by Doctor Aldrich about 1535 and named from the colour of its cover the *Liber Niger* or 'Black Book'. But, though this book purported to treat of the order from the date of its foundation and to be entirely accurate from the year 1416, it was in fact only reliable in its information from about the beginning of the sixteenth century. Thus for not less than the first one hundred and fifty years of its existence the history of the order is founded on guesswork.

Froissart, the earliest and in fact the only contemporary writer on this subject, stated in his *Chronicles*, published about the end of the fourteenth century, that

> In the year 1344 there came into the mind and will of King Edward of England that he would cause to be re-erected the Great Castle of Windsor, where first was established the noble Round Table of which were so many good and valiant Knights, and would make an Order of Knights—*une ordonnance des Chevaliers de luy et de ses enfans et des plus preux de sa terre.*

Froissart was certainly highly qualified to record the facts connected with the founding of this order. He lived from 1327 to 1410, and he came to England in 1360, being even then famous as a narrator of chivalrous deeds.

For several years he held the appointment of Secretary to Queen Philippa of Hainault, wife of King Edward the Third, while later on, about the year 1395, he held a post at the court of King Richard the Second. None the less, it is now thought that when, rather late in life, he wrote a record of those times, he probably confused in his mind the date of the first conception of the order and the date of its actual institution. It is reasonably certain that some of his statements in connection with the order were not accurate. For example, he wrote that 'in 1344 Forty Founder-Knights were elected', whereas it is now universally accepted that there were not more than twenty-five. Selden too, in his *Titles of Honour*, and Anstis in his *Register of the Order of the Garter*, 1724, both give the date of the institution as Saint George's Day, 1344, in the eighteenth year of the reign of Edward the Third. It seems probable, however, that both of them were merely quoting from Froissart's writings. It is thought by most of the historians of the present day that at the earliest the order could not have been founded before 1346, because no person who was not already a knight was eligible for election to the order, and neither the Black Prince nor several others of the original Companions of the Garter received knighthood until the middle of that year. There is reliable proof that the Black Prince (the Prince of Wales) was knighted by his father at La Hogue, near

Barfleur in Normandy, on 12th July 1346, having then just attained the age of seventeen. Two other founder-knights, the Earl of Salisbury and Sir Roger Mortimer (later Earl of March), were also knighted at the same time. Moreover, the King and the Black Prince were actively engaged in the war in France in July 1346, and did not return to England until the 12th October 1347.

Ashmole in his *Institutions and Ceremonies of the Most Noble Order of the Garter*, published in 1672, opines that the order was founded in 1349 or 1350.

Haydn, a more recent historian, in his *Dictionary of Dates*, published in 1810, wrote that:

> Edward the Third, when at war with France and eager to draw the best soldiers of Europe into his interest, projected the revival of King Arthur's Round Table and proclaimed a solemn tilting. On New Year's Day of 1344 he published letters of protection for the safe coming and returning of such foreign knights as would venture their reputation at the Jousts about to be held. A Table was erected in Windsor Castle of 200 feet diameter, and the many Knights who assembled there were entertained at the King's expense.

Other historians, while confirming that a Grand Tournament took place at Windsor in the year 1344, suggest various later dates for the actual foundation of the Order of the Garter. Thus, though the idea of forming the order, based on the rules of King Arthur's Round Table, may well have been conceived in 1344, it would seem that owing to the outbreak of the French war it was not actually instituted until a few years later, after the return of the King and the Prince of Wales from their triumphant victories, including the Battle of Crécy.

During the reign of Richard the Second Lord Walsingham, who, we are told, was 'remarkable for his accuracy', wrote that 'in 1344 King Edward began to build a house in Windsor Castle which should be called the Round Table and which was of circular form and two hundred feet in diameter'. He added that Philip of Valois, King of France, made a similar Round Table. He suggested that though the companions were not chosen nor the details of the order settled until 1348, which was four years after the Great Tournament at Windsor, King Edward might have founded the order in 1344 but have waited until the domicile of the order, namely the College of Windsor, and the Round Table were ready for use before actually choosing the companions or deciding on the habits and ensigns of the order.

It should be noted that, whatever may have been the original signification of the term 'Round Table' and whatever interpretation may be given to it nowadays, in the fourteenth century it was frequently used to describe the place at which jousts were held, and later on it often referred to the tournament itself. Some historians describe the 'Round Table' as a large building and not, as is commonly supposed nowadays, a round piece of furniture at which guests sat in council or at meat.

Perhaps the best authorities for disproving 1344 as the year of foundation of the Garter are the Royal Wardrobe Accounts for 1344–1346, because these do not contain the slightest allusion to the order or to payments for mantles or garters. A possible clue to the cause of the mistaken idea that 1344 was the date of the foundation is that a warrant was issued in that year giving the King's permission for the formation of an Association of Knights of the County of Lincolnshire in connection with a great tournament 'for the practice of arms' to be held at Lincoln. It is possible that the formation of this Association may have put into the King's mind the idea of founding a new fraternity consisting of his own intimate friends and companions of the battle-field. It has now been generally accepted as probable by historians of the present day that the Order of the Garter was founded by King Edward the Third in the year 1348 as a Noble Fraternity consisting of himself and twenty-five knights, to be designated the 'Knights of Saint George' or the 'Knights of the Blue Garter' who were to consist of his children and the bravest in the land. It was his original intention that the order should be reserved as the highest reward for military merit and, though later on there were many diversions from this rule so that at one period the order became confined to the peerage, the great military leaders were frequently appointed to the order in the past. This is the case at the present day, when, exclusive of the Royal Family, the order includes an Admiral of the Fleet, four Field-Marshals and a Marshal of the Royal Air Force.

At the date of institution of the order every knight was commanded to wear on his left leg a light-blue garter inscribed in gold with the motto *Honi soit quy mal y pense*, while at the same time he wore on the left side of his robe or mantle the arms of Saint George, surrounded with a similar garter.

It has been suggested that the blue and gold colours of the garter alluded to the colour of the arms of France, whose crown was claimed by Edward the Third.

It was ordained that the Anniversary Feast should be held each year at Windsor on the day of Saint George. The reason why Saint George was originally chosen as the tutelary saint of England is not clear. It is believed that Saint George was a native of Cappadocia and rose to the rank of military tribune in the reign of Emperor Diocletian, and that, being a man of great courage and equal humanity, he reproached the emperor for his cruel persecution of the Christian martyrs. For this he was imprisoned and eventually executed at Nicomedia on 23rd April in the year A.D. 290. It is worthy of note that it was on this same date in the year 1192 that King Richard the First gained a great victory over Saladin, and it has been suggested that it was from that day that Saint George was officially adopted as the Patron Saint of England. In support of this theory it may be noted that the battle took place near Jaffa, which is only ten miles from Lydda, or Ludd, where Saint George's tomb is supposed to be. It was near Lydda that Perseus was reputed to have rescued Andromeda from a monster, and his heroic feat may possibly have been transferred in imagination to the Christian Saint George. At least we know that as early as the reign of King Edward the First (1272–1307) the badge of Saint George—a red cross on a white ground —was always borne by him in the field. This badge continued to be the national ensign of England until King James the First came to the throne, when it was linked with the arms of Saint Andrew. Later, the badge of Saint Patrick was added to the national ensign.

The soldiers of England, when fighting in France in the fourteenth century, always bore the badge of Saint George on their coats, and their battle-cry was 'Saint George for England'. We find, too, in the Regulations for the Government of the Army, which were drawn up in 1386, in the reign of King Richard the Second, an instruction that 'to avoid confusion on the battle-field every man of whatever estate he may be shall wear a sign of the Arms of Saint George both before and behind'. King Henry the

Fifth issued a similar order before the battle of Agincourt in 1415. None the less, it does not seem that the reason for the selection of Saint George as the Patron Saint was clear to all. Oldmixon in his *History of the Reformation* relates how the youthful King Edward the Sixth, in company with the Knights of the Garter, attended a religious service on Saint George's Day, 1553, at which a sermon was preached in praise of the saint. We read that after the service the young king said to those about him:

'My Lords, pray ye, what Saint is Saint George that we have so honoured him?'

At which question the lords 'were all stunned', not expecting it from so young a king and not well knowing what answer to make. At last the Marquess of Winchester replied:

'If it please Your Majesty, I did never read in history of Saint George, but only in the *Golden Legends* where it is set down that Saint George, mounted on his charger, out with his sword and ran the dragon through with his spear.'

We read that the king fell a-laughing at the thought of a knight mounted on a mettlesome steed wielding a spear with one hand and holding a drawn sword in the other, and he could not for a while speak.

At length he said: 'I pray you, my Lord, and what did he do with his sword the while?'

To which Lord Winchester replied somewhat surlily: 'That I cannot tell Your Majesty.'

It would appear that in the jousts which took place at Windsor in 1348 twelve knights were chosen on the king's side and that they received robes and garters from his wardrobe, while twelve other knights were chosen by the Black Prince as his representatives and received similar gifts from him. At the same time the king extended the ecclesiastical foundation of Windsor Chapel and it was erected into a college which included the twenty-four 'Poor Knights' referred to later in this chapter.

Though regrettably we cannot be certain of the accuracy of the list, the names of the founder-knights are thought to have been:

The Prince of Wales (the Black Prince).
The Duke of Lancaster.
Thomas Beauchamp, Earl of Warwick.

Sir John de Greilley (Captal de Buche—a distinguished Gascon nobleman).

The Earl of Stafford.

William Montacute, Earl of Salisbury (who married Joan, daughter of Edmund of Kent, and of whose mother, the Dowager Countess of Salisbury, it has been suggested that the king was enamoured).

Sir Roger Mortimer (later Earl of March).

Sir John Lisle.

Sir Bartholomew Burghersh (only eighteen years old on election).

Sir John Beauchamp (younger brother of the Earl of Warwick, mentioned above).

Lord Mohun of Dunster.

Sir Hugh Courtenay (son of the Earl of Devon).

Sir Thomas Holand—or Holland (who was said to have married Joan of Kent secretly, before she publicly married the Earl of Salisbury).

Lord Grey of Rotherfield.

Sir Richard Fitzsimon.

Sir Miles Stapleton.

Sir Thomas Wale.

Sir Hugh Wrottesley.

Sir Nigel Loring (sometimes written Nele Loryng).

Sir John Chandos.

Sir James Audeley.

Sir Otho Holand—or Holland (brother of the Earl of Kent and uncle of the Thomas Holand mentioned above).

Sir Henry Eam (previously a subject of the Duke of Brabant).

Sir Sanchet d'Abrichecourt (a French nobleman).

Sir Walter Paveley.

It is believed that all those mentioned above served in the expedition to France and were present at the Battle of Crécy, the three foreigners having previously sworn allegiance to the King of England. Four of these knights had not attained their twentieth year and few of them were much over the age of thirty.

Whatever may be the exact date of the institution of the order, it can be accepted without doubt that the Garter is at the present day the most sought-after and honoured of any order in the world.

It was in 1948 that King George the Sixth gave orders that thenceforth that year was to be accepted as the sexcentenary of its foundation.

It was on Saint George's Day of that year that, accompanied by his queen, his mother (Queen Mary), his daughter (Princess Elizabeth) and his son-in-law (Prince Philip, Duke of Edinburgh), he went in a procession of knights to the chapel of the order (Saint George's, Windsor) to give thanks on this six hundredth anniversary.

The author, like all those who knew what careful investigation that gracious monarch, who took so great an interest in his orders of chivalry, would have made before giving a ruling on this matter, accepts unhesitatingly the correctness of his decision.

The order has never fallen into desuetude, nor has it ever been in a state of 'suspended animation' like many other orders. It should be noted, however, that when the tragic execution of King Charles the First took place the order consisted of only fourteen companions, and two of these perished on the scaffold a few weeks after their royal master.

The Order of the Garter is just as eagerly sought now as it was over six hundred years ago.

However uncertain the exact date of the foundation of the order may be, there is still greater obscurity as to the reason for the choice of its principal ensign, from which it derives its title. As Nicolas, probably the most accurate and meticulous of all writers on this subject, wrote in 1842:

> Neither the cause nor the exact time of the foundation have been discovered and fable and tradition have been called upon to compensate for the lack of facts and records.

A picturesque version is that when a lady, taking part in a ball held at his court near Calais by King Edward the Third in celebration of his victories in France, had the misfortune to drop her garter, it was picked up by the King. Upon observing her great embarrassment and the significant smiles of certain onlookers, 'as if it were an amorous action', he rebuked them with the words *honi soit qui mal y pense*—Dishonoured be he who thinks evil of it. He then tied the garter round his own knee, at the same time saying:

'I will make of it ere long the most honourable garter that ever was worn.'

This anecdote, it will be agreed, is quite in harmony with the sentiments of that age and might well be true. The earliest writer to attribute to this incident the choice of a garter as the ensign of the order was Polydore Vergil, in a document published about 1550. There are various suggestions as to the identity of the lady. Some name her as the Queen Philippa, others as the mother of the Earl of Salisbury, while some suggest that it was the King's cousin, Joan the Fair Maid of Kent, who afterwards married the Earl of Salisbury and, after his death, the Black Prince. Hollinshed, another chronicler, writing in 1587, gave the following version:

> The Queen's Majesty being departed from his Presence, the King, following soon after, happened to find her garter which slacked by chance and so fell from her leg, un-espied. The King's grooms and gentlemen also passed by it, disdaining to stoop and take up such a trifle. But the King, knowing the owner, commanded one of them to reach it up to him and, when the gentleman said 'It is but some woman's garter', said to those about him, 'You, my masters, do make small account of this blue garter, but, if God lend me life for a few months, I will make the proudest of you to reverence the like.'

Another suggests that the words *boni soit qui mal y pense* were Queen Philippa's disdainful answer when the King reproachfully asked her what men would conjecture of her for causing embarrassment by allowing her garter to fall in such a manner.

While Ashmole, Anstis and others agree in repudiating Polydore Vergil's story, and while Heylin (in his *History of Saint George*) described it as a 'vain and idle romance derogatory both to the Order and its Founder', Nicolas thought their 'objections were by no means conclusive, particularly as a garter has frequently been associated with sentiments of gallantry'.

Moreover, he pointed out that to wear a lady's favour, such as her glove or a ribbon from her dress, was a common practice of the age. He wrote: 'At least this version is four hundred years old and, as it is possible, it may well be true.' He agreed that it was not, of course, the primary or only cause of the institution of the order. He thought, though, that if King Edward had previously determined to form this knightly band in imitation of the Round Table of King Arthur and had not fixed upon any particular ensign by which they should be distinguished, he might reasonably have adopted one which was felicitously suited to his purpose, though it had arisen from accident. Moreover, it is well known that from the twelfth century onwards the influence of certain ladies of high birth had introduced into chivalry such ideals as romantic love, gallantry and search for honourable adventure. It is reasonable, therefore, to think that some small object forming part of a lady's attire might well have been chosen as the ensign of a chivalrous order.

At all events it seems probable that Queen Philippa, and the Countess of Salisbury, and Joan, daughter of the Earl of Kent and later a Countess of Salisbury, were all present with the king in his camp before Calais. When Froissart wrote that 'the King was smitten with a sparcle of fyne love for the glorious Countess of Salisbury and danced with her frequently' we do not know for certain whether he was referring to the mother of the young Salisbury who later took the Lady Joan as his countess, or to the Fair Joan herself. Queen Philippa, who was of a particularly kind and generous disposition, had more or less adopted the fair Joan, when her father had been executed on a 'trumped-up charge of treason', and treated her like a daughter. There is considerable argument and confusion in connection with the marriages of this Lady Joan. As stated earlier, some suggest that she married secretly a young man of the name of Thomas Holand (or Holland), who later became a Knight of the Garter, but that this marriage was never announced publicly and that while he was abroad she was forced by her family to marry William Montacute, the young Earl of Salisbury. This same lady became first the wife, and later the widow, of the Black Prince and the mother of King Richard the Second.

Beltz, in his *Memoirs of the Order of the Garter*, considered that the garter was intended as an emblem of the 'tie or union' of warlike qualities to be employed in the assertion of the claim of the founder of the order to the French crown. He thought that the motto might well have been intended as a retort of shame and defiance upon those who should think ill of the enterprise or of those whom the King had chosen to be instruments of its accomplishment. Going further back into history, one writer suggests that the choice of a garter was derived from the legend of Saint George and the Dragon. In this legend the saint, a Christian knight of Cappadocia, having arrived at Silene in Libya, found that the King's daughter was about to be sacrificed to a fierce dragon. Having overthrown the dragon, the knight bade the princess place her girdle round the monster's neck, whereon it followed her as if it were a 'meeke beast and debonnaire'. Others have suggested that the idea came into King Edward's mind when he remembered the story of how Richard the First in the course of his Crusades

> Bethought himself of a new device which was to tie about the legs of a chosen number of Knights a leather thong whereby, being put in mind of the future glory that should accrue to them, they might be roused up to behaving themselves gallantly in the wars.

Another suggestion is that at the Battle of Crécy King Edward gave as the signal for the attack to commence the hoisting of a lance to the top of which his garter had been fixed, and that he remembered this incident later when he was choosing an ensign for his new order.

One thing is sure, namely that it is as arrogant and unsafe to reject all such legends absolutely as it would be rash and unintelligent to accept them implicitly and blindly.

After the end of King Edward the Third's long and glorious reign in 1377, nothing of particular importance happened in connection with the order during the twenty-two years of the reign of King Richard the Second. It is perhaps of interest, though, to note that during this reign there occurred the first instance of a knight resigning from the order. The knight in question was the Sire de Courcy, Earl of Bedford, who courteously renounced his membership as he could no longer retain it consistently with his duty to the King of France, with which country England was then at war.

During the reign of Henry the Fourth (1399–1413) foreign monarchs were appointed to the order for the first time, namely the Kings of Spain, Denmark and Portugal. Until that time, except for a few foreign knights who had sworn allegiance to the King of England, none but subjects of that monarch had been admitted to the order. Since then many foreign monarchs and princes have been elected.

On the accession to the throne by King Henry the Fifth in 1415 the order was distinguished further by the election of most of the great military commanders of the time. We read in the story of this reign, too, of the great grief and disillusionment of the King when one of the Companions of the Garter, Lord Scrope of Masham, who had been a dearly loved boyhood friend, was found guilty of treason. As a Knight of the Garter he received what nowadays seems to be the somewhat doubtful privilege of being merely drawn and beheaded instead of being hanged also. King Henry the Fifth published a new statute ordering that no Knight of the Garter should appear in public without his garter 'unless he were on horseback and booted, instead of which garter he might then wear a silken blue riband within his left boot under the knee'.

When King Henry the Seventh came to the throne, never having been elected a Knight of the Garter, his first admission to that order was as its Sovereign. As a result of the civil war which preceded his accession considerable bitterness existed between the Sovereign and certain noble families, and several Knights of the Garter who had supported King Richard the Third were degraded from the order. Apart from this, the order flourished exceedingly during this reign, and for the first time the words 'Sovereign of the Noble Order of the Garter' were added to the royal title and style. It was this monarch, too, who instituted the collar and the badge (later known as 'the George').

King Henry the Eighth became Sovereign in 1509 and he also 'paid great attention to the Order', and did much to increase its fame and splendour. He ordained that 'the King and his Heirs and Successors should be for ever Sovereigns of the Order' and it was in his reign that for the first time Knights of the Garter were 'classed with Lords'. A little later, in order to remove all ambiguities and doubts touching certain of the ancient rules, the statutes of the order were entirely remodelled. It is of interest to note that in 1510 Wolsey, then the King's Almoner, and later the famous cardinal, was appointed 'Register of the Order'.

An Act of Parliament was passed in 1519 against the wearing of 'costly apparel', and it was laid down that no man under the degree of baron or Knight of the Garter might wear in his gown or coat or any other part of his apparel any 'velvet of the colour of crimson or blue'. It has been suggested, and it is quite possibly true, that this law is the origin of the description of the high nobility as 'blue-blooded'.

The new statutes enjoined that none were to be chosen companions of the order who were not 'Gentlemen of Blood of three Descents of Noblesse of both father's and mother's side'. The 'Points of Reproach' were declared to be three only: Conviction of Error against the Christian Faith Catholic; High Treason; and Cowardice by fleeing away from battle or journey being with his Sovereign Lord or his Deputy. The statutes repeated the earlier rule that if any knight were to be found 'openly without his garter' he would be liable to fine except when he was booted and spurred, in which case he was to wear a 'little blue lace or thread of blue silk over his leg harness'. At the same time it was ordained that certain ceremonies were to be observed on Saint George's Day when all the knights were to meet together within the castle at Windsor. Penalties and fines for failure to attend included the gift of a 'Jewel for the Altar of the value of twenty marks of silver of Troy'.

King Henry the Eighth insisted that the statutes should be adhered to most strictly. For example, when in 1525, after Lord Roos, Warden of the East Marches, had been elected to the Garter and invested, it was found that he had never been knighted, the King declared the election void. The insignia were taken off Lord Roos and he was called before the king again and was knighted. The Knights Companions then proceeded to hold a new election at which he was again chosen, after which he was invested once more with the Garter insignia and installed formally.

In 1522 occurred the execution of a very distinguished knight, the high and mighty Duke of Buckingham, who, as is described in detail later, was degraded publicly from the order. King Henry the Eighth gave orders that in future the 'blotting-out of names' from the register, which had hitherto been done when a knight was degraded, was to be discontinued, as he wished the records to be preserved for posterity free from defacement. He commanded that in future when a knight was expelled from the order it would be sufficient if the words 'Out upon thee, Traitor!' were written in the margin opposite his name.

In 1537 Thomas, Lord Cromwell was elected a Companion in the place of Lord D'Arcy, who had been convicted of high treason. Cromwell, who then held the office of Keeper of the Privy Purse and Principal Secretary, and who afterwards became the Earl of Essex, was the first person of 'mean extraction' to be admitted to the

Engraved by J. Bonner

The Portrait of Sir Richard De la Bere Knight Banneret, receiving his Cognizance from Edward the Black Prince at the Battle of Cressy, 1347.

From an Ancient Painting on Pannel, at Cheltenham.

In the possession of John De la Bere Esq.r To whom this Plate is Inscribed, by his Obliged Humble Serv.t

Rich.d Bigland.

SIR RICHARD DE LA BERE
who was created a Knight Banneret for saving the life of the Black Prince at the Battle of Crecy in 1347.

KING WILLIAM III (1689—1702)
wearing the Sovereign's robes of the Order of the Garter.
Radio Times Hulton Picture Library

order. His election was the first occasion on which the qualification of unblemished gentility at birth was dispensed with. We read from the register's report of the ceremony that Cromwell received the honour 'as being one far above his pretensions and that when he came to the Chapter House he immediately fell down on his knees before the Sovereign giving, with all the eloquence of which he was known to be a master, infinite thanks to the King for vouchsafing so great an honour to him who was so inconsiderable a person.'

On her accession to the throne Queen Mary reappointed to the order all those persons of the Roman Catholic religion who had been dismissed from it during the previous reign, and we read that she did not follow her father's ruling that the register should be defaced as slightly as possible. In fact she caused every insertion which was not in accordance with the Roman Catholic faith to be erased completely. On her marriage to King Philip of Spain in 1554 she appointed him Joint Sovereign of the Order and gave him the badge of this office. Later, in 1560, he returned the sovereign's badge to Queen Elizabeth, the new Sovereign, by the hand of his ambassador. During the sovereignty of Queen Elizabeth there were not many changes in the rules governing the order. Instructions were issued, however, for the provision of appropriate insignia for Garter King of Arms and Black Rod, and certain additional directions were published detailing the occasions on which knights were to wear the Garter robes and insignia. Queen Elizabeth herself appears to have worn only the collar and badge, and those only on very rare occasions when she considered it particularly appropriate to do so. To increase the dignity of the order she commanded, in 1571, that 'Knights of the Garter should go above all other Knights and in the Low Parliament House sit above all other Degrees and next unto the Treasurer and Comptroller of Her Majesty's Household'.

King Charles the First, who came to the throne in 1625, has been described as the 'greatest increaser of honour and renown of the illustrious Order and of the beautification of its insignia'. During his reign, when installation ceremonies took place at Windsor, it was the custom of the knights elect to proceed there in a stately cavalcade with the greatest pomp imaginable and with a vast company of magnificently apparelled friends and mounted attendants. On arrival at Windsor, on the eve of the annual feast, the knights, attired in their mantles, attended a solemn service in the chapel, in the course of which they made their offerings of gold and silver at the altar. Afterwards a great banquet was held in the castle.

Many opinions have been expressed to explain why the riband came to be worn over the left shoulder and in the form of a bandolier about the body, but no authentic reason has been discovered. Ashmole wrote that

> Formerly the ordinary manner of wearing this riband was about the neck but for the more conveniency of riding or action the same is spread over the left shoulder and brought under the right arm where the Jewel hangs.

In Collins' *Peerage* an explanation was given that

> The custom of wearing the riband over the left shoulder arose from the circumstance of Charles, Duke of Richmond, King Charles the Second's natural son by the Duchess of Portsmouth, having been elected a Knight of the Garter. [The explanation continued:] When in 1681 his mother introduced him to the King with his riband over his left shoulder His Majesty was so pleased with this conceit that he commanded that all the Knights should wear it in the same way.

Several historians deny this explanation, but it is at least of interest to note that a few months after the date of this incident, in 1682, a formal instruction was issued by the King to the effect that 'in order that it should be clearly seen the Knights should wear the riband henceforth over the habit beltways put over the left shoulder and coming under the right arm'.

When Queen Anne succeeded William the Third, though she was the fourth Queen Regnant since the foundation of the order, she was the first female Sovereign to wear the insignia of the Garter habitually. Soon after her accession she commanded that a select number of knights should give their opinion as to the manner in which she, as Sovereign, should wear the ensigns of the order. They recommended that when not wearing the collar she should wear the badge pendant to a riband across the body with the garter on her left arm and the star on her left side. There exist portraits of Queen Anne which show her wearing the Garter insignia in this manner.

In 1786 George the Third, desiring to appoint his four sons to the order, promulgated a new statute decreeing that henceforth all the sons of the Sovereign should be additional to the original statutory number of twenty-five knights. In 1805 a further enlargement of the order was made, whereby it was decreed that henceforth the order should consist of the Sovereign and twentyfive knights companions, together with such lineal descendants of George the Second as might thereafter be elected.

In 1821, in the reign of King George the Fourth, a further enlargement decreed that such lineal descendants of King George the First as might be appointed should be counted as 'extra knights' and supernumary to the twenty-five allowed by the statutes.

As explained previously, in the reign of Henry the Fourth the order had admitted various foreign monarchs and these had been included amongst the statutory number of twenty-five knights. At an early date in the nineteenth century it was decreed that henceforth all foreign members should be counted as extra or supernumerary knights. For instance, when in 1813 Alexander the First of Russia was admitted to the order it was as an extra knight. Since that date numerous foreign monarchs and princes have received the order as Extra Knights or Extra Ladies of the Garter. Of these, several were not members of the Christian religion, but this point will be referred to later in this chapter.

> With the Regency, [wrote Nicolas] an era of transcendent splendour dawned upon the Order.

A number of extra knights were appointed, bringing the total number of companions to forty, and on 29th August 1815 the order included two emperors (Russia and Austria) four kings (France, Prussia, Spain and the Netherlands), fifteen dukes and several other great noblemen (including the Duke of Wellington and Earl of Chatham). It is of interest to note that, during this period, when the Duke of Montrose was invested with the insignia of the Garter, he handed back to the Sovereign those of the Thistle, and, as will be shown in Chapters IV and V, there were several other similar examples of return of insignia of junior orders on promotion to the Garter.

When Queen Victoria ascended the throne in 1837 she followed the example of Queen Anne in that she habitually wore some part of the insignia of the Garter, including a miniature collar, to which reference is made later.

As will have been noted from the foregoing, the insignia consisted originally merely of a garter worn round the leg, while the escutcheon of Saint George was embroidered on the left side of the mantle of the order. These garters were made of light-blue silk, with the motto embroidered thereon with gold thread, and they were fastened with a gold buckle. Later it came to be the custom for knights to provide themselves with garters of their own design and frequently to ornament these with precious stones in such a way that the letters of the motto were formed of diamonds, rubies or pearls. We read that the garter sent to the King of Portugal in 1455 was adorned with 'exceedingly precious jewels', while the Spanish ambassador, when writing to his sovereign, King Philip, stated that the garter which Queen Mary was sending him as a wedding gift was 'very richly jewelled and had cost eight thousand crowns'. The garter worn by King Charles the First on the scaffold was ornamented with over four hundred diamonds, while that worn by King Charles the Second had his miniature, surrounded by diamonds, in the hinge of the buckle with a jewelled engraving on the back of the pendant.

The garter described above which was worn by King Charles the First at his execution was seized by a Captain Preston, one of Cromwell's Captains of Horse. He sold it later to a Lord Mayor of London, from whom it was bought back eventually by King Charles the Second, and it is now in the Royal Collection.

As far as is known to the author, no jewelled garters or jewelled copies of other Garter insignia have been manufactured for knights under private arrangements during the last thirty years. Such insignia, having been made at the personal expense of knights, are their own property and are not returnable on the death of the holders. From time to time these jewelled insignia are offered for sale at auction by those into whose legal possession they have come, and this is quite permissible. A comparatively recent sale of jewelled Garter insignia was that made in London in 1959, when a garter, star and Lesser George made in diamonds for the late Lord Lonsdale were sold for £2,300. These are now in the Royal collection. Certain Garter insignia decorated with jewels by his grandfather, the eleventh

duke, were also sold by the present Duke of Bedford in 1962 for
£3,800.

The garter with which a knight is formally invested by the Sovereign
at the present day is made of very dark blue velvet about one inch
wide and having the letters of the motto attached thereto in gold
of the highest quality.

It has been remarked that, though the companions normally
wore the garter at all times, the monuments of both King Edward
the Third and the Black Prince do not portray them as wearing
a garter. This was obviously a deliberate omission because the
sculptured figures are dressed in armour.

In Hereford Cathedral, however, there is a garter on the effigy
of Sir Richard Pembrugge who was appointed a Companion of the
Garter in the reign of King Edward the Third. Similarly, in Saint
Paul's Cathedral there is a garter on the effigy of Sir Simon Burley,
a Knight Companion who was beheaded in 1388, while in Saint
Mary's Church in Warwick, a garter is shown on the tomb of the
celebrated earl of that name.

As stated earlier, originally the escutcheon of the patron saint
was embroidered, with a garter around it, on the left side of the
mantle which was presented to the Knight by the Sovereign at the
time of his election and installation. Later on it became the custom
for this escutcheon to be embroidered also on the habit or coat of
the knight.

King Charles the First caused 'Radii of Silver' to be added to
the embroidered badge so that they issued from the centre of the
cross making what was described as a 'Glory'. When first introduced these radii were of silver thread, and this Sovereign decreed
in 1625 that 'the escutcheon' must not be 'enriched with precious
stones'. But very soon afterwards he changed the embroidered star
to a metal one of gold and silver which was described as a 'cut star'.
The cross was superimposed on the star in enamel in a manner
similar to that used at the present time, and not many years later
some of the knights began to ornament their stars with diamonds
and rubies, in the same way as their garters were sometimes embel-
lished.

As stated earlier, it was King Henry the Seventh who introduced a collar for the order together with an appendant badge
which came to be known as the George. The George was of gold

and enamel and was a representation of Saint George, in armour, and in his right hand a spear with which he was piercing the throat of a dragon which lay prostrate beneath the feet of his horse. Later some knights had the George ornamented with precious stones according to their individual tastes, but, though it has varied from time to time in size and in the colour of the enamelling, its general design has remained almost unchanged throughout. A few portraits of the seventeenth century show Knights of the Garter wearing a George which is surrounded by a representation of a garter, but there is no record of such an addition ever having been authorised by statute. Queen Anne gave the Duke of Marlborough a particularly large and beautiful George set with magnificent diamonds. Later this George came into the hands of the Prince Regent and he gave it to the great Duke of Wellington. It is now in the possession of the present holder of that title, who lent it to Sir Winston Churchill so that he might wear it at the Coronation of Queen Elizabeth the Second. There are many fine specimens of these jewelled insignia in the Royal Collections. King Charles the First commanded, however, that though the George might be 'garnished and enriched at the pleasure of the Knight', the collar must never be 'made richer with stones or other things', and this has never been done.

The statutes published by King Henry the Eighth not only ordained that the weight of the gold collar should be thirty ounces Troy weight, but they also made a significant addition to the design as introduced by King Henry the Seventh. They ordered that in future the collar was to be 'composed of pieces in the fashion of garters in the midst of which garters were to be two double roses'. The first was to be 'a red rose with a white rose within' and the second 'a white rose with a red rose within'. Previously all the roses in the collar had been red in colour. King Henry the Eighth thus changed the Badge of Lancaster into his own 'Union Badge' of the Houses of Lancaster and York, declaring that he was in right of his mother the representative of York, while he and his father were of Lancaster. Edward the Sixth, the Boy King, for some reason that is not clear, altered all the roses of the collar back to red again. It is thought that this omission of the white roses was quite accidental and that he had no wish to dissociate himself from the 'Union of the Roses'. But the statutes of the order were never altered, and even at the present day they still ordain that the roses of the collar shall be alternately red and white, though in fact all the collars now in use contain only red roses. It is believed that the only collar made since the reign of King Edward the Sixth with alternate red and white roses is one which was made specially for Queen Victoria in the early part of her reign. This collar was made of an especially small size and of very light weight, and in later years was worn occasionally by Queen Mary (the consort of King George the Fifth), thus giving rise to an inaccurate story that a collar of this pattern, correct according to the statutes, was made specially at the request of Queen Mary.

As it was often inconvenient to wear the collar and the George, authority was given by King Henry the Eighth in 1519 for knights instead of these to wear on suitable occasions a small gold badge bearing a representation of Saint George slaying a dragon. This badge was worn from a thin gold chain or a blue riband in such a manner that it rested on the breast. After a time the design and fashion of this small badge, or, as it came to be known, the 'Lesser George', was left to the personal choice of the knight. Sometimes it was cut in Onyx, Agate, Garnet or precious stones. These thin gold chains, too, varied in design, according to the taste of the owner and the fashion of the time. The Lesser George worn by King Charles the First at his execution was made of onyx 'set with twenty-one large table-diamonds in the fashion of a garter', while on the back was a picture of Queen Henrietta Maria set in a case of gold and 'surrounded with another garter adorned with diamonds of equal size to those on the fore-side'.

It is believed that immediately before he was beheaded King Charles handed this Lesser George and the riband from which it was suspended to Bishop Juxon, who was in attendance on him. At the same time he pronounced the injunction 'Remember' to remind the bishop that this badge was to be delivered to the King's eldest son with the command that no effort was to be made in later days to take revenge on those responsible for his father's execution. Some say that one of Cromwell's adherents seized this badge from the bishop and that it was not until some time afterwards that it came into the possession of King Charles the Second, while others say that the bishop delivered it without delay safely into his hands. But it is universally agreed that either immediately after his father's execution or later on this badge did come into King Charles the Second's possession and was worn by him until his death, when it passed to King James the Second. There is reason to believe that when the latter gave up the throne he took this badge with him and that eventually it came into the possession of Prince Charles Edward, who was commonly known as the Count of Albany.

From the *History of the George Worn on the Scaffold by King Charles I*, written by Sir R. Payne-Gallwey, Bt., we learn that Sir Ralph Payne went to Italy in 1788, and it would seem that he endeavoured to purchase this badge for the Prince of Wales from the Duchess of Albany, the daughter of Prince Charles Edward, who had inherited all his 'jewels'. Sir Ralph's efforts, however, do not appear to have been successful. Some thought that this badge was sold in about 1796 by the residuary legatee of the Duchess of Albany to Lord Hertford, but investigation has shown that the badge bought by Lord Hertford was of eighteenth century foreign workmanship and did not contain the motto of the Order as all correctly-made Lesser George Badges did. Later, in 1951, this badge was sold by auction in London. The genuine royal badge came into the possession of the Marquis of Wellesley in 1811, and was in the hands of the Duke of Wellington in 1843 and has been kept as an heirloom by that ducal family ever since.

As explained previously, the Lesser George, pendant from a broad blue riband, from the time of King Charles the Second, came to be worn across the body 'belt-wise'. It is worn in this manner at the present day, when the collar and George are not being worn. The Lesser George is now made of high-quality gold without any other adornment and does not now vary in design or size.

At its first introduction it would seem that the riband of the Garter may have been black in colour, but later it changed from time to time to various shades of blue. In the year 1622 King James the First decreed that 'whereas the colour of the riband had not been particularly expressed in any article of the Statutes it should for the future always be of a sky-blue colour'. Though James the Second ceased to be King of England at the Revolution in 1688, neither he nor his descendants in the Stuart line relinquished either their pretensions to the crown or the sovereignty of the Order of the Garter. They not only continued to wear the Garter insignia themselves, but also continued to appoint new knights to the order.

The House of Stuart and those they had appointed knights always wore the riband of the sky-blue colour which was in use when that royal house held the throne of England. Therefore, soon after the accession of King George the First, in the early part of the eighteenth century, it was decided to distinguish the knights appointed by the real Sovereign from those who were receiving an appointment from the Pretender by changing the colour of the riband, the mantle and the actual garter to a dark blue colour. Unfortunately, the statutes of the order were not clearly altered to that effect, and even at the present day the mantle is described in the statutes as a 'Robe of Heavenly Blue'.

In 1950, on the instruction of King George the Sixth, the shade of blue then in use for the riband was changed slightly so that it should henceforth resemble exactly the 'kingfisher blue' colour of the riband preferred by Queen Victoria, a sample of which was produced by the crown jewellers concerned and approved by the king.

For the same reason as the colour of the riband and the garter were changed by King George the First to distinguish his knights from those of the Stuart princes, the shape of the star was at the same time also changed by him to a somewhat squarer pattern.

King George the Sixth, however, greatly preferred the shape of the Stuart Star and in 1946 he gave orders that all stars of Georgian pattern were to be altered to the Stuart pattern when they were handed back on the death of the holders.

It would appear that by the personal order of King Edward the Third at the time of the institution of the order the Garter mantles were made of 'sanguine-coloured' woollen cloth rather than any richer material so that attention might be specially drawn to this famous English-made commodity.

In the statutes published by King Henry the Fifth the colour of the mantle was described as blue, but during the reigns of King Henry the Sixth and King Henry the Seventh it was ordained that mantles should be made of 'sanguine-coloured velvet'. Though the clear and detailed statutes published by King Henry the Eighth ordained that the mantles should be of 'blue velvet of Heavenly colour', it seems that in fact the blue was of so deep a shade that it was close to purple, so much so that in King Edward the Sixth's reign the colour was described as 'blue-purple'. In 1636, in King Charles the First's reign, the colour was restored to what the king considered to be the correct shade, namely, 'not purple but a rich celestial blue'. The mantle in use at the present day is made of very dark blue velvet lined with white taffeta, having on the left side the badge of the order, namely, a silver escutcheon charged with a red cross and encircled with the garter and motto. The sealed pattern for this mantle is held at the Central Chancery (St. James's Palace). Though now a quite useless appendage to the mantle, the hood, which is made of red velvet, was in earlier times an essential part and was used as a covering for the head. It originally hung down the back of the mantle in a manner similar to the hood of a modern duffle-coat. In 1556 the hood was replaced as a head covering by a flat velvet cap adorned with ostrich feathers, and it was decreed that thenceforth the hood should be attached to the right shoulder so that the badge on the left shoulder would be clearly seen. In Queen Elizabeth's reign the flat cap became considerably more elevated, but King Charles the Second changed it to the velvet hat of the pattern worn nowadays, with an ostrich feather and with a metal badge in the form of the badge of Saint George on the side.

It was not until 1661, in the reign of King Charles the Second, that a scarlet undercoat, to be worn under the mantle, was introduced. This undercoat was not worn for very many years, and in the reign of King George the First it was replaced by a silver or white lace and linen doublet worn with knee-breeches and trunk-hose.

For a considerable time after the foundation of the order neither the mantle nor any of the insignia were handed back on the death of a knight companion, particularly as some of them were made of a special design at the expense of the knight himself. These valuable mementoes were often handed down as heirlooms or bequeathed in other ways. We find that the Earl of Southampton by his will in 1542 bequeathed to the King 'my great ship with all her tackle and my Collar of the Garter with my best George beset with diamonds'. About the same time the Duke of Suffolk left instructions in his will that a gold cup should be made out of his collar of the Garter and given to the King; while in 1555 Sir John Gage bequeathed his collar to be sold for charitable bequests and left his mantle to the College of Windsor.

None the less, it is clear that later on the insignia began to be returned on the death of the holders, for we find that on 19th April 1637 King Charles the First decreed that 'the Old Law be restored whereby all Persons receiving the Order of the Garter do take care that the ensigns be returned to the hands of the Sovereign after their deaths'. A little later, too, another instruction was issued decreeing that 'the Collar may not be sold, engaged, aliened or given for any need, cause or necessity whatever it be'.

Though the records show that in the seventeenth century a considerable quantity of Garter insignia was returned to the Sovereign, in some way a custom crept in whereby the insignia of deceased knights were claimed as his property by the Chancellor of the order, in the same way as Garter King of Arms apparently claimed as his perquisites the crests of deceased knights when they were taken down from the stalls of Saint George's Chapel, Windsor. In 1825 it was ordained that the Chancellor should receive one hundred pounds on the death of a knight in lieu of retaining his collar and badge, which were thenceforward to be returned to the crown so that they might be renovated and given to a newly appointed knight. Nowadays it is the custom on the death of a knight for the badge and star with which he was formally invested to be handed back to the Sovereign personally by the nearest male relative of the deceased knight. At the same time, the collar and George and the garter are returned informally direct to the Central Chancery, St. James's Palace. However, if there is no son or grandson of this knight living, then all the insignia of the order are usually returned informally direct to the Central Chancery of the Orders of Knighthood. Nevertheless, there have been occasions when for some special reason the Sovereign has graciously permitted the widow of a knight to retain some piece of the Garter insignia as a family heirloom. Included amongst these are the present Princess Royal, Princess Alice, Countess of Athlone, and the late Countess of Clarendon. Similarly, it has not, always been possible to recover at the time from foreign knights, whose countries were waging war against England, the insignia which should have been surrendered when their appointments were cancelled and annulled. Usually, however, unless they had become lost in some way, these insignia have eventually been recovered after the death of the foreign holders, including Kaiser Wilhelm of Germany.

Some insignia have been lost by fire or theft and, in the case of Field-Marshal Lord Kitchener, through enemy action when the cruiser in which he was travelling to Russia during the 1914—1918 war sank, presumably as a result of hitting an enemy mine.

From time to time insignia of the Garter, Thistle and Saint Patrick have been offered for sale by auction. If these insignia are the official, or as one might say 'ration', insignia with which the knight was formally invested on his appointment to the order in question, their return is demanded by the Central Chancery unless it can be proved by the would-be vendors that special authority was given by the Sovereign either to the knight or to his relatives for the insignia to be retained after his death as family heirlooms or for some sentimental reason.

Unfortunately, it was not until 1948 that any accurate record was kept to show by whom particular collars had been worn in the past, but now collars of all British Orders are marked by the Central Chancery in such a way that in future the names of former holders will be known. The object of this is to endeavour, if such an occasion should arise, to make it possible, when a new knight is appointed, for him to be invested with the collar which was worn by one or more of his ancestors. An interesting example of this is that the present Sovereign in May 1959 was able to give to King Olav the Fifth of Norway the Garter collar which had been worn by his father, King Haakon, for over fifty years. The present Marquess of Salisbury also wears the Garter Collar worn formerly by his father.

The Knights Companions elected at the time of the foundation of the order were chosen personally by King Edward the Third. After his initial selection, the system adopted during the remainder of his reign was that the existing knights submitted recommendations from which new knights were chosen to fill vacancies in the order. On the death of a knight a Quorum of not less than six knights presented for the consideration of the sovereign a list of nominees to fill the vacancy. Each knight submitted nine names. In theory the King chose the name with the greatest number of votes, but in fact the person eventually chosen was usually that one whom the Sovereign 'esteemed to be most profitable to the Crown and the Realm'. It is not certain exactly when this system of recommendation by a quorum of knights was discontinued. It would appear that, after a time, the choice of new companions became for several hundred years an entirely personal selection by the Sovereign, as it has now become once more.

The Stuart Sovereigns certainly seem to have filled the vacancies in this way and we know, for instance, that King Charles the Second gave the Garter to at least one of his illegitimate sons and to some of his favourites who in the general estimation were quite unworthy of the honour.

During the Hanoverian régime the political party in power claimed the right to choose new knights and to submit their names for the purely formal approval of the Sovereign. The reason for this change in procedure was that King George the First really knew nothing about the English aristocracy and the suitability of candidates for appointment to the Garter. He was therefore forced at the start of his reign to rely almost entirely on the recommendations of his ministers. Eventually an unwritten rule developed under which no appointments were made by the Sovereign unless they had been recommended by the Prime Minister. Thus appointment to the Garter became largely a political honour. Gradually the order began also to lose a good deal of its Christian character as a result of the appointments thereto for political reasons of certain non-Christian monarchs. For example, two Shahs of Persia were elected, one in 1873 and one in 1902, two Sultans of Turkey, one in 1876 and one in 1886, and three successive Emperors of Japan, in 1905, 1912 and 1929 respectively. None the less, when the King of Siam paid a state visit to London in 1907, King Edward VII absolutely refused to give him the Garter which he was expecting. Instead he offered the Victorian Chain, but the Siamese Government strongly advised their King not to accept it as they considered that he should not receive an award lower than that given to a Sultan or a Shah.

Under present regulations the Garter is never given to any person who is a non-Christian. Rather an extraordinary incident occurred in 1962. The Emperor of Japan, who had been a Knight of the Garter until his country went to war with Great Britain in the 1939—1945 war, had automatically forfeited this honour then. However, when Princess Alexandra visited Japan, permission was sought by his government for him to wear the Garter Star when the Princess attended a State Banquet in Japan. For some reason permission was given for him to wear the Garter insignia though he has never been restored to his companionship in the Order. According to the statutes these Garter insignia should have been surrendered, but, presumably for political reasons, this was not done. King George the Sixth was most anxious that the Garter and the Thistle (like the Order of Merit and the Royal Victorian Order) should be in the personal gift of the sovereign. In December of 1946 Mr. Attlee (then the leader of the Socialist Party in power) agreed with Mr. Winston Churchill (at that time H.M.'s Leader of the Opposition Party) that thenceforth those two great orders should be non-political honours and should in future be conferred by the Sovereign without any previous formal submission tendering the advice of the Prime Minister. It was understood, however, that prior to the publication of any new appointments the Sovereign would inform the Prime Minister.

Originally on his election to the order the banner, helmet-crest and sword of a knight were placed over his stall in Saint George's Chapel, Windsor, and these were taken down at his death, when, in exchange, a stall-plate bearing a representation of his arms and with his 'description' was placed at the back of the stall. This procedure was altered by King Henry the Eighth, who ordered that the stall-plate must be put up within a year of the knight's election to the order and that it was to remain there after his death as a permanent memorial. This procedure is still followed at the present day. Knights were at one time allowed to have these stall-plates made of whatever metal they themselves preferred, but we are told that 'unfortunately many of these noble and remarkable memorials were by sacrilegious hands torn off and embezzled'.

The only crimes for which a Knight of the Garter could be degraded were heresy, treason and cowardice. Felony was not an offence which justified degradation, and there is certainly at least one case in which a Knight of the Garter committed murder and yet was not degraded from the order.* The ceremony of degradation is described by Ashmole as follows:

When a Knight Companion is found guilty of any of the offences named in the Statutes of King Henry the Eighth the Sovereign commands Garter King of Arms to attend such Knight Companions as are appointed to go to the Convict-Knight and to take from him the George and Riband and the Garter. Publication of his crimes is then made by Garter King of Arms, after which one of the Heralds who will be placed ready on a ladder set to the back of the Convict-Knight's Stall shall take his Crest and violently cast it down into the Choir and after that his Banner and Sword.

* Lord Somerset in 1606.

All the Officers of the Order then spurn these achievements out of the Choir, into the Body of the Church, so out of the West Door, thence to the Bridge and over into the Ditch.

This form of degradation was carried out in the case of the Duke of Buckingham in 1522, in the thirteenth year of King Henry the Eighth's reign. Owing to the somewhat frequent charges of high treason which were made and upheld in earlier days degradation and subsequent execution of Knights of the Garter was not a particularly rare occurrence. Such degradation has not occurred, however, for a long time, and the most recent instance of deprivation was that of the Duke of Ormond in 1715.

When at the outbreak of the 1914–1918 war it was first suggested to King George the Fifth that the German Emperor and eight other foreigners who were Knights of the Garter and whose countries were at war with Great Britain should have their British honours cancelled, his first decision was that no action should be taken until they had themselves resigned their appointments and returned their insignia. The editors of certain newspapers, however, clamoured so excitedly for the immediate cancellation of the awards and the tearing-down and destruction of their banners and stall-plates in Saint George's Chapel, Windsor, that the King eventually gave approval for the unostentatious removal of the banners. He also commanded at the same time that the names of other enemy aliens should be removed from the lists of members of all other British orders of chivalry. The King was adamant, however, that the stall-plates at Windsor were to be allowed to remain as historical records, and, thanks to his foresight, these interesting memorials still exist.

Some of the insignia held by those who were enemies of this country in the 1914–1918 war was eventually recovered without undue publicity, notably those worn by the ex-Emperor of Germany, Kaiser Wilhelm the Second, while certain Garter insignia which were offered for sale by auction in London were claimed back by the Central Chancery, Saint James's Palace.

At the outbreak of the Second World War in 1939 action was taken to cancel and annul the appointments of all those whose countries were at war with Great Britain. A notable exception was King Carol of Roumania. Although his country became an enemy, he was not then on the throne there or even domiciled in

Roumania, and King George the Sixth allowed him to continue as a Knight of the Garter and to retain the insignia of other British orders of chivalry of which he was a member. Prince Paul of Yugoslavia also remained a Member of the Order of the Garter. In 1946 it proved impracticable for the King of Italy to return the Garter insignia worn formerly by his father, King Victor Emmanuel, as, except for the George, all the insignia had been stolen by looters during the German occupation of Rome. At his request, King George the Sixth permitted him to retain this George for sentimental reasons as a reminder of happier and friendlier days.

We learn from the writings of the early historian Bertrand Caprioli that:

> Anciently it was customary for Emperors to take under their more immediate care and protection such of the best, most experienced and valiant soldiers of gentilitial birth as had been either grievously wounded or maimed in the wars and to provide them with victuals and all sorts of necessaries for their support.

Similarly, when the Order of the Garter was founded, provision was made for the same number of 'poor or decayed' knights as there were companions of the order. King Edward the Third created an establishment of twenty-six 'deserving veteran knights' who, as a result of the wars, including sometimes the payment of large sums in ransom, found themselves 'inclining to poverty'. It was the intention of this monarch to provide a 'place of retirement and honourable asylum' for certain knights who had rendered outstandingly brave service in the wars and who through no fault of their own were now distressed financially and in some cases infirm through wounds and unable to support themselves. An additional object of the establishment was to provide suitable representatives of the Knights of the Garter so that when they were absent from Windsor their places might be taken at daily worship in the chapel for the 'honour of God and Saint George'. These representatives were designated *Milites Pauperes*, and they were originally chosen by the Knights of the Garter, each of whom was entitled to nominate his personal representative. Later these *Milites Pauperes* were selected by the Sovereign and that is the procedure at the present day, a list of suitable candidates being maintained by the Secretary of State at the War Office. Soon after this establishment had been formed, the description of these knights was changed to the 'Alms or Poor Knights'; but since 1833, in the reign of King William the Fourth, they have been more honourably described as the 'Military Knights of Windsor'. Since the fifteenth century it has not been essential for these Military Knights actually to have received the accolade.

Although for a brief period retired naval officers were eligible for appointment as military knights, those appointed now are always retired army officers of distinguished record. The present establishment is thirteen, including their 'Governor'. Under the will of Henry the Eighth a sum of money was settled on the Dean and Canons of Windsor so that suitable living accommodation adjacent to the Chapel might be provided for the 'Poor Knights'. A further amount was bequeathed so that a moderate financial allowance might be paid to each knight. The payment of this allowance is still made. A special uniform is still provided and the military knights still receive a free residence. These knights formerly wore mantles somewhat similar to those worn by Knights of the Garter, but they now wear a scarlet tail-coat with a white cross-sword-belt, a crimson sash and a cocked hat with a plume. Their duties are simple and entail very little beyond regular attendance at Saint George's Chapel and participation in certain ceremonies and processions such as installation ceremonies for Knights of the Garter and funerals of members of the Royal Family when these take place at Windsor. The present establishment consists of a Governor (Major-General Hakewill Smith) and eleven military knights.

As is the case with so many matters connected with the Garter, it is impossible to ascertain with accuracy the conditions under which ladies became associated with the order.

Some historians opine that ladies were entirely forgotten in the original constitution; but though there is no positive proof, it would appear probable that at its foundation there was a sort of quasi-admission to the order. The Queen and the wives of the knights certainly attended the annual banquets in Windsor Castle, and it would appear that they frequently wore dresses of the same material and colour as those of the mantles of the knights, and that these dresses were often embroidered with numerous small garters. On many occasions, too, it would appear that ladies wore on the left arm a garter similar to that worn on the left leg by a knight. They were described as 'Ladies of the Society of the Garter' or '*Dames de la Fraternité de Saint George*'. We read in the Chronicles of the order that Queen Philippa, the Founder's Consort, in 1351 made her offering at the annual service at Windsor, while it is recorded in the Wardrobe Accounts for 1358 that she attended the annual Feast of Saint George and 'for her attire on this occasion the King set aside five hundred pounds'. Again in 1379 the Wardrobe Accounts show that materials were issued for making 'Robes for the King and the other Knights of the Society of the Garter and also a robe of scarlet cloth for the King's mother and other Ladies recently received into the Society of the Garter, against the Feast of Saint George'. There are many other entries in the Wardrobe Accounts which give proof of the provision of robes for royal ladies in connection with Garter ceremonies. For instance, in the record of the Grand Feast in 1488 the Queen and the King's mother are described as wearing 'gowns of the Garter, the same as the King and the Lords were in'.

We read, too, of the provision during the reign of King Edward the Fourth of garters for certain ladies, similar in colour and design to those of the knights, except that they were 'to be worn on the left arm a little above the elbow'.

Additional proof that ladies wore these garters on the arm is to be found in the monumental effigies of ladies in various cathedrals and churches. Examples are the effigy in Ewelme Church of Alice Chaucer, wife of the Duke of Suffolk, K.G., and that of Margaret Byron, wife of Sir Robert Harcourt, K.G., in the Church of Stanton Harcourt, both in the County of Oxfordshire.

The romantic spirit of chivalry, including homage to ladies, faded greatly as a result of the bitter feelings brought about during the Wars of the Roses.

King Henry the Eighth is described by Nicolas as being 'altogether un-genial' to the continuance of participation by ladies in the Garter ceremonies. Nor did that monarch invite any ladies to wear the habits of the Garter, as had been the custom previously. His daughter, Queen Elizabeth, was equally opposed to the re-introduction of ladies, which is not surprising as notoriously she had little respect for her own sex and in fact often appeared to dislike and despise them. From certain records of this time it would appear that the artistic and courteous King Charles the First 'had it in mind to restore the former courtesys and honours' to ladies in connection with the Order of the Garter, but no doubt the troublous distractions caused by the distressing wars during his reign prevented him from doing so. From that time, except in the case of queens regnant, no ladies seem to have been admitted to or to have worn the habits of the order until the reign of King Edward the Seventh. At the time of his coronation he appointed his consort, Queen Alexandra, a Lady of the order. Both King George the Fifth and King George the Sixth conferred a similar honour on their respective consorts.

King George the Sixth also honoured his daughter, the Princess Elizabeth, similarly in 1947, and she and her husband, the Duke of Edinburgh, were invested with the insignia and installed at Windsor on Saint George's Day of the following year. At the same time a ruling was given that no letters in signification of this honour were to be placed after the names of ladies who had been invested with the Garter insignia, but that in formal documents they were to be described as 'Ladies of the Garter'.

In this connection it is interesting to note that, except when they have been appointed Ladies of the Garter or the Thistle, or Dames Grand Cross, or Dames of the Royal Victorian Order or the Order of the British Empire, very few Royal ladies other than Queen Mary have received the insignia of any British Order of Chivalry. Though the statutes of that order made no provision for the admittance of Ladies, Queen Mary was appointed a Knight Grand Commander of the Order of the Star of India in 1911 in celebration of her visit with King George the Fifth to India in that year, and occasionally Indian Princesses were appointed to the Indian Orders. Included among these were H.H. the Begum of Bhopal, G.C.S.I. in 1872 and later her daughters in 1904 (G.C.I.E.) and in 1910 (G.C.S.I.). Both of these ladies also received the Badge of the Order of the Crown of India which was the customary reward for very important Indian Princesses and senior wives of Rajahs.

It was a great day in the history of the Order of the Garter when King George the Sixth, who took so deep an interest in the orders of chivalry and who performed his part as Sovereign of these orders in so dignified and distinguished a manner, decided to revive fully and hold regularly the complete ceremonies of investiture and installation of the Order of the Garter. Processions in connection with the installation services at Saint George's, Windsor, had not been held as public spectacles for a considerable time.

On 7th December 1946 a chapter of the order was held at Buckingham Palace and six new knights, including four great service leaders—Alanbrooke, Portal, Montgomery and Mountbatten—were invested with their insignia. Field-Marshal Lord Alexander of Tunis would also have been invested that day if he had not been out of England because he was then holding the appointment of Governor-General in Canada. As stated earlier, the first installation service of the reign was held at Windsor on Saint George's Day, 1948.

It may be of interest to draw attention to the fact that there was in 1946 some criticism of the fact that another great war leader, Admiral of the Fleet Viscount Cunningham of Hyndhope, was not at the same time as those mentioned above elected a Knight of the Garter. It was, however, thought particularly suitable that, as a distinguished Scotsman, he should be appointed to the Order of the Thistle and this was done in 1945. There were precedents for such action, as Field-Marshal Earl Haig, the Scottish Commander-in-Chief of the British armies in France in 1918, had been made a Knight of the Thistle, while his predecessor, Field-Marshal Lord French, who was an Irishman, had been made a Knight of Saint Patrick. Many people, too, at that time felt regret that it had not been found practicable to keep the Order of Saint Patrick alive by appointing to it Field-Marshals Alanbrooke, Alexander, Montgomery and Dill, and certain other distinguished men who were members of ancient Irish families. But, as is explained in the chapter which deals with the Order of Saint Patrick, the position was somewhat 'delicate' and there was reason to believe that new appointments to that order would have caused considerable annoyance to the Government of the Irish Free State.

Since 1948 it has been customary, when any Knights of the Garter are due for installation, for an investiture ceremony to be held in the Throne Room at Windsor Castle on the morning of some date within a month or so of Saint George's Day—often on the first day of the Royal Ascot Week in June when the Court is at Windsor. This ceremony is attended by all Knights Companions of the order, and also by their wives. The wordings of the oath sworn by the new knights at this ceremony and of the Admonitions addressed to them in turn by the prelate and chancellor of the order when the several items of insignia are placed upon them are exactly the same as they were at the time of Henry the Eighth, and probably even earlier than that. The Admonitions are as follows:

Upon Putting on the Garter
To the honour of God omnipotent and in Memorial of the blessed Martyr Saint George, tie about thy leg, for thy Renown, this most noble Garter: Wear it as a symbol of the most illustrious Order never to be forgotten or laid aside, that hereby thou mayest be admonished to be courageous, and having undertaken a just war, with which thou shalt be engaged, thou mayest stand firm, valiantly fight, courageously and successfully conquer.

Upon Putting on the Riband and Lesser George
Wear this riband, adorned with the image of the Blessed Martyr and Soldier of Christ, Saint George, by whose imitation provoked thou mayest so overpass both prosperous and adverse encounters, that having stoutly vanquished thine enemies, both of body and soul, thou mayest not only receive the praise of this transient combat, but be crowned with the palm of eternal victory.

Upon Putting on the Mantle
Receive this robe of heavenly colour, the livery of this most excellent Order, in augmentation of thine honour, ennobled with the shield and red Cross of our Lord, by whose power thou mayest safely pierce troops of thine enemies and be over them ever victorious, and being in this temporal warfare glorious, in egregious and heroic actions, thou mayest obtain eternal and triumphant joy.

Upon Putting on the Collar and George
Wear this Collar about thy neck, adorned with the image of the blessed martyr and soldier of Christ (et cetera, as in the second Admonition above.

At the investiture ceremony the Admonitions are read in turn by the prelate and chancellor of the order and the several insignia are offered on a cushion to the Sovereign by Garter King of Arms, Black Rod, and the secretary of the order, in turn, so that the Sovereign may perform the ceremony of investiture. Two senior knights of the order assist the Sovereign in these ceremonies by placing the garter round the left leg of the new knight and by assisting the Sovereign in the fastening of the riband and Lesser George about the body of the new knight, and in the adjustment of the mantle and the collar.

In connection with the first investiture ceremony for the Order of the Garter held at Windsor Castle by King George the Sixth in 1948, the author was placed in a most awkward predicament. It is customary at an ordinary investiture held at Buckingham Palace, when the Sovereign is investing a knight by placing round his body the riband and badge of an order, for the hook and eye which fasten the ends of the riband to be very tightly clamped together beforehand, so that they cannot possibly come unfastened when the Sovereign is placing the riband over the head and shoulder of the knight. But, as at this special investiture at Windsor the King had arranged that he would have two Knights of the Garter standing there to assist him in putting on the ribands, he had decided that the hook and eye fastening each riband should not be clamped together, but should be left undone so that he himself could fasten them at the actual moment of investiture.

Unfortunately, no one had mentioned this arrangement to the author, who was responsible for providing the insignia at the appropriate moment. As a result, when the King endeavoured to manipulate the hook-and-eye fastening of the first riband, these were so tightly clamped that it was extremely difficult for him to undo them so that the riband could be placed round the body of Princess Elizabeth, who was the first to be invested. Luckily the riband which was being used for the princess was not new, and had come with the badge from the King's private collection, with the result that the hook and eye were reasonably pliant, and after some difficulty the King succeeded in unfastening them so that the riband might be placed round the princess and then re-fastened. But the author had on the table in front of him six more ribands with brand-new hooks and eyes which were all so tightly clamped that it seemed impossible to separate them without a suitable implement. By the greatest good luck the author discovered in his pocket a particularly thin sixpenny piece with which he succeeded in prising open the hooks and eyes just in time to place the insignia on the cushions held by the appropriate officer of the order so that these might be offered to the King. The look of disapproval which the author received from Queen Mary, who was sitting immediately next to the insignia table, at this apparently inexcusable mistake will never be forgotten. It was not until a year or so later that an opportunity came to explain the incident. To the author's great relief, Her Majesty, unlike Queen Victoria on another occasion, 'was amused'.

After the investiture ceremony at Windsor is concluded, a state luncheon is held in the Banqueting Room. This is attended by the Royal Family, by all the Companions of the Order and their ladies, and by the Officers of the Order. The beauty and magnificence of the banqueting-table with its priceless gold plate, antique china and beautiful table appointments have to be seen to be believed.

After the banquet all the knights and ladies of the order, together with the prelate, chancellor and other officers of the order, all robed in their mantles, move in procession, watched by a great crowd of spectators, from the castle, down the hill, which is lined with troops, to Saint George's Chapel, where the formal installation service takes place.

It should be noted that the Prince of Wales has always been a constituent part of the order. Though Prince Charles, the present Prince of Wales, has not yet received knighthood or been invested with the insignia of the Garter, his name was entered on the official list of Companions from the date on which the Queen announced his title as Prince of Wales, namely 26th July, 1958. He will be invested in due course on some date selected as being particularly appropriate by the Queen.

George the Fifth appointed the then Prince of Wales a Knight of the Garter on 10th June 1911, at the age of seventeen, so that he could wear the mantle and insignia of the Garter at his father's coronation. The reason for this was that, as he had not yet reached the age of twenty-one, he was not entitled to take his seat in the House of Lords or to wear the robes of a peer. The prince's younger brothers, Prince Albert (later King George the Sixth), Prince Henry (later the Duke of Gloucester) and Prince George (later the Duke of Kent) were not made Knights of the Garter until they attained the age of twenty-one.

At this point it may be of interest to note that in earlier days children of the Sovereign sometimes received the insignia of the Garter at a very young age. We read that in 1525 King Henry the Eighth gave the Garter to Sir Henry Fitzroy, the king's natural son by Lady Elizabeth Talboys, the boy being then seven years of age.

In 1603 King James the First appointed his son, Prince Henry (afterwards Prince of Wales), to be a Companion of the order at the age of eleven years, while in 1611 he also made his second son, Charles, Duke of York (afterwards King Charles the First), a Companion at the age of eleven. King Charles the First gave the Garter to his son in 1638, he being then eight years of age.

For a greater part of its existence the Garter was the perquisite of the higher nobility, and, though this was not so at the time of its institution, for a considerable period afterwards admission was limited to members of the Peerage. Its value in the estimation of the world lay in its rigid exclusiveness. It was—and still is—coveted not only by the heads of the noblest families in England, but equally desired by foreign monarchs and princes. A biographer of Lord Chesterfield wrote of his ambition to become a Knight of the Garter and quoted a remark by him to Sir Robert Walpole, the Prime Minister, to the effect that so great was its reputation abroad that 'the blue riband would add two inches to his size when he entered a drawing-room in a foreign country'. There have been a certain number of exceptions in whose cases, though they were 'Commoners', the Garter has been given, particularly in Tudor times. Samuel Pepys mentions in his Diary also two 'Commoner Recipients', namely General Monk, who was instrumental in restoring Charles the Second to his throne, and Admiral Montagu, whose fleet in the same year provided the escort from Holland to Dover. Another commoner to receive the Garter was Sir Robert Walpole, in 1726. He was the first commoner to receive it after the Restoration and did not become an earl until much later. In more recent times Sir Edward Grey received the Garter in 1912 (some four years before he became Viscount Grey of Fallodon), while Arthur Balfour received the Garter in 1922, being created an Earl two months later. Sir Austen Chamberlain received the Garter in 1925. Then, of course, more recently it was given to Sir Winston Churchill in 1953 and Sir Anthony Eden in 1954. Even more recently Sir Gerald Templer was appointed a Knight of the Garter on 16th September, 1963.

In spite of its great reputation, however, there have been from time to time some uncomplimentary remarks about the order. Lord Palmerston is reported to have remarked somewhat cynically that the knights were usually chosen 'more because of their social standing than for any great thing they had achieved'.

Then there is the frequently quoted remark of Lord Melbourne: 'I like the Garter. There is no damned merit about it.'

Again, in 1851, a certain Lady Ashburton, the relative of a Garter knight, is reported to have boasted that 'the Garter is the only honour which cannot be earned merely by talent or hard work'.

None the less, examination of the list of Companions of the order at the present day will prove that criticisms of that kind now would be as inaccurate as they would be unkind. All the present knights have rendered outstanding service either as successful military leaders, or as eminent statesmen, or by long and valuable, though sometimes unspectacular, service as Lieutenants of Counties or in some similar office of importance to this country or to the British Commonwealth.

The order, with the dates of appointment now consists of the following:

Sovereign
The Queen

Lady of the Garter
Queen Elizabeth the Queen Mother, 14 December, 1936

Royal Knights Companions
Duke of Edinburgh, 19 November, 1947
Prince of Wales, 26 July, 1958
Duke of Gloucester, 31 March, 1921
Duke of Windsor, 12 December, 1936

Knights Companions
Earl Stanhope, 1 January, 1934
Duke of Norfolk, 11 May, 1937
Duke of Beaufort, 11 May, 1937
Marquess of Salisbury
Admiral of the Fleet Earl Mountbatten of Burma
Marshal of the Royal Air Force Viscount Portal
   of Hungerford   3 December, 1946
Field-Marshal Earl Alexander of Tunis
Field-Marshal Viscount Montgomery of Alamein
Duke of Portland
Earl of Scarbrough   12 May, 1948
Duke of Wellington, 9 April, 1951
Sir Winston Spencer-Churchill, 24 April 1953
Earl of Avon, 20 October, 1954

Earl of Iveagh, 23 April, 1955
Earl Attlee, 7 April, 1956
General Lord Ismay ⎫
Lord Middleton ⎭ 23 April, 1957
Field-Marshal Viscount Slim, ⎫
Duke of Northumberland ⎭ 23 April, 1959
Earl of Radnor, 23 April, 1960
Lord Wakehurst, 23 April, 1962
Field-Marshal Sir Gerald Templer, 16 September, 1963
Earl Alexander of Hillsborough ⎫
Viscount Cobham ⎭ 9 April, 1964

Extra Knights and Ladies of the Garter

King Leopold III (formerly King of the Belgians), 2 Dec. 1935
King Paul of Yugoslavia, 19 July, 1939
Prince Frederik IX of Denmark, 8 May, 1951
King Gustav VI of Sweden, 28 June, 1954
The Emperor Haile Selassie of Ethiopia, 14 October, 1954
Queen Juliana of the Netherlands, 25 March, 1958
King Olav V of Norway, 29 May, 1959
Baudouin, King of the Belgians, 14 May, 1963
Paul, King of the Hellenes, 9 July, 1963

Officers of the Order

Prelate	Bishop of Winchester
Chancellor	Marquess of Salisbury
Register	Dean of Windsor
Garter King of Arms	Sir Anthony Wagner
Gentleman Usher of the Black Rod	Air Chief Marshal Sir George Mills
Secretary	Hon. Sir George Bellew

At some periods in the past it seems to have been the custom to admit to the order somewhat automatically the heads of certain aristocratic families. Amongst the families which during the past six hundred years seem to have been represented most frequently are the following: Howard, Percy, Grey, Stanley, Neville, Talbot, Cavendish, Cecil, Lennox, Manners, Mortimer, Somerset, Russell, Bohun, and Mowbray.

It is of interest, in this connection, to note that the comparatively recent appointment to the order of the present Duke of

Northumberland (on 23rd April 1959) brought to seven the total of members of that family who have been Companions of the Garter during the past two hundred years.

The appointment of Lord Cranborne in 1946 provided an example of a father (the Marquess of Salisbury) and son both being Knights of the Garter at the same time. There was an earlier example of this in the Woodville family, as the father-in-law and brother-in-law of King Edward the Fourth were both Companions of the order at the same time. The third Duke of Norfolk and his son, the Earl of Surrey, were also both K.G.s in the period 1541–1547.

Rarely have brothers, apart from members of the Royal Family, been knights at the same time, but at the foundation of the order, the Earl of Warwick and his brother, Sir John Beauchamp, were both made Companions of the order, as were the Earl of Salisbury and his brother Lord Fauconsberg in 1441 and two sons of the Earl of Salisbury in 1462.

Also at the foundation of the order, an uncle and a nephew were both made Knights Companions, namely Sir Thomas Holand and Sir Otho Holand, while in 1937 Viscount Fitzalan of Derwent and his nephew, the Duke of Norfolk, were both Companions.

Writing about a hundred years ago, Nicolas reckoned that less than seven hundred knights, including foreigners, had been appointed to the order since its foundation. Probably, therefore, it is reasonably accurate to state that only about one thousand persons have received this high award during a period of over six hundred years.

In the early days of the order, a Garter knight had to pay certain fees 'proportioned according to his state and dignity', ranging from very high charges for a monarch or prince downwards through the various grades of nobility to a 'simple knight' who escaped with payment of comparatively moderate fees. But in addition to these 'fees' there were many officers of the order and others, including servants, who had to be rewarded either financially or by other means described somewhat vaguely as 'benevolences'. Amongst these were the registrar and usher of the order and numerous marshals of the hall, vicars, vergers, sextons, choristers and others. As they usually do, these fees and benevolences had a tendency to increase steadily, and by the time of the reign of King Charles the First it had become a very expensive matter to become a Knight of the Garter. The fees payable nowadays however do not amount to much more than

£100, this being the sum required to pay for the knight's banner, crest and stall-plate in the chapel of the order at Windsor.

There have been several instances in which a Prime Minister has refused the Garter, the earliest-known case being that of William Pitt the Younger. Sir Robert Peel also declined the honour. Mr. Asquith refused the offer of the Garter by King George the Fifth when it was made to him at the time of his resignation of the premiership in December 1916. He is reported to have written:

> I have had the honour of serving Your Majesty continuously from the first day of your reign. Through times of much difficulty and peril Your Majesty has honoured me with unstinting confidence and unwavering support. I desire no higher distinction.

King George renewed the offer to him when, as Lord Oxford, he was defeated in an election for the Chancellorship of Oxford University, and on that occasion the offer was accepted gratefully.

The Garter was also offered to Mr. Neville Chamberlain on his resignation as Prime Minister in 1940, but he was by then a very sick man and beyond interest in anything of that nature. Mr. Winston Churchill also 'begged leave to decline the offer' of the Garter when his party was defeated in the general election of 1945, as he felt it would not be appropriate for him to accept an honour of any kind at that time. He also declined a second offer on a later occasion, but when the Garter was no longer a political honour and was offered to him a third time by Queen Elizabeth the Second on the occasion of her Coronation in 1953 he was proud to accept it. On the occasion of the first refusal, it was suggested to the King that he might consider offering this honour to Mr. Anthony Eden, but when he was 'sounded' by the King's representative he too begged leave to decline it as he did not feel that it would be right for him to receive it when the chief of his party had thought it correct not to accept it. Mr. Eden eventually accepted a second offer when it was made to him by Queen Elizabeth in the year following that in which it had been accepted by Sir Winston Churchill. Mr. Harold Macmillan, a former Prime Minister recently begged leave to decline this honour.

There have only been a few known occasions when members of the peerage have refused the Garter. One of these was when Lord

Shaftesbury, the great philanthropist, who, as modest as he was charitable, declined the honour when it was first offered to him by Queen Victoria, as he did not feel 'worthy of it'. Eventually, however, he too accepted it when it was offered a second time.

In 1937, the Coronation Year of King George the Sixth, as the retirement of the Bishop of Oxford, who was then the holder of the office of Chancellor of the Order of the Garter, was imminent, the Bishop of Salisbury submitted to the King his petition that this great office might be restored to the See of Salisbury. The Bishop of Salisbury based his claim on the Charter of King Edward the Fourth in 1476, granting the office of Chancellor of the Order of the Garter to the occupants of the See of Salisbury 'for ever'. As a result of this petition the King ordered that a full investigation of the facts should be made by Garter King of Arms. The investigation yielded the following facts:

The office of Chancellor was created by King Edward the Fourth by letters patent under the Great Seal on 10th October 1475, in favour of Richard Beauchamp, Bishop of Salisbury, and to his successors. When Bishop Beauchamp died in 1482 his successor as Chancellor was the new Bishop of Salisbury, who held the appointment until his death in 1485. There is considerable uncertainty as to how many Bishops of Salisbury subsequently held the office of Chancellor. Ashmole, in his writings, stated that successive Bishops of Salisbury continued in that office until 1553, when Sir William Cecil, then Principal Secretary of State, was made Chancellor.

Sir Harris Nicolas, however, in his history, asserted that no Bishop of Salisbury held the office after 1485, and he quoted from a letter from Cardinal Wolsey to King Henry the Eighth wherein it was shown that in 1523 the Chancellor of the Order was the Lord Chamberlain of that time, namely the Earl of Worcester.

Moreover, when the statutes of the Garter were rewritten in 1519, it was ordained that 'as the office of Chancellor is very noble and of great charge it is necessary that it shall be held by an honourable and eminent person who must be either a Prelate of the Church or, if a secular person, a Knight of Noble Blood of great learning, reputation and experience.' These statutes prove clearly that the office was not then thought to be vested in the See of Salisbury, and there is no doubt that, as stated above, in 1553 in the reign of King Edward the Sixth, Sir William Cecil (afterwards Lord Burleigh) was appointed Chancellor.

On her accession, Queen Mary (the daughter of King Henry the Eighth) dismissed Lord Burleigh, but she appointed another layman, Sir William Petre, in his place. After his death in 1572, the office of Chancellor was held by a number of other laymen, the last of whom, Sir Edgar Dyer, died in 1608.

In that year the Bishop of Salisbury submitted a petition to King James the First requesting that the office of Chancellor might be restored to the See of Salisbury in accordance with the Charter of King Edward the Fourth, which is referred to above. However, on the advice of the judges, the King refused this petition.

In 1669 Dr. Seth Ward, Bishop of Salisbury, again submitted a petition to King Charles the Second, who referred it for consideration by a chapter of the knights. On their recommendation the King ordained that the Bishop of Salisbury and his successors should in future hold the office of Chancellor, and this they did until 1837. In that year the county of Berkshire was detached from the diocese of Salisbury and included in the diocese of Oxford, and at the command of King William the Fourth the office of Chancellor was transferred from the See of Salisbury and attached permanently to the See of Oxford, by which it was held until 1937. In this year King George the Sixth ordained that this appointment was not the perquisite of any prelate and should henceforth be held by a Knight Companion of the Order of the Garter. Accordingly he appointed the Duke of Portland, who held the appointment until his death in 1943, when he was succeeded by the Earl of Halifax, who died in 1959. The present Chancellor is the Marquess of Salisbury.

One of the rights of the Knights of the Garter is that at coronations they play a special part in the Ceremony of Anointing.

As has been the procedure at similar ceremonies in the past, at the coronation of the present Queen, after Her Majesty had been disrobed of her crimson robe by the Lord Great Chamberlain, assisted by the Mistress of the Robes, she proceeded to the altar. She was then seated in King Edward's Chair wherein the ceremony of anointing was performed by the Archbishop. During this ceremony four Knights of the Garter held over her a rich silken canopy.

CHAPTER IV

The Most Ancient and Most Noble Order of the Thistle

Abbot Justinian, an eminent Scottish historian of ancient days, stated in his *Chronicles* that the Order of the Thistle, sometimes known as the Order of Saint Andrew, was founded in the year 809 when King Achaius made an offensive and defensive league, or alliance, with the Emperor Charlemagne. Andrew Favine, in his *Theatre of Honours and Knighthood*, and various other historians have also suggested that the order was founded by an ancient King of Scotland, about A.D. 800. Some opine that it was instituted to celebrate the amity between Scotland and France in the reign of Charles the Seventh of France. There is, however, no real proof of this legendary antiquity. None the less, as will be explained later, when the order was placed on a regular foundation in 1687 it was emphasised most definitely that it was not being instituted as a new order, but that what was being effected was the revival of a very ancient Companionship of Knights. In 1578 John Lesley, Bishop of Ross and a famous Scottish antiquary, wrote in his *History of Scotland* that Hungus, King of the Picts, being attacked by Athelstan, King of the West Saxons, called to his aid Achaius, King of the Scots, who joined him with ten thousand fighting men. Bishop Ross narrated how, while the night was being spent in supplication to the Almighty, Saint Andrew appeared to Hungus in a vision and promised him complete victory over his enemy. The Bishop told how at the dawn of day there appeared in the heavens a representation of the Cross on which Saint Andrew had suffered martyrdom—a cross in the shape of an ✗. Hungus and his armies were so 'uplifted and encouraged' by this promise that they attacked fiercely and confidently and completely routed their enemy at Athelstan's Ford in East Lothian.

To celebrate this glorious victory, so runs the legend, King Hungus built a temple in honour of Saint Andrew, and thenceforward bore on his standard the cross of that saint. Many antiquaries cast doubt on this legend because they say that King Achaius died some time before the reign of King Athelstan (A.D. 924 to 940). It would be unwise, however, to condemn this legend on that point alone, because the period of the reign of Achaius is somewhat uncertain. Nisbet in his *System of Heraldry*, published in the sixteenth century, was another who favoured the belief that King Achaius was the founder of the Order of the Thistle and he claimed that it was among the most ancient orders of chivalry in Europe and that it should certainly take precedence over the Order of the Garter to which it was senior by date of institution. Other Scottish historians have argued similarly that, as the order was instituted earlier than the Garter, it should, at least in Scotland, rank as the senior order of the two kingdoms. In this connection it is of interest to note that at the time of the Coronation of King George the Second in 1727 the Knights of the Thistle presented a petition to the Sovereign requesting that, in the same way as the Garter was the chief order in England, the Thistle, which had been instituted before the union of the two kingdoms, should be ranked as the chief order in Scotland. History does not provide us with the answer to this petition, but it seems clear that it did not meet with royal approval, as the Garter everywhere retained its place at the head of the Order of Precedence and there were after this date several instances of Knights of the Thistle handing back the insignia of this 'junior' order on 'promotion' to the Garter. Examples of this are the Earl of Bute in 1762, the Earl of Carlisle in 1793 and the Duke of Buccleuch in 1801, while the Marquess of Queensberry and the Duke of Montrose handed back their Thistle insignia during the Regency. The most recent case of handing back Thistle insignia on election to the Garter is that of the Earl of Zetland in 1872.

Except for members of the Royal Family, during the early part of the nineteenth century only one Knight of the Thistle was given written authority to retain his Companionship of that order after he had been elected to the Garter. This was the Duke of Roxburgh, who was given this privilege as a special mark of favour. More recently, however, the Marquess of Linlithgow, who was elected to the Garter in 1943, was allowed to retain his appointment to the Thistle, which had been made in 1928.

It was an almost unknown event, except for royalty, for a person who was a Knight of the Garter to be made subsequently a Knight of the Thistle, though this did occur occasionally; a former Earl of Rosebery, for instance, who had been elected to the Garter in 1892, was made a Knight of the Thistle in 1895, while the Earl of Strathmore (father of Queen Elizabeth the Queen Mother) held both the Garter and the Thistle. It would be most unlikely nowadays for any person other than a member of the Royal Family or a foreign monarch to be appointed both to the Garter and the Thistle, though it may be noted that during the past sixty years two field-marshals who were already Knights of Saint Patrick also became Knights of the Garter. These were Lord Roberts, in 1902, and Lord Kitchener, in 1915, while even more recently the Duke of Abercorn, who had been made a Knight of Saint Patrick in 1922, was made a Knight of the Garter in 1928. As explained, the normal rules for wearing insignia have not always been followed by members of the Royal Family. King William the Fourth, for instance, at his accession and at the funeral of his brother (King George the Fourth) wore the collars of the Garter and the Thistle, while a portrait of King George the Fourth, hanging in the State Dining Room at Buckingham Palace, shows him wearing the collars of three British orders. It should be noted that under present rules not more than one collar of an order is ever worn at one time.

Though we know that Saint Andrew (who was said to have been martyred by crucifixion in A.D. 69 at Patrae in Achaia) was from ancient days accepted as the tutelar saint of Scotland, there is nothing to prove that the thistle was adopted as the national badge in equally early days.

Whereas the gold coins of Robert the Second (1371–1390) and of several of his successors bore a representation of Saint Andrew and his cross, a representation of a thistle did not appear on coins until the latter part of the fifteenth century. In fact it was not formally declared to be the official badge and symbol of Scotland until that time, when it was selected by King James the Third as being 'a native Scottish plant of which the self-protective qualities illustrated most aptly the Royal motto *In Defence*'.

Support of this theory is provided by the fact that there was included in the effects of King James the Third, who died in 1488, 'the jewel of Saint Andrew bearing the badges of Thissils and a Unicorne'.

We find another version in Pinkerton's *History of Scotland*, however, wherein we read that in the year 1503 King James the Fourth of Scotland instituted a 'Badge of the Order of Saint Andrew or the Thistle, which was considered by some antiquaries to have been a national badge in much earlier times'. It is not clear, however, whether or not this badge was to be worn solely by the monarch and his successors or whether it was the Sovereign's badge of a fraternity of knights.

We read that when King James the Fifth of Scotland went to France in 1535 to marry Magdalen, daughter of King Francis the First, he bestowed insignia of the 'Order of the Burr or Thissil' on the French king and also on a certain Count de Montmorency. Another chronicler states too that later in his reign King James the Fifth created Lord Seaton a Knight Companion of the Order of Saint Andrew.

That the collar of an order was worn by the Kings of Scotland at least as early as the sixteenth century is proved by the fact that on his 'Gold Bonnet pieces', which were struck in 1539, King James the Fifth is portrayed as wearing a collar of what were described by a contemporary writer as 'Thistle heads and knots alternately'. It has been suggested that about the year 1532 King James the Fifth instituted this collar as part of the insignia of his Scottish Order in imitation of the collars of the Golden Fleece and the Garter, both of which he had received at about that time.

It may be noted that the Great Seal of Queen Mary, made in about 1558, included a collar fashioned of alternate Thistles and 'S's'.

In Haydn's *Book of Universal Information* the foundation of the Order of Saint Andrew was stated to have occurred in about the year 1535, and that it consisted of the King himself as Sovereign, and twelve other knights in 'respectful imitation of Christ and his Twelve Apostles'. He stated also that 'in 1542 King James died and the Order was discontinued about the time of the Reformation'.

On the whole it seems probable that, though some kind of Scottish order of chivalry existed in the fifteenth and sixteenth centuries and possibly much earlier, the Order of the Thistle did not become an organised association of knights and an established order of chivalry with a statutory foundation until it was revived under new rules by King James the Second of England (and the Seventh of Scotland) on 29th May 1687. A careful scrutiny of the records of earlier times has failed to reveal any mention of a person being officially styled a 'Knight of the Order of the Thistle' before this year. According to Haydn, on the date of its revival in 1687 the following were appointed knights of the order:

Duke of Gordon
Marquis of Atholl
Earl of Arran
Earl of Moray
Earl of Perth
Earl of Seaforth
Earl of Dumbarton
Earl of Melfort

Joseph Edmondson (Mowbray Herald) in his *Complete Body of Heraldry*, published in 1780, agrees that this list was correct, though he places them in a different order of seniority.

It must be repeated, however, that in the new statutes which were published on 29th May 1687 it was stated very clearly that King James

Desired to make mention of the fact that he was merely reviving the order and that it was his royal predecessor, Achaius, King of the Scots, who had actually instituted this most ancient and most noble Order of the Thistle which had consisted and was now to continue to consist of the Sovereign and twelve Knights-Brethren in allusion to the Blessed Saviour and his Twelve Apostles.

The statutes stated also that the order had been founded under the protection of 'Our Blessed Lady and the Holy Apostle Saint Andrew, Patron of Scotland, for defence of the Christian religion and in commemoration of the signal victory gained by King Achaius over Athelstan, King of the Saxons. The statutes confirmed that:

It was most certain by the consent of ancient and modern historians and by several other authentic proofs that the Order of the Thistle had existed in great glory and splendour for many hundreds of years.

The statutes declared also that numerous foreign kings and princes had been knights of the order which had 'always been held in great honour in all places wherever Christian valour advanced the glory of the Cross, until the unfortunate rebellion against His Majesty's great-grand-mother, Mary, Queen of Scots'. They explained that on that sad occasion the splendour of the monarchy fell into contempt while the Ancient Order of the Thistle, with all its rites and ceremonies, was extinguished owing to the rebellious desertion of some knights and the necessity for others to fly to foreign countries to save their lives.

It was decreed that the habits were to be a doublet and trunk hose of cloth of silver, stockings of pearl-coloured silk, white leather shoes, garters and shoe-strings of blue and silver, the breeches and sleeves of the doublet to be 'decently garnished' with silver and blue ribands. A surcoat of purple velvet lined with white taffeta was to be worn, girt about the middle with a purple sword-belt edged with gold with a sword in a purple scabbard.

Over all this was to be worn a mantle of green velvet embroidered with thistles of gold, while on the left shoulder was to be embroidered in silver the image of Saint Andrew with his cross.

The collar was to consist of thistles and sprigs of rue with a gold badge appendant, showing Saint Andrew, enamelled with his gown green and the surcoat purple, bearing before him his cross, enamelled white or 'if in diamonds consisting of the number of thirteen just'.

The cap was to be of black velvet adorned with jewels and with a large 'plume of white feathers and with a black Egret or Heron's top in the middle'.

The Statutes ordained that 'whereas it had been the ancient custom for the Sovereign and Knights to wear the Badge of the Order pendant from a chain of gold or precious stones round the neck, now that the use of ribands had been brought in since the ancient order had been left off, in future the Badge was to be worn from a purple-blue riband'. The badge was to have on one side the image of Saint Andrew, enamelled or in precious stones, and on the other a thistle, enamelled in gold and green and round it the motto *Nemo me impune lacessit*. Upon the left breast of the coat an embroidered star was to be worn with the motto of the order surrounding a thistle of gold on a blue field.

It was decreed that before anyone could be admitted to the order he must have been dubbed, and the knights had to swear to defend the Christian religion and their Sovereign and the other brethren of the order.

There is one particularly interesting point contained in these statutes, namely, an instruction that 'in all time coming His Majesty and his Royal Successors shall wear the badge of the Order of the Thistle on the riband of the Order of the Garter or in whatever other ways His Majesty shall think fit'.

After the abdication of King James the Second in 1688 it is clear that the order fell into desuetude and it remained in abeyance during the reign of King William and Queen Mary (1689–1702).

However, when Queen Anne came to the throne in 1702 the Order of the Thistle was resuscitated and remodelled on the lines of the Garter. The statutes, which were re-published on Queen Anne's instructions on 31st December 1703, repeated in full the story of the institution of the Order by King Achaius, as given in the statutes published by King James the Second of England in 1687. They emphasised the Queen's desire to revive and restore the order as evidence of her appreciation of the duty and affection shown by the ancient kingdom of Scotland to her father and to herself.

The number of knights was, as before, to be twelve, but she changed the colour of the riband to green instead of purple and decreed that it was to be worn in a manner exactly similar to that for the Garter, namely 'over the left shoulder across the body and tied under the right arm'. The new statutes also repeated the interesting instruction contained in the statutes of King James the Second, namely, that the Queen and her royal successors should 'in all time coming, as they might think fit, wear the Badge of the Thistle on the Riband of the Garter'. If this rule were to be revived now it would give great pleasure to the Queen's Scottish subjects.

One portrait of Queen Anne shows her wearing a somewhat unusual badge from a Garter Riband. According to a description written at that time this badge bore on one side a representation of Saint George within a garter, while on the other there was a representation of Saint Andrew.

The statutes decreed that in future all insignia must be returned to the Sovereign on the death of a knight.

The fees appointed as payable by knights on admission to the order were as on the following page.

	£	s.	d.
To Secretary of the Order	55	11	1⅓
To Commissioner's Servants	8	6	7⅔
To Sextons, Ringers of Bells, etc.	5	11	1⅓
To the Usher of the Order	8	6	7⅔
To the Queen's Usher	5	11	1⅓
To Lyon's Office, Heralds and Trumpeters	27	15	6⅔
	111	2	2

Under a statute published on 17th February, 1714, by the command of King George the First, a star was instituted. This was to be worn in the form of an embroidered 'paste-board and tinsel' star which was sewn on the coat. At the same time the collar-badge was enlarged, with rays of gold going out from it, making the form of a 'Glory'. It should be noted that it was not until about 1864 that a metal star, made of silver and enamel, was introduced.

A statute published on 17th July 1717 ordained that in future new knights selected to fill vacancies should be chosen by a chapter of the knights which must consist of 'three Knights at least besides the Sovereign'.

Up till 1720 the fees remained unchanged, but in February of that year it was ordained that 'as it had been represented that the fees formerly appointed were too mean and not suitable to the dignity of the Order', they were to be increased as follows:

	£
To the Secretary	100
To Lyon King of Arms	70
To the Usher of the Green Rod	70
To the Six Heralds	30
To the Six Pursuivants	18
To the Six Trumpeters	9
	297

It will be observed that even two hundred years ago the cost of living was rising rather sharply—for Knights of the Thistle at least!

On 17th July 1821 King George the Fourth, to mark his coronation, increased the number of knights temporarily to sixteen, while in 1827 it was permanently increased to that number. Under a number of statutes published from time to time by order of Queen Victoria various members of the Royal Family were admitted as Extra Knights in addition to the statutory number of sixteen.

By the year 1905 the admittance fees paid by a knight had increased to £347, but in that year, as these fees were considered excessive, new arrangements were made to meet certain expenses from an official source, and it was ruled thenceforth that a knight would only have to pay the sum of £50 *in toto*.

The chapel of the order is in Saint Giles Cathedral, Edinburgh, and when practicable a service of the order is held each year.

In 1962 no foreigners had been admitted to the order for over two hundred years. It caused some surprise therefore when King Olav V of Norway, who was already a Knight of the Garter, was appointed an Extra Knight of the Thistle in October of that year.

Although in the official order of precedence a Knight of the Thistle ranks next after a Knight of the Garter, there are still some in Scotland who claim that the Thistle is not only a more ancient order than the Garter but also more exclusive.

The Anniversary Day of the order is the 30th November, Saint Andrew's Day.

The insignia of the order are now as follows: a mantle of green velvet bound with taffeta and tied with tasselled cordons of green and gold and having on its left side a figure of Saint Andrew bearing his cross, surrounded by a circlet of gold bearing the motto of the order—*Nemo me impune lacessit*: a collar of gold made in the form of alternate thistles and sprigs of rue, enamelled in proper colours, and pendent from the collar the badge or jewel, a golden image of Saint Andrew in green gown and purple surcoat, bearing before him the cross, enamelled in white, the whole surrounded by rays of gold: a star in silver in the shape of Saint Andrew's cross, with other rays issuing between the points of the cross, and in the centre, on a gold background, a thistle enamelled in proper colours surrounded by a green circle bearing the motto, and a plain gold badge to be worn when the Riband is worn.

When the collar is not being worn, the plain gold badge is attached to a dark green riband which passes over the left shoulder so that this badge rests on the right hip.

The order now consists of the members listed overleaf.

Sovereign of the Order

The Queen

Lady of the Order

Queen Elizabeth the Queen Mother, 11 May, 1937

Royal Knights

Duke of Edinburgh, 21 April, 1952
Duke of Gloucester, 3 June, 1933
Duke of Windsor, 23 June, 1922

Knights (16)

Earl of Elgin and Kincardine, 3 June, 1933
Viscount Thurso, 12 June, 1941
Earl of Airlie, 11 June, 1942
Earl of Rosebery, 17 June, 1947
Duke of Buccleuch and Queensberry, 1 November, 1949
Duke of Hamilton and Brandon, 8 December, 1951
Earl of Haddington, 8 December, 1951
Earl of Crawford and Balcarres, 22 March, 1955
The Lord Bilsland, 22 March, 1955
Sir John Stirling of Fairburn, 8 May, 1956
The Lord Mathers, 8 May, 1956
The Lord Kinnaird, 14 May, 1957
The Lord Rowallan, 14 May, 1957
Sir Alec Douglas-Home, 15 October, 1962
Sir Robert Menzies, 12 March, 1963

Extra Knight

King Olav V of Norway, 15 October, 1962

Officers of the Order

Chancellor	Earl of Airlie
Dean	The Very Rev. Charles Warr
Lyon King of Arms	Sir Thomas Innes of Learney
Usher of the Green Rod	Sir Reginald Graham of Larbert, Bt., V.C.

CHAPTER V

The Most Honourable Order of the Bath

In former days, as explained in Chapter II, except on the battlefield, the honour of knighthood was not conferred until the candidates had prepared themselves by various ceremonies and symbolic rituals. Having purified his inner soul by fasting, vigils and prayer, the knight also cleansed his body by immersing himself in a bath. The signification of this was that henceforward, both inwardly and outwardly, all his intentions would be pure and honest, or, as it might be summed up, *Mens sana in corpore sano.*

Initiation of a knight by bathing goes back at least as far as the eleventh century, and it was certainly included in all ceremonies of this nature during the next few centuries.

The earliest mention in an official document, after the crowning of William the Conqueror, of the ceremony of bathing at the creation of a knight was that of Geoffrey, son of the Count of Anjou, in 1128, when at the age of fifteen he was betrothed to Matilda, daughter of Henry the First. It is recorded that:

After the customary religious ceremonies, Geoffrey immersed his body in a bath and was afterwards habited by the attendants in crimson robes, while a sword was girded about his body and golden spurs placed upon his heels.

Similar descriptions are to be found in the annals of the reigns of King Henry the Third and Edward the First.

In a document written by Matthew of Westminster we read that in 1306:

The King, meditating an expedition against the Scots and being desirous of increasing his retinue, conferred Knighthood of the Bath on three hundred youths at Westminster.

We also read that, on the Saturday before his coronation, in 1399, Henry the Fourth went from Westminster to the Tower of London 'with many followers and all the Esquires who were to be made Knights of the Bath, who watched all night, each in his chamber, where he bathed'. Though Froissart, describing the same occasion, merely wrote that 'forty-six Esquires kept vigil and were bathed prior to being knighted', there are some who assume that the institution of the ancient Companionship of the Bath occurred in that year—1399.

We read, too, that, at the coronation of King Henry the Fifth in 1413 'Fifty gallant young gentlemen, candidates for Knighthood of the Bath, according to custom went into the baths prepared severally for them' and accounts of many similar ceremonies can be found in the chronicles of that period. In the Wardrobe Accounts of King Henry the Fifth there is an entry recording the purchase of 'divers items for Chevaliers de Bath'. Below is an extract from an old manuscript, of the fourteenth century, printed by Anstis and entitled *The manner of making Knights after the custom of England in time of peace and at the time of the Coronation of the King, that is Knights of the Bath.*

When an Esquire cometh into the Court to receive the Order of Knighthood he shall be led to his chamber and there shall his beard be shaven and his head rounded. Then shall the King command his Chamberlain to go into the Esquire's chamber with certain wise Knights to the intent that they shall the same esquire truly counsel, and teach wisely of the Laws of Knighthood. When the minstrels shall have ceased their singing and dancing and there shall be no noise for the time, they shall make naked the young esquire and shall put him into the bath, saying secretly to him 'Right dear brother, great worship be this Order unto you and Almighty God give you the praising of all Knighthood. Be ye strong in the faith of Holy Church and in the protection of all widows and oppressed maidens. And above all earthly things love the King thy Sovereign Lord and his right defend unto thy power.' And when the squire is thus counselled, the

Knight Counsellor shall take in his hand water of the bath and shall put it upon the shoulders of the squire and, this done, his servants shall take their master from the bath and lay him softly in his bed to dry. And when he is well dried, they shall clothe him warm for the watch of the night.

After this the Knights Counsellors, with minstrels playing on their instruments, shall lead the squire into the Chapel where shall be spices and wines, but, as he must fast, the squire shall not partake of these.

All this done, the squire shall thank them for their labours and shall divide his garments amongst those who have attended him. Then shall the door be shut till the dawning wax clear. In this wise shall the squire all night abide in his prayers. And when the dawning comes he shall have a priest and be confessed of his sins and trespasses, which thing ended, he shall go to Matins.

Then his Counsellors shall lead him again to his chamber and there he shall take rest. Then rich under-garments, silken hose and a blue robe shall be placed upon him with a white girdle about his body and white gloves and he shall be placed on horseback and led into the King's Hall. When the King cometh and perceiveth the squire ready to take the Order in due wise, he asketh for the sword and spurs, and two of the Knights shall place the spurs upon the squire's heels. Then the King shall himself gird the squire with the sword and shall put his arms round the neck of the squire and lifting up his right hand shall smite the squire upon the neck, saying: 'Be a good Knight' and kissing him. After that the Knight shall be led into the Chapel with melody and there he shall un-girt him and shall offer his sword to God and Holy Church to be laid upon the Altar by the Bishop.

Some of the chronicles of those days record that when he returned the sword to the knight it was customary for the bishop to lay the blade upon his neck. It may be that from that procedure originated the idea that a new knight was 'dubbed' by a bishop or some other high ecclesiastic.

Though, as has been shown, it was usual for a new knight, as a part of the ceremony, to receive a robe and a sword, it was not until many years later that he was invested with a badge or any other insignia. Eventually the investiture with insignia took the place of the girding with a sword.

By the end of the fifteenth century many of the ceremonial rituals were beginning to disappear, but at coronations the custom of making a number of young gentlemen 'Knights of the Bath' was still continued.

The first record of any insignia or badge of the 'Bath' being worn is to be found in the chronicles of the early part of the seventeenth century. In a work published in 1613 Mennenius wrote:

> In the year 1605 the Knights of the Bath wore as their Badge 'Three golden Crowns within a golden circle and surrounded by the inscription *Tria in Unum*'.

A hundred years or so later the motto became—perhaps somewhat more grammatically—*Tria Juncta in Uno*.

Andrew Favine, writing in 1619, stated that Knights of the Bath were sometimes known as 'Knights of the Crowns'. He thought that the three crowns were symbolical of the Union of England, France and Scotland. This may well have been the correct interpretation, though some later writers have suggested that the motto referred to the Union of England, Scotland and Ireland, while others opine that it referred to the Holy Trinity.

In 1625, immediately after the coronation of King Charles the First the Earl Marshal of England published an ordinance stating that it was the will and pleasure of the King that all Knights of the Bath should continually wear the ensign of that order as a mark of honour. The badge appears to have been worn at that time round the neck and pendent from a red riband. A little later on, though exactly when is doubtful, Knights of the Bath imitated the Knights of the Garter in wearing the riband belt-wise about the body, except that the Bath riband was worn over the right shoulder instead of the left.

The ancient forms of making knights were discontinued after the reign of King Charles the Second, during which reign we read of an occasion on which sixty-eight young men were made Knights of the Bath with 'the usual ceremonies and rites'.

Thereafter the order fell into desuetude and it was not until 1725 that it was revivified and placed on a quite new establishment by King George the First. It was in this year that this monarch decided that, 'as it had become necessary to provide additional means of gratifying candidates for the favour of the Crown and of rewarding services to the State', the ancient Knighthood of the Bath should be errected into a regular military order, to consist of the Sovereign, a Great Master and thirty-six Knights Companions.

The revival of the order was the measure of Sir Robert Walpole, the King's First Minister. By appointments to it he was able to obtain the political support of certain influential noblemen of great wealth who were not desirous of receiving new titles or any sort of financial reward. It was described by his celebrated son, Horace, as 'an artful bank of thirty-six ribands to supply a fund of favours in lieu of places', while it also 'assisted the Prime Minister in staving off demands for the Garter'. Thus the majority of the original knights were supporters of Walpole, either in the House of Lords or the Commons.

In fact this plan was not acted upon for long, and the custom of awarding the order as a reward for parliamentary support soon ceased.

Below is a list of the Knights appointed in 1725, at the revival of the order:

First and Principal Companion:

Prince William Augustus (second son of the Prince of Wales and afterwards Duke of Cumberland)

Great Master:

Duke of Richmond	The Duke of Montagu
Duke of Manchester	Lord De La Warr
Earl of Burford	Lord Clinton
Earl of Leicester	Lord Walpole (son of Sir
Earl of Albemarle	Robert Walpole)
Earl of Deloraine	Sir Spencer Compton
Earl of Halifax	Sir William Stanhope
Earl of Sussex	Sir Coniers Darcy
Earl of Pomfret	Sir Thomas Sanderson
Earl of Inchequin	Sir Paul Methuen
Lord Nassau Paulett	Sir Robert Walpole (after-
Viscount Tyrconnel	ward Earl of Orford)
Viscount Torrington	Sir Robert Sutton
Viscount Malpas	Sir Charles Wills
Viscount Glenorchy	Sir John Hobart
Sir Robert Clifton	Sir William Gage

Sir William Yonge	Sir Michael Newton
Sir Thomas Wentworth	Sir William Morgan
Sir John Monson	Sir Thomas Coke

Two of those who were offered the Bath by Sir Robert Walpole were the young Duke of Marlborough, grandson of the high and mighty Sarah, and the Duke of Bedford, who had married her granddaughter. The formidable dowager duchess, however, on their behalf indignantly refused the offer, saying that 'they would take nothing but the Garter'. To this Walpole replied somewhat curtly:

'Madam, they who take the Bath will the sooner have the Garter'.

It was in fact intended by King George the First that henceforward particularly eminent and distinguished service should be rewarded by appointment to the Bath, known as 'the Red Riband', and that the Bath should be the stepping-stone to the Garter, the Blue Riband. The nineteenth statute of the order stated:

> We do hereby declare and order for the great love, favour and confidence we bear towards the Knights of the Most Honourable Order of the Bath that from henceforth a special regard shall be had in preferring, advancing and presenting them to be Companions of the Most Noble Order of the Garter.

To some extent it might be said that it was the intention that the conditions of admission to the order were to be merit and service as compared with those for the two existing orders (Garter and Thistle), which were really birth and nobility.

In fact, comparatively few K.B.s became K.G.s, though what Sir Robert Walpole predicted became true in his own case, for within a year he, together with the Duke of Richmond, was promoted to the Garter. Others who similarly resigned the Bath on promotion to the Garter were the Earl of Wilmington (in 1733) and the Earl of Albemarle (in 1749). The royal dukes of Cumberland and York, who were promoted to the Garter in 1730 and 1771 respectively, in accordance with the custom for members of the Royal Family, were allowed to retain their appointments in, and continued to wear the insignia of, the Order of the Bath.

We shall see later in this chapter how in 1813 Lord Wellington (later the famous Duke) was required to resign from the Bath and hand back its insignia on election to the Garter.

The statutes of the Bath were based to a considerable extent on those of the Garter. It should be realised that when George the First revived the Knighthood of the Bath he not only reorganised the existing institution but in fact altered it into a new 'military order'. The wording of his statutes gives proof of his. They stated that:

> Whereas in case of a war in Europe we are determined that this Realm should be in a posture of defence against the attempts of our enemies, We do hereby ordain that from henceforth every Companion of the said Military Order in case of any danger of invasion from foreign enemies or from rebellion at home shall maintain at his own cost four men-at-arms for any number of days the Sovereign shall think proper.

The first installation of knights, after the revival of the order, took place in 1725, in King Henry the Seventh Chapel, in Westminster Abbey, which had been selected as the chapel of the order. The ceremony of bathing was not included at this installation, and the former customs which had included vigils and fasting were also omitted.

At the conclusion of the installation the knights moved in procession to the Chapter House where, as has been stated earlier, the Sovereign's Master-cook, 'standing at the outside of the door of Westminster Church', warned each knight that if he did anything contrary to the Laws of Chivalry, he would cut away the spurs from his heels.

Following the installation ceremony a great banquet was held in the 'Court of Requests' at Westminster.

The insignia of the order at that time consisted of a collar of gold, a red riband and badge and the ensign or star of the order which was not then made of metal but of gold and silver thread and with a 'paste-board' back. This star was sewn on the left side of either the coat or the mantle which was of crimson satin. Rays made of tinsel issued from the centre of the star making what was described as a 'Glory'. It was customary in those days for knights to have the star embroidered on all the uniform coats which they possessed. There are, for instance, in existence at least two coats which were worn formerly by Lord Nelson, and each of these has the star embroidered on the left side. Though at this period the knights were not invested with a metal star of silver, some of them purchased privately for themselves stars fashioned in diamonds and other precious stones.

It was ordained that banners for knights should be erected in King Henry the Seventh Chapel over their stalls and that their escutcheons should be placed at the back of their respective stalls.

From 1725 until just after the end of the eighteenth century an accurate record of knights was preserved by means of these stall-plates, and among the latest of those erected during that period are the memorials for Lord Clive (dated 1779), and Lord Nelson, the Duke of Wellington and Sir William Pitt (all dated 1803). Unfortunately the erection of these beautifully produced memorials of distinguished leaders of the armed services or eminent political leaders or ambassadors was discontinued in 1812. It was not until the end of the nineteenth century that the erection of stall-plates was reintroduced and amongst those erected about this time are the memorials for Field-Marshal Earl Roberts, V.C., and Field-Marshal Viscount Wolseley (both dated 1880), Field-Marshal Sir Evelyn Wood, V.C. (1891), and Field-Marshal Earl Kitchener (1898). Great military leaders of the 1914–1918 war are represented by the plates for Field-Marshal Earl Haig and Admiral of the Fleet Earl Jellicoe (both dated 1915) and for Admiral of the Fleet Earl Beatty (dated 1916).

There is no plate for a Sovereign earlier than that for King George the Fifth.

Originally, when a knight died, the banner and stall-plate of the next senior knight were moved up, but this procedure was discontinued because the constant removal and re-affixing of stall-plates caused considerable damage to the woodwork. Moreover, many knights preferred to keep the same stall throughout their lives.

As stated previously, by the end of the eighteenth century many of the great naval and military leaders were included in the order, and the remaining members consisted mainly of eminent ambassadors and plenipotentiaries. The order was not, however, always given to successful admirals and generals who had been commanders-in-chief. It was often used as a less valuable or secondary reward. For instance, when a commander-in-chief received a peerage or baronetcy the 'Red Riband' was frequently given to more junior leaders. Thus in connection with the great naval battle on the 'Glorious First of

INSIGNIA OF A KNIGHT GRAND
CROSS OF THE ORDER OF ST.
MICHAEL AND ST. GEORGE
The mantle with star embroidered there-
on, and collar with badge appendant.
A. C. K. Ware

INSIGNIA OF A KNIGHT OF THE
THISTLE
Star section of collar with St. Andrew
badge.
Zanton House

INSIGNIA OF A KNIGHT GRAND
CROSS OF THE ORDER OF THE
BATH (MILITARY DIVISION)
The star and a section of the collar
with badge appendant.
Harrison and Sons

INSTALLATION OF KNIGHTS
GRAND CROSS OF THE ORDER
OF THE BATH AT WESTMINSTER
ABBEY IN 1956
The Queen wearing the Sovereign's
robes makes her offering of gold and
silver at the altar in King Henry VII's
Chapel, while the Knights stand beneath
the banners and the officers (in white
mantles) stand near the Sovereign.
The officers were as follows: in front
of the altar receiving the Queen's
offering, the Dean of Westminster
(Dr Alan Don); on the Queen's right,
Bath King of Arms (Air Chief Marshal
Sir James Robb), the Deputy Secre-
tary (the author), and the Genealogist
(Hon. Sir George Bellew); on the
Queen's left, the Secretary (Major-
General D. Wimberley) and Scarlet Rod
(Rear-Admiral R. Sherbrooke, V.C.).
The Times

June' in 1794, none of the admirals were appointed Knights of the Bath because Earl Howe had been promised the next vacancy in the Garter, while the second and third in command received Irish peerages and the three next senior flag officers were created baronets. Similarly, in celebration of the great victory off Cape Saint Vincent in February 1797, the commander-in-chief, Sir John Jervis, received an earldom, the two next senior admirals received baronetcies, while Commodore Nelson, who was at the time the fifth senior officer, was appointed a Knight of the Bath. He was created a peer later, after the Battle of the Nile.

Many people disapproved strongly of the methods used for rewarding successful admirals and generals. They considered that those who were responsible for winning great military victories ought to be rewarded by being appointed to the highest military order of their country, even though they were given also a peerage or baronetcy. Their argument was that in most European countries it was the custom to reward great military leaders in this fashion. For instance, in Russia and Austria respectively the highest objects of an officer's ambition were appointments in the military orders of Saint George and Maria Teresa.

We read that when, after the battle off Cape Saint Vincent, a friend remarked to Nelson that he would certainly receive a baronetcy, he replied:

'No! No! If they want to mark my services it must not be in that manner. If these services have been of any value let them be noticed in a way that the public may know of them by appointment to the Bath.'

As described above, he was in fact made a K.B. for his outstanding service in this important battle.

It must be realised that in those days orders and medals, both of which were then given very rarely, often meant more to distinguished commanders than titles or gifts of money. In a letter sent to his wife after the Battle of Trafalgar, Admiral Collingwood wrote:

'To possess riches is not my ambition, but I am in hope to get another medal: of that indeed I am ambitious, for I am the only officer in the Service with three.'

Unfortunately, though he received a medal for Trafalgar, he did not receive appointment to the Bath but was created a peer instead, and in fact he was never appointed to the order.

The following anecdote which was related by the Right Honourable William Wynn in a speech in the House of Commons is of interest in that it shows how great a value was placed on the winning of insignia by those of humble rank.

'After the Battle of the Nile a patriotic individual caused a number of medals to be struck and distributed among the seamen who were present in the conflict. I have heard from several officers that the effect produced was of the most gratifying kind, and that many of these gallant men, when dying in a foreign land, had expressed in their last moments the most anxious solicitude about the disposition of these medals. Some wished that their medal should be buried with them: others that it should be carefully transmitted to their families: but all of them placed more value on their small medal than on any other property they happened to possess.'

How different is the value placed on war medals now when it was possible during each of the two Great Wars of this century for a man to qualify for three or more medals by service in branches of the services which were seldom in a position of any danger. Many thousands who were qualified to receive war medals have never even taken the trouble to apply for them. Medals and Stars given for service during the war of 1939–1945 did not even have the names of the recipients engraved thereon and this economy made these tokens of service even less valuable.

In 1804, though there was no statutory vacancy in the Order of the Bath, Major-General Arthur Wellesley (afterwards Duke of Wellington) was appointed a K.B. as a reward for his outstanding services at the Battle of Assaye. There was no real vacancy until a year later when Lord Nelson was mortally wounded at Trafalgar. Several historians have drawn attention to the interesting fact that the greatest admiral of the day was succeeded in his Bath stall by a person who later became the greatest general of his time. A few years later, as there were no regular vacancies and as it was essential to provide suitable rewards for a number of distinguished generals of the Peninsular War, a special statute was published authorising the making of such additional appointments as were deemed necessary during times of war. More than a hundred years later, under the authority of the statute, a great many additional appointments were made in respect of service in the wars of 1914–1918 and 1939–1945.

In March 1813, as the Prince Regent desired to give to the Marquess of Wellington 'a new proof of his gratitude for his glorious conduct which was beyond all human praise and for which no language in all the world could give suitable expression', he conferred on him the Order of the Garter. We find in the records of the order of the Bath letters showing that, in accordance with the instructions contained in the statutes, Lord Wellington made arrangements for handing back the insignia of that order. But when this became known, it caused great distress and concern to many of Lord Wellington's companions in arms who had received their own Bath insignia from his hand. They wrote to complain most strongly that, in their opinion, if their great commander should cease to be a member of the Order of the Bath it would lose much of its prestige and honour. After much persuasion and with the greatest reluctance Lord Wellington was induced to write to the Prime Minister in the following terms:

> Some of my brother officers have expressed an anxious desire that I should continue as a Knight of the Bath into which I have admitted most of them and all of whom owe this honour to action performed under my command. Under these circumstances I desire you to consider whether it would not be better if I should keep it. I feel great reluctance in suggesting that I should keep this Order and I should not have done so if it had not been suggested to me by some of the Knights. God knows I have plenty of Orders and I consider myself to have been most handsomely treated by the Prince Regent and the Government and shall not consider myself the less so if you should not think it proper that I should retain the Order of the Bath.

Many senior army officers were bitterly disappointed when the Prime Minister took no action to submit Lord Wellington's suggestion to the Prince Regent. It was certainly most unfortunate that in the special circumstances of the case the greatest and most famous military leader of the day was not allowed to remain a member of the only military order of his country while he was authorised to wear many military orders of foreign countries.

Fortunately when, as is described below, the Order of the Bath was enlarged, Lord Wellington was reappointed to its First Class as a Knight Grand Cross.

After the Peninsular War had been brought to a successful conclusion, it became essential to introduce some new means of rewarding the many officers who had distinguished themselves in battle but who were not of sufficiently high rank to be admitted into any of the four existing orders, all of which were of one class only.

After considerable discussion, instead of instituting a completely new order, it was decided to enlarge considerably the existing Order of the Bath. On 2nd January 1815 new statutes were published introducing two new military classes. The reason given was 'to commemorate the auspicious termination of the long and arduous contests in which the Empire had been engaged and to mark in an especial manner the magnificent perseverance and devotion manifested by the Officers of His Majesty's forces on sea and land'. Though the Prince Regent agreed rather reluctantly, provision was made also for the admission of a small number of particularly distinguished persons as 'Civil Knights Grand Cross'.

Thus the order was placed on an entirely new foundation, and for the first time in England an order was made to consist of more than one degree of rank, namely, more than one class of members. This innovation was copied from the other countries of Europe, most of which possessed several orders of chivalry divided into three or more classes.

There was very little enthusiasm amongst existing K.B.s for this vast extension of the order—just about as much as there would be now amongst Knights of the Garter or the Thistle if several hundred new admissions were made to those orders by the introduction of two new junior classes.

Many thought that the order had been made almost valueless by this great number of new holders of whom some at least had very faint claims to distinction.

Admiral Earl Saint Vincent was particularly hostile to the new designation of the senior knights and refused to wear the new insignia except in the presence of the Sovereign. Undoubtedly the importance of the order was much diminished. Not the least part of this feeling was caused by the fact that whereas formerly only persons of great position had held a British order, there were now several hundred holders, some of whom were of quite unimportant rank and social position.

Though of course in the latter case the numbers were far greater, the situation may be compared to a measure taken during the 1914–1918 war, when, after a '1914, or Mons, star' had been given to those who had genuinely been in action with the enemy during the first desperate months of the war, an almost identical star* and ribbon, the '1914–1915 star, was given to thousand of troops who had merely disembarked in France prior to the end of 1915 and who had not necessarily taken part in any action or even served in an area of any danger.

The Order of the Bath in its new form was to consist of seventy-two Knights Grand Cross (exclusive of the Royal Family) and this number was to include all existing K.B.s who were thenceforth to be styled G.C.B.s, or Knights Grand Cross.

Of these seventy-two Knights Grand Cross, twelve were to belong to a Civil Division, and no member in the Military Division was to be of a rank below that of rear admiral or major-general.

In the Second Class the maximum number of Knights Commanders permissible was one hundred and eighty, and these were to take precedence next above knights bachelor. In this class all had to hold a regular commission in the Navy or Army and be not below the rank of post-captain or lieutenant-colonel.

In the Third Class the number of Companions was unlimited and they were to be selected from regular officers not below field rank (major) or its equivalent naval rank, and it was a condition of appointment that the recipient must have distinguished himself by valour against the enemy. It should be noted that the Duke of Wellington disapproved strongly of the rule which prevented army officers below the rank of major from qualifying for an award in the new order. He wrote in his despatches to the Duke of York:

> I do not concur in the limitation of the Order to Field Officers. Many Captains in the Army conduct themselves in a very meritorious manner and deserve it.

He would have liked the order to consist of four classes so that junior officers could be eligible for it. He also favoured the reviving of the rank of 'knight banneret' for knights of the first class, thus giving them precedence above baronets, as is the rule nowadays.

Each class was provided with distinctive insignia and there were some differences in design from those given previously.

---

*It is true that a silver emblem was worn by some holders of the 1914 star and that the 1914 star had '1914' in the design while the 1915 star had '1915', but apart from those differences the stars were identical, as were the two ribbons.

Those few former K.B.s who were civilians retained their former insignia, and insignia of the same pattern were given to those newly appointed civilians who were included in the number of twelve Knights Grand Cross of the Civil Division.

The badges and stars of members of the three classes of the Military Division were distinguished by the superimposition of a wreath of laurel encircling the motto and issuing from an escrol inscribed *Ich Dien.*

From the date of the enlargement of the order a new rule was introduced whereby it became no longer essential for the insignia of the Bath to be handed back on election to a senior order, but, as is shown in the records at the Central Chancery, until the latter part of the nineteenth century the insignia of all classes of the order were normally returned on the death of the holder, though in some cases this was not practicable because the badges had been lost or disposed of in some other way.

Below is given a list of the Knights Grand Cross who were appointed in 1815:

Military Knights Grand Cross

1. The Sovereign
2. His Royal Highness the Duke of York (acting as Great Master)
3. Admiral Earl St. Vincent
4. General Sir Robert Abercromby
5. Admiral Viscount Keith
6. Admiral Sir John Warren, Bt.
7. General Sir Aluved Clarke
8. Admiral Sir John Colpoys
9. General Lord Hutchinson
10. Admiral Sir John Duckworth
11. Admiral Sir James Saumarez
12. General Sir Eyre Coote
13. General Sir John Cradock
14. General Sir David Dundas
15. Field-Marshal the Duke of Wellington, K.G.
16. General the Earl of Ludlow
17. Vice-Admiral Sir Samuel Hood
18. Admiral the Earl of Northesk
19. Vice-Admiral Sir Richard Strachan

20. Vice-Admiral Hon. Sir Alexander Cochrane
21. Lieutenant-General Sir John Stuart
22. Vice-Admiral Sir Richard Keats
23. General Sir David Baird
24. General Sir George Beckwith
25. Lieutenant-General Lord Niddry
26. Lieutenant-General Sir Brent Spencer
27. Lieutenant-General Sir John Sherbrooke
28. Lieutenant-General Lord Beresford
29. Lieutenant-General Lord Lynedoch
30. Lieutenant-General Lord Hill
31. Lieutenant-General Sir Samuel Auchmuty
32. Lieutenant-General Sir Edward Paget
33. Lieutenant-General Lord Combermere
34. Admiral Hon. Sir George Berkeley
35. General Sir George Nugent
36. General Sir William Keppel
37. Lieutenant-General Sir John Doyle, Bt.
38. Lieutenant-General Lord Cavendish-Bentinck
39. Lieutenant-General Sir James Leith
40. Lieutenant-General Sir Thomas Picton
41. Lieutenant-General Hon. Sir Galbraith Cole
42. Lieutenant-General Lord Stewart
43. Lieutenant-General Hon. Sir Alexander Hope
44. Lieutenant-General Sir Henry Clinton
45. Lieutenant-General Earl of Dalhousie
46. Lieutenant-General Hon. William Stewart
47. Major-General Sir George Murray
48. Major-General Hon. Sir Edward Pakenham
49. Admiral Sir William Young
50. General the Prince of Orange
51. Admiral Viscount Hood
52. Admiral Sir Richard Onslow
53. Admiral Hon. William Cornwallis
54. Admiral Lord Radstock
55. Admiral Sir Roger Curtis, Bt.
56. Admiral George Montagu
57. Lieutenant-General Earl of Uxbridge
58. Lieutenant-General Robert Brownrigg
59. Lieutenant-General Harry Calvert
60. Lieutenant-General Rt. Hon. Thomas Maitland
61. Lieutenant-General William Clinton

Civil Knights Grand Cross

1. Sir Robert Gunning
2. Earl of Malmesbury
3. Lord Henley
4. Lord Whitworth
5. Sir Joseph Banks, Bt.
6. The Right Hon. Sir Arthur Paget
7. Sir Philip Francis
8. Sir George Barlow
9. Viscount Strangford
10. The Hon. Sir Henry Wellesley
11. The Right Hon. Sir Charles Stuart

When the order was enlarged, in addition to the disapproval of a number of the former Knights of the Bath at the addition to the order of two extra classes involving the appointment of a considerable number of Knights Commanders and Companions of the Military Division, there was a considerable amount of grumbling by politicians because two similar extra classes had not been introduced for civilians.

The Prime Minister wrote to the Prince Regent recommending that a greater number of civilians should be admitted to the order by the institution of extra classes for civilians, but this suggestion was not viewed favourably by the prince, as will be seen from the wording of the following letter to Lord Bathurst:

Carlton House,
7th December, 1819.

My dear Lord,

When I first contemplated the present extension of the Order of the Bath, my desire was strictly to avoid all Political Considerations.

Lord Liverpool happening to have an audience of me, I named my intention to him, mentioning the Individuals whose Characters and Professional Merits appeared to me to point them out as proper and fit persons for this Mark of Royal Favor.

After a full consideration of the subject contained in your last letter, I confess myself quite at a loss how to give the magnitude of importance, which your Lordship is disposed to give, to the Heart-Burning and Disappointments which the Measure in question as you state, cannot fail to create: On the contrary, I am of opinion that the measure itself is calculated to heal those deep wounds which have been inflicted upon a most deserving and meritorious Class of Officers, the Services of whom have not only been by the late Regulations neglected and shut out from this Reward, but, I grieve to add, have almost been insulted; and it is to this meritorious Class of Officers that my honor now stands committed.

With respect to the modern Rules and Regulations that I was, in the hurry of the whole proceeding, induced to adopt in the year 1815, they formed a severity of Code that did not leave me the power of alteration in any of its principles: Yet, I had scarcely sanctioned those positive enactments before I was desired to dispense with them in favor of Cases for whose Merit I nevertheless entertained an high consideration and which dispensation I most willingly granted.

I cannot however avoid observing that these enactments have since proved to be both embarrassing and objectionable. Upon the further names that have been submitted to me I defer making my decision at present; feeling strongly that the intermixture of the Government in this Measure is an infringement of the Statutes and only admissible with reference to the position of Grand Crosses which have been set apart for Political Civil Service.

George P. R.

When the rules and regulations were rewritten in 1815 it was ordained that in future the rites of bathing, vigils and preparative ceremonies, which in fact had not been followed since the reign of Charles the Second should be abolished.

The Great Master was authorised in the absence of the Sovereign to 'supply his place' and 'to take especial care that the statutes should be observed with great exactness'. It was his duty in the absence of the Sovereign to preside over all chapters and ceremonials, to confer the honour of knighthood on the knights-elect and to invest them with their insignia. He was to signify all vacancies in the order to the Sovereign, and take His Majesty's Pleasure as to the persons who should fill these vacancies. He was also to appoint all the officers of the order except the dean, who was to be selected by the Sovereign on the advice of the Prime Minister. The office of Great Master was not honorary because at that time every knight on his appointment paid £138, and it would appear that the first Great Master, the Duke of Montagu, received some £5,000 on the re-establishment of the order in 1725 and a further £5,000 between that date and his death in 1749.

For a considerable time no Great Master was appointed to succeed the Duke of Montagu as the Government intended to keep the order entirely under their own control, and there was only an Acting Great Master.

For many years thereafter the appointment of Acting Great Master was held by a prince of the royal blood—namely the Duke of York in 1815 and the Duke of Clarence in 1827 (who on becoming Sovereign on his accession in 1830 decided to continue also as Great Master). He was followed in the appointment of Great Master by the Duke of Sussex in 1838. In 1841 the Prince Consort was appointed Great Master by Queen Victoria. The appointment was left vacant for some time after his death, but it was given to the Duke of Connaught in 1901, while he was followed by the Duke of Gloucester (the present holder) in 1942. None of these royal princes, however, were ever concerned with the appointment of the officers of the order, nor were any fees ever paid to a Great Master after the death of the Duke of Montagu in 1749.

The Order of the Bath, like the Thistle, did not have a prelate, but it was ordained in the statutes that the Dean of Westminster for the time being should be for ever dean of the order and its highest officer.

As in earlier days, advancement in the Army depended largely on the ability of those concerned to pay a considerable sum to purchase promotion, the new statutes prevented those who could not afford to do this from receiving appointments in the order. This was manifestly unfair and placed a premium on the possession of wealth.

For other reasons the creation of this large new military order came in for a good deal of criticism in the House of Commons and some members expressed their desire to 'repress rather than encourage any attempt to give too great a military character to this country.' They considered that 'Great Britain not being a Military Nation was differently circumstanced from those foreign States where Military Orders had been found beneficial'. It was not only in Parliament that antagonism was shown towards the new order. We read that the College of Heralds complained that 'their privileges had been invaded' and they took steps to vindicate their rights. They informed all Knights Commanders that certain fixed fees were payable to ensure that their pedigrees were traced and brought up to date. It will be shown later how the fees demanded by the holders of various offices increased steadily and how refusals to pay them were made until they were first very greatly reduced and eventually made entirely voluntary.

Another totally unfair rule was introduced. Though it had been clearly laid down at the of time the expansion of the order that all Knights Commanders should receive identical insignia, a marked distinction was suddenly introduced prior to the holding of the first investiture on 12th April 1815. It was then announced that no Knight Commander who held a rank below that of rear-admiral or major-general would receive a star, and while all Knights Commanders of these ranks were invested with both star and badge, those who held the rank of post captain or lieutenant colonel were not only merely presented to and knighted by the Prince Regent without being invested with a star, but did not even receive their badges from his hand and had these sent to them afterwards in a quite informal manner.

In 1837, however, King William the Fourth, who took a remarkably keen interest in the order, revoked this particularly snobbish and unfair rule and invested with stars all those Knights Commanders who had not previously received them. He directed also that thenceforth all Knights Commanders, irrespective of rank, were to be invested with both the star and badge. As stated previously, King William also showed his great esteem for the order by appointing himself to be its Great Master. He invariably wore the riband, badge and star at Levées and Reviews, and on all state occasions he wore the Bath collar as well as that of the Garter. It was this Sovereign who sent a message to the House of Commons complaining of the high charges which were being levied against recipients of the Bath by the offices of the Earl Marshal and Lord Chamberlain. These charges even included a fee of £6 to the 'Royal Barber' for some imaginary services rendered at a ceremony of initiation—a ceremony which had long been abolished. These charges for the senior knights amounted to nearly £400 each. Moreover, though in their case the fees were much less, it was quite impossible for those members of the junior classes who depended on their pensions or pay to meet the charges demanded of them.

It is true that when the order was re-established in 1725 it had been intended that the knights should themselves remunerate the officers of the order, as was the arrangement in the Orders of the Garter and Thistle. As one historian wrote:

> The members of these ancient Orders came from the higher nobility so that the payment of a few hundred pounds was to them a matter of comparatively slight importance.

But when the Bath was enlarged to such an extent that many somewhat impoverished naval and military officers were concerned, the claiming and payment of these fees became a very different matter.

As explained, a proposal was put forward to reduce drastically the number of officials by whom fees could be claimed and to pay some of the charges from government funds.

Considerable opposition, however, was offered in Parliament to the latter suggestion on the ground that, as it was the sovereign who had the power to confer an unlimited number of honours, he could not expect the Government to foot the bill for maintaining the machinery for making these awards.

Mr. Hume declared in the House of Commons: 'Let Royalty with its princely allowance bear the charge and do not levy it from the poverty-stricken people of England.'

He went on to protest that in any case the system was wrong because practically all honours went to military men and 'we had not in England, as there were on the Continent, Orders of Chivalry available as rewards for men of genius, intelligence and merit in Civil Life'.

Another member—Admiral Sir Edward Codrington—supported the proposal to dispense with the excessive fees demanded.

'I hold in my hand,' he said, 'a bill of fees which was presented to me in consequence of my having had the honour of being made a Knight Grand Cross of the Order of the Bath. I was quite shocked at seeing this bill—not on my own account, because I was determined never to pay one farthing of the money. But I was shocked to find that any officer having received such an honour from his Sovereign should be called upon to pay for it. This honour was conferred on me gratuitously. I never asked for it, nor would I have had it if I could only have obtained it by asking for it.

'Indeed the Order itself was lessened in my estimation from the moment I received this bill, for I did not receive it until some three years after the Honour had been conferred upon me. Upon receiving this bill I showed it to the First Lord of the Admiralty, who observed that it was very hard upon me to have such a sum to pay.

' "Not the least," I replied, "for I don't mean to pay a farthing."

'I was told that there was an Order in Council that everybody must pay the customary fees: but my reply was that I had nothing to do with the Order in Council and that I wished that all the officers on whom the Order had been conferred had done the same thing as I, as it would have upheld the distinction very much. Among the items which struck me most forcibly was the charge of £122 to the King's Household. What patent right can they have to entitle them to this sum? I am told that part of these fees are appropriated to paying salaries and that another portion goes to a Fee-Fund. But there can be no justification whatsoever for calling upon the Officers of the Army and Navy to pay for their honours. At the end of the war a great number of officers were given this distinction and they went to Court in consequence of such honour being conferred upon them. And what was it they did? All of them having received a bill of Fees, they laid them in a heap on the table at the Palace for the King to do as he pleased with them, for they were determined not to pay a shilling themselves. The bill which I hold in my hand is as follows:

	£	s.	d.
The Secretary of State's Office	16	17	6
The Seven Officers of the Order	164	17	2
The King's Household	122	2	0
The Lord Chamberlain's Office	26	14	6
The College of Arms, for supporters	55	16	0
	£386	7	2

After a time I was informed by the First Lord of the Admiralty that I should hear no more of this claim.'

Another Member of Parliament, supporting Admiral Codrington, stated that the practice appeared to him to be absolute piracy.

Sir Robert Peel also stated that in his opinion service officers who received honours should not have to pay for them.

In spite of the fact that a large majority of the members of the House of Commons agreed that new rules should be introduced to put an end to this unfair obligation on officers to pay for their honours, nothing was done in the matter for many years. While some recipients refused to pay, some of those who were better endowed financially paid up to avoid trouble. Nowadays, apart from the fact that those who accept quite voluntarily stalls in the chapels of the various orders od chivalry have to pay a contribution towards the cost of their banners and stall-plates, there is no obligation on any recipient to pay anything at all, though most newly appointed recipients voluntarily make one small contribution towards the upkeep of the chapel of their order and the cost of religious services there. Those Knights Grand Cross who desire to have supporters added to their arms, or to have their arms brought up to date, still have to pay for these privileges, but this is by private arrangement with the College of Arms, and there is no compulsion on any person to make any contribution unless he so desires.

At the coronation of King George the Fourth a dress was laid down for wear by Knights Commanders, namely the members of the second class, of the Order of the Bath. They were authorised to wear a mantle of crimson satin of about half the length of the mantle worn by Knights Grand Cross of the first class. However, the use of this mantle for knights of the second class was discontinued shortly afterwards, and it has not been mentioned in the statutes of the order for well over a hundred years.

Though it was obviously impossible, through lack of space, to allot stalls in the King Henry the Seventh Chapel in Westminster Abbey to the numerous knights of the second class of the order, for some reason an ordinance was published in January 1815, to the effect that the escutcheons and banners of these Knights Commanders were to be erected in the chapel. As a result a considerable fee was demanded by and in many cases was paid to certain officers of the order.

Similarly, it was proposed to erect the escutcheon of every Companion of the third class of the order and fees were demanded from many of these Companions also.

In fact no stall-plates for those members of the order lower than the first class, or Knights Grand Cross, were ever erected in the chapel, but a certain number of plates were erected for the esquires in attendance on the earliest Knights Grand Cross at the time of their installation.

The reason for this was that when the ceremony of installation of knights was performed in 1725, and in the following years up till 1812, each knight installed was attended by three esquires, who carried his robes, sword and accoutrements. The seats of the esquires, with their plates, were immediately below the stalls of the knights whom they severally attended. For instance, amongst a considerable number of others there are to be found in King Henry the Seventh Chapel plates for the following esquires:

To Prince William Montagu, Duke of Manchester (1725)
    Charles Edwin, Savill Cust, François Hildesley
To Prince Charles Lenox, Duke of Richmond (1725)
    Matthew Snow, Martin Folkes, Thomas Hill
To Vicomte et Baron Nelson du Nile (1803)
    Horatio Nelson, Thomas Bolton, John Tyson.

The wearing of special under-habits, which were formerly worn beneath the mantle of the order, has been discontinued for many years now. The under-habit consisted of a white satin doublet and it was worn with white hose, boots of white kid leather with red heels and turned over at the top with crimson satin, gilt spurs with white leathers and a sword in a scabbard of white leather with gilt 'furniture'. A crimson satin sash was worn about the waist with long ends fringed with gold. A lace ruff was worn about the neck, and those Knights Grand Cross who were privy counsellors wore a blue silk sash round the right arm.

The hat or cap of the Knights Grand Cross has been changed from time to time. Originally it was made of white satin adorned with a plume of ostrich feathers, but later the colour was changed to black.

On 6th March 1840 the Prince Consort, although he was already a Knight of the Garter, was invested by Queen Victoria with the insignia of a Military Knight Grand Cross of the Bath, but no formal ceremony was held as no installations of knights were held during her reign. As stated previously, a little later he was appointed Great Master of the order.

As explained, there was at the time of the first enlargement of the order considerable criticism not only of the increased number of holders, but also of the inclusion of Civil Knights Grand Cross in what was originally intended to be a military order of chivalry. However, in course of time the changes in the construction of the order came to be accepted as being both wise and useful, and in 1847 Queen Victoria, on the advice of her Prime Minister, was able to add two new civil divisions—one of Knights Commanders and another of Companions—without causing undue controversy or criticism. She introduced these changes 'with a view to the altered state and circumstances of Society'. As Nicolas writes in his *History*:

> Probably the greatest disability that the Order suffered under Queen Victoria's reign was the prosaic attitude adopted towards all honours. The dignified and impressive ceremonies at one time associated with the great Orders of Chivalry had been discontinued.

We read from the letter of a senior officer that at the conclusion of the Crimean War

> When many French and Sardinian Officers were decorated with the Order of the Bath the English Officers were placed in a humiliating position in that while they saw the foreign officers receive the Star in silver it was given to them in tinsel and paste-board.

In May 1858 Lord Hotham drew attention in Parliament to the subject of military awards. He complained that the Bath star delivered to an English officer was 'of so mean and miserable a description that no officer could wear it in the state in which it was handed over and that the very first thing he did after the investiture was to go to his own jewellers to purchase a silver decoration'.

It was not until about 1860 that it became the custom to issue to all knights stars made of silver, though, as stated above, stars of this kind had been presented earlier to certain foreigners such as the commanders and other senior officers of allied armies. Silver stars had also been given at the same time to members of the Royal Family.

Promotion in the Order of the Bath now began to be made more because 'it was Buggins' turn' rather than because 'Buggins was the most deserving of a high honour'. We read in a letter from General Lord Wolseley of his request for permission to refuse a G.C.B. when it was first offered to him. He preferred not to accept promotion in the order over the heads of various officers who

INSIGNIA OF A KNIGHT GRAND
CROSS OF THE ORDER OF THE
BRITISH EMPIRE (MILITARY
DIVISION)
Collar, riband and badge, and star.
British Combine

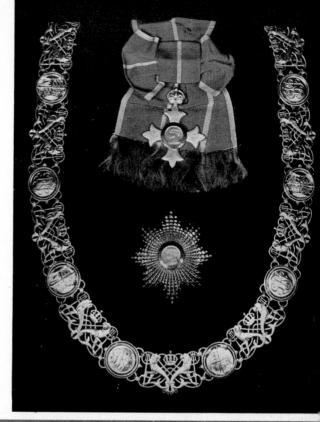

THE CHAPEL OF THE ORDER
OF THE BRITISH EMPIRE IN
THE CRYPT OF ST. PAUL'S
CATHEDRAL
John Maltby

MILITARY KNIGHTS OF WINDSOR IN ST. GEORGE'S CHAPEL
Formerly known as the 'Poor or Veteran Knights'.
Harold White

were senior to him in rank in case they might be offended thereby, and in case his advancement in the army might be adversely prejudiced by their hostility to him.

However, after the institution of junior orders such as that of Saint Michael and Saint George and the Royal Victorian Order, the Bath slowly began to regain its former position in the public estimation. Gradually a C.B., which had originally been considered a suitable award for a major, began to be used as the appropriate award for a major-general or a rear-admiral.

It was not until the reign of King George the Fifth that the magnificent ceremony of installing Knights Grand Cross was revived in Westminster Abbey. For this revival a great deal of credit is due to the Great Master at that time, the Duke of Connaught, who took an enormous personal interest in the order. The records of the order include innumerable lengthy letters in his own handwriting in connection with the business of the order and the conduct of its ceremonies.

It was in 1913 that King George the Fifth commanded that 'the ceremony of installation which had been omitted for so many years should be revived' and a service was held on 22nd July 1913, at which forty-six Senior Knights Grand Cross were installed. The custom of erecting banners and stall-plates was also revived. Installation services were also held in 1920, 1924, 1928, 1935, 1951, 1956 and 1960. At the most recent service, held on 27th October 1960, vacancies in the stalls which had occurred since 1956 were filled. The next installation service is to be held on 29th October 1964.

In the course of the service on 24th May 1951 King George the Sixth formally installed his brother, the Duke of Gloucester, as Great Master of the Order. This was the first service which it had been possible to hold during his reign because of the war of 1939–45 and the necessity after the war to carry out extensive repairs in the King Henry the Seventh Chapel.

It was the King himself who planned the whole service and all the details of the ceremony of the installation of knights. As he had not prior to his accession been made a member of the Order of the Bath, he insisted on 'offering his sword'—the sword which his father had given him when he was first commissioned as a naval officer in 1915. The sword was accepted by the Dean of Westminster, the Dean of the Order, laid upon the altar and blessed, and then returned to the king. After the death of King George the Sixth in 1952, this sword was presented by Their Majesties the Queen and Queen Elizabeth the Queen Mother to Westminster Abbey, and it now stands in a dignified exhibition-case in King Henry the Seventh Chapel. The service of 1951 is particularly memorable as it was the last public ceremony attended by King George the Sixth. On the day of the service he was, to the great distress of all present, particularly the officers of the order who were attending him, obviously ill and in such pain that the procession had to be considerably curtailed in an endeavour to spare him fatigue. None the less, at the end of the ceremony, when the dean and other officers of the order took farewell of His Majesty, the King, being aware that none of these officers had ever previously taken part in arrangements for a service of the order, turned to them, and in spite of his fatigue showed his approval with the words:

'Not so bad for a lot of new boys'—a remark which, together with the smile which accompanied it, will never be forgotten by those who had the honour to be in attendance that day.

In addition to the Queen and the Duke of Gloucester, the following are the present occupants of stalls in the King Henry VII Chapel:

General Sir John Shea
Marshal of R.A.F. Sir John Salmond
Admiral of the Fleet Lord Chatfield
Marshal of the R.A.F. Sir Edward Ellington
Admiral of the Fleet Earl of Cork and Orrery
Air Chief Marshal Lord Dowding
Sir Frank Smith
Sir Horace Hamilton
Field Marshal Earl Alexander of Tunis
Admiral of the Fleet Lord Tovey
Admiral Sir William James
General Sir George Giffard
Lord Bridges
General Sir Frederick Pile, Bt.
Field Marshal Sir Claude Auchinleck
Admiral Sir Charles Little
Field Marshal Viscount Montgomery of Alamein
Marshal of the R.A.F. Sir Arthur Harris, Bt.
Admiral Sir Henry Moore

General Sir Ronald Adam, Bt.
General Sir Thomas Riddell-Webster
Marshal of the R.A.F. Lord Douglas of Kirtleside
Air Chief Marshal Sir Edgar Ludlow-Hewitt
Lord Hurcomb
General Lord Ismay
Admiral of the Fleet Sir Algernon Willis
Admiral Sir Neville Syfret
Marshal of the R.A.F. Sir John Slessor
Sir Ulick Alexander
Sir Ernest Gowers
Sir Thomas Gardiner
Sir John Maud
Sir Harold Emmerson
Sir Ivone Kirkpatrick
Lord Normanbrook
Admiral Sir Harold Burrough

In earlier days the ceremony of investiture of Knights of the Bath was frequently delegated to commanders of the royal fleets and armies. We read, for example, in the *Naval Chronicle* of 1801 how Admiral Lord Nelson invested his second-in-command, Rear-Admiral Thomas Graves:

A throne covered with the Union Flag was placed on the quarter-deck with the Royal Standard suspended over it. Guards provided by Royal Marines and the Rifle Corps were ranged on each side. Lord Nelson came up the ladder and made three reverences to the throne. Rear-Admiral Graves was then introduced between two senior officers and kneeled down, when Lord Nelson, in the name of His Majesty, laid on his shoulders the ceremonial sword which had been presented to him by the Captains of the Fleet who had fought under his command at the Battle of the Nile. The new Knight then rose and Nelson placed the Riband and Badge over his right shoulder and the Star on his left breast.

Though in the case of armies in the field the ceremonial was not quite so elaborate and often took place in a camp or bivouac, Field-Marshal the Duke of Wellington invested many senior officers with the insignia of the Bath.

As has been explained in an earlier chapter, there were frequent occasions in the past on which, when a recipient was domiciled in a foreign country and unlikely to return to his own country for a considerable time, investitures with British insignia were performed by a foreign monarch who was of the Christian faith. It was, however, a curious anomaly when a Mohammedan prince was delegated to invest a Christian knight. This occurred, however, when Admiral Sir John Lyster, who was Minister Plenipotentiary to the Great Mogul, was invested with the insignia of the Bath by the Nabob of the Carnatic. This ceremony was arranged for political reasons and was carried out with the greatest magnificence and splendour at a Durbar held at Madras in 1771. On a later occasion a similar ceremony was carried out by the Nabob of Arcot, who invested Sir Hector Munro.

From written descriptions of these ceremonies it is manifest that the settings and arrangements were most striking and elaborate. A solemn procession was formed in which the 'Letters Patent from the King-Sovereign', authorising the Mohammedan potentate to perform the investiture on his behalf, were borne on a state elephant, magnificently caparisoned and surrounded by a large armed escort. After the highly ceremonial firing of the royal salute, the investiture was carried out in the presence of a huge concourse and before thousands of troops, and at the close of the ceremony there was a public feast and a display of fireworks.

Just as was laid down in the statutes of the Garter, the statutes of the Bath ordained that knights who were found guilty of the crimes of heresy, high treason or cowardice were to be degraded from the order. It is of interest to note that, though felony came next to treason in the 'precedence of crimes', it was adjudged in a chapter of the Garter held in 1606 that conviction of felony did not also entail degradation from an order of chivalry.

For instance, after the Earl of Somerset had been convicted of murder in that year it was ruled that 'Felony comes not within the compass of the Statutes as not being particularly specified among the Reproaches there reckoned up', and in fact he continued as a Knight of the Garter until his death.

Though provision was made in the statutes for such degradations as might be deemed necessary, apart from foreigners whose countries were at war with Great Britain, there have only been two cases of degradation or expulsion of knights from the Bath.

The first case was that of Lord Cochrane, K.B., in 1814, and it is difficult to understand why the harsh sentence of degradation was enforced. Though he was found guilty of 'having conspired to injure and aggrieve divers of our subjects', his crime appears to have been little more than a 'misdemeanour'.

It would seem that most historians of that time felt that his outstanding bravery and distinguished record of service should have been allowed to redeem the crime imputed to him. None the less, in a warrant, which was signed by the Prince Regent on behalf of the sovereign on 15th July 1814, it was ordained that:

Sir Thomas Cochrane commonly called Lord Cochrane shall no longer be deemed a Knight Companion of the Order of the Bath but shall be declared to be removed and degraded from that most honourable Order and from all immunities and advantages appertaining thereto.

There is a note in the records of the order that on 11th August of that year his banner and other achievements were removed by Bath King of Arms from his stall in King Henry the Seventh Chapel.

In 1831 this Lord Cochrane, on the death of his father, succeeded to the Earldom of Dundonald, and in 1832 King William granted him a free pardon under the Great Seal. In May 1847 Queen Victoria nominated him to be a Knight Grand Cross of the Order of the Bath and he was thus restored to the order and was invested with the insignia by Her Majesty on 13th July following.

Except for one or two cases in the Order of the Garter when Queen Mary ascended the throne in 1553, this is the only case known in which a knight who had been degraded from an order of knighthood in England was subsequently restored to that order.

In 1816 occurred the second and, except for foreign enemies, the last instance of a knight being expelled from the Bath. The knight was General Sir Eyre Coote, at one time Governor of Jamaica. He died in 1823 and should not be confused with another General Sir Eyre Coote, also a G.C.B., at one time Commander-in-Chief in India, who died in India in 1783. He was degraded by royal warrant dated 25th July, 1816, for dishonourable conduct, and his banner and achievements were removed from his stall with the customary marks of dishonour.

It is of interest to note that, though Lord Cochrane and Sir Eyre

Coote lost their appointments as Knights of the Bath, they were not deprived of the dignity of knighthood, and to this day there is no statute which would authorise such deprivation.

Though it was strictly laid down on the re-establishment of the order that its records should be kept accurately and carefully preserved, in fact it was not until the beginning of this century that these records began to be kept in such a way that they could be referred to and checked easily. They are now maintained with meticulous accuracy.

As the Order of Saint Patrick is now to all intents and purposes obsolete, the Order of the Bath now ranks next after the Garter and the Thistle.

As appointments to these two "great orders" are nowadays seldom, if ever, given to the heads of the military services in times of peace, it can be assumed that appointment to the first class of the Order of the Bath is the highest military honour available.

In earlier days when those who had been appointed members of the order attended an investiture to receive from the Sovereign the insignia due to them, their names were read out by the Bath King of Arms, but nowadays this duty is performed by the Lord Chamberlain, as is the case for all the orders of chivalry when those who have been appointed thereto attend an investiture at Buckingham Palace.

The salient points of the present-day statutes are as follows:

The Kings and Queens regnant of the United Kingdom are and for ever shall be Sovereigns of the Order and to them shall belong all power of annulling or augmenting every part of the Statutes.

A Prince of the Royal Blood being a descendant of King George the First, or such other exalted person as the Sovereign may appoint, shall hold the office of Great Master and shall be the First or Principal Knight Grand Cross of the Order, and to his custody shall be confided the Great Seal of the Order.

The order shall contain three Classes, Knights Grand Cross, Knights Commanders and Companions. Each of these Classes shall contain two subdivisions—one Military and one Civil—and each of these subdivisions shall be composed partly of Ordinary, partly of Additional (those made in time of war, or at a Coronation or on some other special occasion) and partly of Honorary Members (who shall be persons of Foreign Nationality).

The number of appointments now permissible in the various classes of the Order are now as follows:

CLASS AND DIVISION	CLASSES, DIVISIONS, AND SUB-DIVISIONS	NUMBERS ALLOWED BY STATUTE	
	KNIGHTS GRAND CROSS		
1st Class			
Military Division	Navy and Marines (1 p.a.)	20	
	Army (3 in 2 years)	32	
	Air Force (1 p.a.)	14	68
	Forces of Member Countries of the Commonwealth, overseas	2	
Civil Division	Civilian Services (3 in 2 years)		27
	TOTAL (5 p.a.)		95
	KNIGHTS COMMANDERS		
2nd Class			
Military Division	Navy and Marines (4 p.a.)	65	
	Army (7 in 2 years)	48	
	Air Force (3 p.a.)	54	173
	Forces of Member Countries of the Commonwealth, overseas	6	
Civil Division	Civilian Services including Territorial Army and Territorial Army and Air Force Associations (6 p.a.)		112
	TOTAL (16 p.a.)		285

CLASS AND DIVISION	CLASSES, DIVISIONS, AND SUB-DIVISIONS	NUMBERS ALLOWED BY STATUTE	
	COMPANIONS		
3rd Class *Military Division*	Navy and Marines (39 in 2 years)	291	
	Army (17 p.a.)	358	
	Air Force (15 p.a.)	244	943
	Forces of Member Countries of the Commonwealth, overseas	50	
Civil Division	Civilian Services including Territorial Army and Territorial Army and Air Force Associations 30 p.a.)		555
	TOTAL (81 p.a.)		1,498

The mantles of the Knights Grand Cross are of crimson satin lined with white taffeta, and on the left side of the mantle is embroidered a representation of the star of the order.

The insignia for Military Knights Grand Cross consist of a collar of gold, weighing thirty ounces troy weight, and composed of nine royal crowns, eight roses, thistles and shamrocks issuing from a gold sceptre and enamelled in their proper colours, linked together with seventeen knots, enamelled argent: from the collar is suspended a gold badge in the shape of a Maltese Cross of eight points, terminating with small gold balls, having in each of the four angles a lion passant, and in the centre the rose, thistle and shamrock issuing from a sceptre between three royal crowns, within a circle gules inscribed with the motto *Tria Juncta in Uno,* encompassed by two laurel branches issuant from an escrol whereon is inscribed *Ich Dien* in letters of gold. The star is composed of rays of silver, charged with a gold Maltese Cross of which the centre shall be charged and inscribed similarly to the badge. It is worn on the left side.

The collar for Civil Knights Grand Cross is similar to that of the Military Division, but the badge and star differ in the following manner:

The badge is of gold and of an oval shape composed of a rose, thistle and shamrock issuing from a sceptre between three royal crowns, the whole surrounded by the motto *Tria Juncta in Uno*.

The star is composed of rays of silver issuing from a centre and is charged with three royal crowns, charged and inscribed similarly to the badge.

The collars are returnable on the death of the holder.

The insignia of Knights Commanders of the Military and Civil Divisions are similar to but smaller than those for the Knights Grand Cross of these divisions. The badge is worn round the neck and the star is placed on the left side.

The badges for Companions of the Military and Civilian Divisions are similar to but smaller than those worn by the Knights Commanders of these divisions. The badge is worn round the neck.

The ceremony of installation of Knights Grand Cross is performed in King Henry the Seventh Chapel in the Abbey Church of Westminster.

For the greater splendour and dignity of the order it is lawful for Knights Grand Cross upon all occasions to bear and use supporters to their arms.

The officers of the order take precedence in the following order:

The Great Master (the Duke of Gloucester)
The Dean (the Dean of Westminster)
The King of Arms (at present Air Chief Marshal Sir James Robb, G.C.B.)
The Registrar and Secretary (at present Major-General D. Wimberley, C.B.)
The Genealogist (at present Garter King of Arms)
The Gentleman Usher (at present Rear-Admiral A. St. V. Sherbrooke, V.C., C.B.)
The Deputy Secretary (the Secretary of the Central Chancery of the Orders of Knighthood).

Services of the Order of the Bath are usually held in Westminster Abbey once in every four years. In the course of these services all Knights Grand Cross, wearing their crimson mantles, move in solemn procession from the choir of the Abbey to King Henry the Seventh Chapel—the actual chapel of the order. On arrival there, a most dignified ceremony takes place in the course of which those Knights Grand Cross who are due to be installed are placed in their respective stalls by the Great Master. Before being installed these knights swear an oath of loyalty to the Sovereign. The senior knight, on behalf of those installed, offers the ceremonial sword of the order to the dean who places it upon the altar and then returns it to the knight. This sword was purchased by a legacy from Air Vice-Marshal Sir Charles Longcroft who was for many years an Officer of the Order.

The service is attended by the State Trumpeters, detachments of the Gentlemen-at-Arms (the Bodyguard) and of the Queen's Bodyguard of the Yeomen of the Guard. Members of all classes of the order are eligible to be present at this service.

CHAPTER VI

The Most Distinguished Order of Saint Michael and Saint George

Shortly after the assumption of the sovereignty of the Island of Malta by the King of England in 1814, when the seven Ionian islands were also placed under the protection of Great Britain, for political reasons it became necessary to institute a new order of chivalry.

The purpose of this order was to provide a means of conferring a mark of royal favour on the most meritorious of the Ionians and Maltese who had showed outstanding loyalty to the Crown. It was also to be given to those British subjects who were serving in an official capacity in the Mediterranean area and who had rendered distinguished service in those parts.

The order was founded on 27th April 1818 by the Prince Regent on behalf of his father, King George the Third. The Lord Commissioner or, as he became later, the Governor and Commander-in-Chief of this new independent state was *ex officio* the Grand Master of the order and its first or principal Knight Grand Cross. The order, like the Bath, was to consist of three classes, and the statutory maxima were fixed at:

    8 Knights Grand Cross
  12 Knights Commanders
  24 Companions (or *Cavalieri* when the holders were Maltese).

At first the intention was that members of all three classes should be entitled to be styled 'Sir' and that the third class should take precedence above knights bachelor. Confusion was caused, however, by the extraordinary idea that, though they could use the title Sir, the *Cavalieri*, or third class, were not to receive the accolade of knighthood.

Accordingly, in 1832 new statutes clarified this point by ordaining that only the two senior classes were to be knighted. At the same time the statutory maxima were increased to:

15 Knights Grand Cross
20 Knights Commanders
25 Companions (or *Cavalieri*).

In 1850 the number of Knights Grand Cross was increased further to twenty.

In 1864 the Ionian Islands were ceded to Greece, and in 1868 the order was entirely remodelled so that all British subjects who were either serving in foreign countries overseas or who were domiciled in any of the British Possessions overseas were made eligible for appointment to it. The statutory maxima were increased further to:

25 Knights Grand Cross
60 Knights Commanders
100 Companions.

In 1861 the order was placed in the scale of precedence next below the Order of the Star of India, which had been instituted in that year. In the course of the next thirty years the statutory maxima were steadily increased, and by 1902 they had reached the following numbers:

100 Knights Grand Cross (G.C.M.G.)
300 Knights Commanders (K.C.M.G.)
600 Companions (C.M.G)

During the first two years of the 1914–18 war the order served to some extent as a kind of junior Order of the Bath, and many officers of the armed services, from the rank of lieutenant-colonel, and equivalent naval rank, upwards, received appointments therein. Appointments to the third class of the order were greatly reduced after the institution of the Order of the British Empire in 1917, and thereafter it became the policy to reserve appointments in the Order of Saint Michael and Saint George for diplomats, members of the Foreign Service and for those who had performed valuable administrative service in connection with the Colonies and the British Dominions, or, as they came to be described, the Countries of the Commonwealth Overseas.

The order now consists of:

The Sovereign and Chief and of the Order (the Queen)

The Prelate (the Bishop of Birmingham)

The Grand Master (Field-Marshal Earl Alexander of Tunis, K.G. G.C.B., O.M., G.C.M.G., C.S.I., D.S.O., M.C.)

The Chancellor (Lord Norrie, G.C.M.G., G.C.V.O., C.B., D.S.O., M.C.)

The Secretary (the Permanent Under Secretary of State, Colonial Office)

The King of Arms (Lord Inchyra)

The Registrar (the Permanent Under Secretary of State, Commonwealth Relations Office)

The Gentleman Usher of the Blue Rod (Sir George Stooke, K.C.M.G.)

The statutory maxima of ordinary members of the three classes are now:

G.C.M.G.—100 (not more than 7 per annum)

K.C.M.G.—355 (not more than 24 per annum)

C.M.G.—1,435 (not more than 103 per annum)

Princes of the blood royal who are descendants of the body of King George the First may be appointed Extra Knights Grand Cross, and foreign princes and such other foreign persons or members of a republic within the Commonwealth as the sovereign may think fit to appoint to the order are classed as honorary members. Neither extra, nor additional, nor honorary members count towards the statutory numbers prescribed for the various classes.

The qualification for ordinary members is that they must be subjects of the British Crown or such British protected persons as are connected with any of the territories under the protection and administration of the British Sovereign. They must either hold or have held high and confidential offices or have rendered extraordinary and important services (other than military service) within or in relation to any part of the Commonwealth beyond the seas or in territories under British protection or administration. Those who have rendered important or loyal services in relation to foreign affairs are also eligible for appointment to the order.

As the Order of the Star of India is now obsolescent, in due course the Order of Saint Michael and Saint George will follow the Order of the Bath in the official order of precedence. It is ordained in the statutes that the Sovereign and the Knights Grand Cross on all great and solemn occasions shall wear mantles of saxon-blue satin lined with scarlet silk. On the left side of the mantle is a representation of the star of the order, which is composed of seven rays of silver between each of which a small ray of gold issues, and over all is the Red Cross of Saint George. In the centre of the star, within a blue circle inscribed in gold with the motto *Auspicium Melioris Aevi*, is a representation of the Archangel Saint Michael, holding in his right hand a flaming sword, and trampling upon Satan.

The collar of the order is composed of lions of England (royally crowned), of Maltese crosses and of the cyphers 'S.M.' and 'S.G.'. In the centre of the collar there is an imperial crown over two winged lions, each holding in his fore-paw a book and seven arrows. The whole of the collar is of gold, excepting the crosses, which are enamelled white and edged with gold.

From the collar hangs the badge of the order, which is an enamelled white cross of fourteen points, having on one side the same design as that of the star, and on the other side a representation of Saint George, on horseback and in armour, armed with a spear and encountering a dragon.

On those occasions when the collar is not worn the Knights Grand Cross wear the badge suspended from a saxon-blue riband of the width of four inches, with a scarlet central stripe, passing from the right shoulder to the left side. The collar is returnable on the death of the holder unless he received it prior to 14th December, 1948, in which case it became his personal property. Knights Grand Cross are entitled to bear and use supporters to their arms.

Except that they receive no collars, the insignia of Knights Commanders are similar to the badges and stars of the Knights Grand Cross, but they are of smaller size. The badge of a Companion is similar to that of a Knight Commander, but it is of smaller size.

Both Knights Commanders and Companions wear their badges round the neck. Further details as to the method of wearing the insignia are to be found in Chapter XII.

The chapel of the order is in the south-west corner of Saint Paul's Cathedral, having been placed there on 15th January 1904. Services of the order are held there annually. Banners and stall-plates for Knights Grand Cross are erected there; and while his banner is taken down after the death of a knight, his stall-plate remains in the chapel as a permanent memorial.

Though in the earlier years of this century numerous foreigners were appointed honorary members of the order, it is now only on comparatively rare occasions that appointments are given to those not of British nationality or British protected persons.

Amongst comparatively recent honorary appointments to the first class was that made to Doctor Adenauer, Chancellor of West Germany, in 1958, and that to the President of Pakistan in 1960. Amongst other distinguished persons who have received the insignia of the G.C.M.G. during the past fifty years are the Emperor of Ethiopia in 1916, King George the Second of Greece and the Sultan of Zanzibar in 1936, Monsieur Henri Spaak in 1937, Messieurs Edouard Daladier and Georges Bonnet in 1938, and Doctor Salazar of Portugal in 1950.

CHAPTER VII

The Royal Victorian Order and the Royal Victorian Chain

Towards the end of the nineteenth century the Prime Minister had almost entire control over the award of all honours of an official nature.

When, early in 1896, the Premier of that time (Lord Salisbury) was asked by Queen Victoria's Private Secretary to give his views on a proposal by Her Majesty to institute an order which would be entirely in her personal gift he offered no objection. He made the proviso, however, that the Government must not be asked to contribute to the expenses incurred thereby.

He thought it would be an excellent idea to keep the new order entirely in the hands of the Sovereign, and he considered that recipients of its insignia would value the honour all the more because it was a personal gift which had not only been paid for by the Sovereign but which expressed in a most gracious manner Her Majesty's own feelings towards them and her appreciation of their personal service.

Thus the Royal Victorian Order was instituted on 21st April 1896, on the strict understanding that the Government would not be expected to contribute towards its cost.

The purpose of the order was to reward personal service to the Sovereign, and the statutes ordained that those admitted as ordinary members of the several classes of the order were to be such persons as might have rendered extraordinary or important or personal services to the Sovereign or who might thereafter merit the royal favour. The statutes ordained also that the honorary members of the several classes of the order were to consist of foreign princes and foreign persons on whom the Sovereign might think fit to confer the honour of being received into the order for personal services.

At the time of the institution of the order, while its Knights Grand Cross and Knights Commanders ranked junior to the equivalent ranks in other existing orders of chivalry, members of the third class, namely Commanders, ranked senior to members of the third class, or Companions, of the Order of the Bath, of the two Indian orders and of the Order of Saint Michael and Saint George. In addition, the Commanders of the Royal Victorian Order wore their badge round the neck, while the Companions of all the other orders wore their badges on the breast together with breast-decorations and campaign and commemorative medals.

As has always been the case in the past, appointments to the order are still at the present day very much the personal gifts of the Sovereign.

The order consists of five classes (Knights or Dames Grand Cross, Knights or Dames Commanders, Commanders, and members of a fourth and fifth class), and it includes also a medal in three grades—silver-gilt, silver and bronze. There have never been any limitations to the number of appointments, and these are made entirely at the discretion of the Sovereign.

Queen Victoria bestowed awards in the order sparingly and only on those who were either relatives or close to her personally or who had rendered service of a personal nature or in connection with her private affairs.

King Edward the Seventh has been described as being far 'less rigorous' in his interpretation of the words 'important personal service' and it would appear that he quite often put a case containing an M.V.O. badge into the hand of one who had rendered some comparatively small service which had added to his pleasure and comfort. As he did not always remember to tell those responsible for keeping the records of the order that he had made these gifts, it was not always easy to maintain an accurate note of the names and descriptions of all recipients of junior awards. He used the order very much as a personal 'present', and it was once jokingly said that it depended on his ability as a cook whether the head chef at the place where the king was spending a holiday received a silvergilt, silver or bronze medal of the Royal Victorian Order. We read in Lord Hardinge of Penshurst's fascinating book *Old Diplomacy* that

'King Edward had rather foreign ideas about decorations. He liked people to be plastered with them'.

It was not until the reign of King George the Fifth that the order began to justify its position in the order of precedence of British orders and decorations, and soon after his accession it came to enjoy a unique prestige as a high honour and a valuable personal gift from the monarch.

King Edward the Eighth opened the ranks of the order to ladies, and his first action thereafter was to make his mother a Dame Grand Cross therein. He made no other appointments in the order, but after his abdication one or two of those who had assisted him personally at that sad and difficult time received appointments to the order from his successor on the throne.

King George the Sixth treated the order in a manner similar to that adopted by his father, but possibly in an even more personal manner, and certainly no one received any appointment therein without his most careful consideration. The present Sovereign, as in so many other matters, has followed the wise and careful rules laid down by her beloved father. As a result, by many persons who cannot aspire to the Garter, Thistle or Order of Merit, the Royal Victorian Order is looked upon as the most desirable honour, preferable to all others, even the Order of the Bath. It must be pointed out, however, that it has become the custom to give foreigners an increasingly large number of honorary awards of Royal Victorian Order insignia in connection with the state visits of the Sovereign abroad, and similar visits to this country by the Sovereigns or heads of states of foreign countries. This procedure, though no doubt difficult to curtail, tends to decrease the value of appointments to the order, and it is suggested that many of these foreign recipients, instead of receiving appointments in the Royal Victorian Order, should receive awards in the Order of the British Empire, particularly as many state visits are matters of government policy and international politics. Presumably it is considered more economical to give Orders and Medals rather than a large number of presents. This may be so, as we read in the journal of Queen Victoria's visit to Napoleon III in Paris in 1855 that she presented £1,000 to the 'poor of Paris', £1,500 to the palace servants, while she gave to other members of the Imperial Household presents costing well over £4,000.

The chapel of the order is the Queen's Chapel of the Savoy,

which is unique in that it is the private possession of the Sovereign in his or her right as the Duke of Lancaster. It is not within the jurisdiction of any archbishop or bishop.

It was King George the Sixth who ordained that from the date of his coronation it should be regarded as the chapel of the order. It was once the principal of one of the three chapels serving a hospital or alms house founded by Henry VII. By some it is thought that the chapel may have formed part of the Palace of the Savoy, the residence of John of Gaunt, which was described as 'the finest palace in all the land'. When this palace was burnt down in 1381, in the course of Wat Tyler's rebellion, at least a part of this chapel fortunately escaped damage.

The first service of the order was held on 22nd October, 1946, when a particularly beautiful set of silver altar plate of a modern pattern, which had been presented by the Sovereign and other members of the Royal Family, was handed by King George the Sixth to the chaplain of the order (the Rev. Cyril Cresswell, K.C.V.O.) for formal dedication.

Further services were held in 1949 and 1958, the first for the unveiling by King George the Sixth of a tablet commemorating those members of the order who lost their lives during the Second World War and the second for the dedication in the presence of the Queen of a number of commemorative windows.

Queen Elizabeth the Queen Mother is the Grand Master of the order and the officers are the Chancellor (the Lord Chamberlain), the Secretary (the Keeper of the Privy Purse), the Registrar (the Secretary of the Central Chancery of the Orders of Knighthood) and the Chaplain. There is an Honorary Genealogist of the order and this appointment is held at present by Lord Sinclair.

Owing to lack of space, no banners are hung in the chapel, but many members of the Royal Family and other Knights and Dames Grand Cross of the order have had stall-plates erected there to show their arms, to which they are entitled to add supporters.

The anniversary of the institution of the order is 20th June, this being the day of the accession to the throne of England of Queen Victoria.

The mantles of Knights and Dames Grand Cross are of dark-blue silk, edged with red satin and lined with white silk, and fastened by a cordon of dark-blue silk and gold. On the left side of the mantle is a representation of the star of the order, which is a silver chipped star of eight points in the centre whereof is a representation of the badge described below.

The collar of the order is of gold, composed of octagonal pieces and oblong perforated and ornamental frames alternately, linked together with gold; the said pieces being edged and ornamented with gold, and each containing upon a blue enamelled ground a gold rose jewelled with a carbuncle. The frames are of gold, and each contains a portion of the inscription *Victoria ... Britt. Reg. ... Def. Fid. ... Ind. Imp.* in letters of white enamel. In the centre of the collar is an octagonal piece, enamelled blue, edged with red, and charged with a white saltire, thereon being a gold medallion of the effigy of Queen Victoria, from which hangs the badge of the order. The badge consists of a white enamelled Maltese Cross of eight points, in the centre of which is an oval of crimson enamel with the royal and imperial monogram of Queen Victoria, in gold, and encircling this is a blue enamelled riband inscribed with the motto of the order, *Victoria*, in letters of gold, and above this is the imperial crown enamelled in proper colours.

When the collar is not worn, the badge is worn suspended from a dark-blue riband, with a narrow edge of three stripes (red, white and red) on each side, the riband being of the breadth of three and three-quarter inches in the case of Knights Grand Cross and of the breadth of two and a quarter inches in the case of Dames Grand Cross, passing from the right shoulder to the left side.

Knights Commanders wear around their neck a riband of the same colours and pattern as that of the Knights Grand Cross, of the breadth of one and three-quarter inches and pendent there-from the badge of a Knight Commander which is of similar form and pattern to that appointed for the Knights Grand Cross, but of a smaller size. They also wear on the left side of their coats a silver star composed of a Maltese Cross, with smaller rays issuing from the centre between the angles of the cross, and in the centre the badge of the order, as before described, except that the cross is of frosted silver instead of white enamel. Dames Commanders wear a badge of similar form and pattern to that appointed for Knights Commanders, attached to a similar riband tied in a bow and worn on the left shoulder. They also wear a similar star.

Commanders of the order wear a riband and badge of similar

form and pattern to those appointed for the Knights and Dame Commanders of the order, but they are not entitled to wear a star of the order.

Members of the fourth class wear a badge of similar pattern to that appointed for the Commanders, but of a smaller size, pendent from a riband of the breadth of one and a quarter inches, attached to the left side of the coat or dress as may be appropriate.

Members of the fifth class wear in a like manner a riband and badge similar to those appointed for the fourth class, except that the cross is of frosted silver instead of white enamel.

The Royal Victorian Medal, for which both men and women are eligible, is of either silver-gilt, silver or bronze, having on the obverse the effigy of the reigning Sovereign and on the reverse the royal cypher upon an ornamental shield within a wreath of laurel and below a scroll bearing the words *Royal Victorian Medal.*

Further meritorious services by holders of any one of the Royal Victorian Medals may be recognised by the award of clasps to these medals.

It should be noted that in order to distinguish between British recipients of the Royal Victorian Medal, who normally have to render very long service before gaining the award, and foreign recipients, who may gain it in recognition of participation in a state visit of a few a days' duration, King George the Sixth in 1951 ordained that when awarded to foreigners the ribbon of the medal should be distinguished by the superimposition of a central white stripe one eighth of an inch in width.

The miniature badges to be worn by Knights and Dames Grand Cross, Knights and Dames Commanders, Commanders and members of the fourth class are replicas of the badges of the respective classes, the size being half that of the badge of the members of the fourth class.

The miniature badge to be worn by a member of the fifth class is a replica of his badge, but of half its size.

THE ROYAL VICTORIAN CHAIN

This chain does not form part of the Royal Victorian Order, and it confers no precedence or any addition to the style, title or description of the recipient. It was instituted by King Edward the Seventh in 1902, as 'a pre-eminent mark of the Sovereign's esteem and affection towards such persons as his Majesty specially desired to honour'.

The bestowal of this chain upon ladies was introduced by King George the Sixth in 1937 in consequence of the instruction given by King Edward the Eighth in 1936 which authorised the admission of ladies to the Royal Victorian Order.

At the present day the gift of this chain indicates a rare mark of the highest distinction and special esteem on the part of the Sovereign.

Male holders wear the chain round the neck in a manner somewhat similar to that in which the collar of an order is worn, except that the chain does not hang at an equal distance at the back and in front, but hangs from round the neck and rests upon the chest. In the day-time the chain should be worn on all occasions when British orders of chivalry are worn, and ladies should wear it pinned to the left side of the dress. With evening dress ladies should wear the chain above miniatures and badges and stars of orders. In evening dress male holders should shorten the chain and wear it as the neck badge of an order is worn in evening dress, but, as not more than one neck badge is worn at one time in evening dress, the chain should not be worn if the holder possesses a neck badge of a higher grade, such as the Order of Merit or that of a Grand Master or Chancellor of a British order.

The chain, which is returnable on the death of a holder, is of gold, composed of lotuses, trefoils, thistles and roses. It is linked together with a double chain, and in the centre, within a wreath, is the cypher *E.R. II*, enamelled in red, surmounted by the imperial crown, and pendent from a wreath is the badge of the Royal Victorian Order. In addition to Queen Elizabeth the Queen Mother, and the Dukes of Gloucester and Windsor those who hold the chain are, in order of date of appointment:

The Nizam of Hyderabad, 1 January, 1946
Lord Fisher of Lambeth, 1 January, 1959
Sir John Weir, 9 June, 1949
The Duke of Norfolk, 1 June, 1953
The Duke of Beaufort, 1 June, 1953
Rt. Hon. Vincent Massey, 22 July, 1960
The Earl of Scarbrough, 1 January, 1963
The Duke of Hamilton and Brandod, 28 February, 1964

while foreign holders of the chain include the following, in order of date of appointment:

King Gustav VI of Sweden, 4 June, 1923
The Emperor of Ethiopia, 30 October, 1930
Prince Paul of Yugoslavia, 26 November, 1934
King Leopold III (formerly King of the Belgians), 16 November, 1937
The Shahanshah of Persia, 21 July, 1948
Queen Juliana of the Netherlands, 21 November, 1950
King Olav V of Norway, 24 June, 1955
General Francisco Lopes, (formerly President of Portugal), 18 February, 1957
King Frederik IX of Denmark, 21 May, 1957
General Charles de Gaulle, (President of the French Republic), 5 April, 1960
The King of Thailand, 19 July, 1960
The King of Nepal, 2 March, 1961

CHAPTER VIII

The Most Excellent Order of the British Empire

During the 1914–18 war there was a total mobilization of man and woman-power in the British Isles. It was quite a new situation and entirely different from anything that had happened before in the British Empire. Such wars as those in the Crimea and South Africa had hardly affected the ordinary life of the nation because the numbers fighting were comparatively low and only a small proportion of the population suffered personal loss through deaths of relatives in battle. The situation was very different in 1917. There were few families then who were unaffected by the war and many had suffered bereavement.

Thus, in that year, when casualties on the battle-front were immense and when large numbers, both in the British Isles and in other parts of the Empire overseas, and in allied countries, were helping in the war-effort, the necessity arose for a new award of honour which could be given on a generous scale. King George the Fifth was faced with a problem somewhat similar to that which was posed to the Prince Regent in 1814 and which he solved by enlarging the Order of the Bath. But the problem facing King George in 1917 was far greater. It was not feasible to solve it by enlarging certain existing orders with the addition of two extra classes, namely, a fourth and fifth class to the Orders of the Bath and Saint Michael and Saint George, though suggestions on these lines received the consideration of the Sovereign and his advisers.

As far as the armed services were concerned there was no existing decoration which could suitably be awarded to the less senior ranks for administrative services at the headquarters of formations, at the many installations and camps at home or at ports on the lines of communications both at home and abroad, and at places such as base hospitals. For such services neither the Distinguished Service Order nor the existing decorations and medals for gallantry could properly be awarded without altering greatly the character of these awards. To have done so would have destroyed their value not only in the eyes of those who had received them for bravery in battle, but also in the opinion of the relatives of recipients who, later, had been killed in battle. Some so-called gallantry awards had already been greatly lessened in value by the incorrect and unfair manner in which they had been awarded to certain staff-officers, aides-de-camp and other ranks employed in comfortable, or, as they were styled, 'cushy' posts in safe areas. It must be realised that in the 1914–18 war a brigade headquarter, and of course the headquarters of higher formations, were normally quite safe areas. It was thus very galling at that time for those who had served for long periods in the filth and danger of the front-line trenches to see during their brief periods of release from the battle area immaculately dressed staff officers and A.D.C.s, with red bands round their caps, with the ribbon of the Distinguished Service Order or the Military Cross sewn on their uniform jackets. Nor was there at that time any existing award suitable for the general recognition of the wonderful work of women, not only in official women's services, but also in munition factories, war depots and hospitals—work which was little different from or less arduous than that performed by men in similar places.

Again, there was no award which could appropriately be given to those persons who, being outside the Civil Service, were ineligible for the Imperial Service Order and whose positions and occupations were such that their services did not qualify them for an award in the Order of the Bath or the Order of Saint Michael and Saint George. The outstanding requirement was that the new honour had to provide suitable awards for all classes and ranks of the community—from members of the most aristocratic families in the land down to those in quite humble walks of life. In that respect the new order was not required to resemble the more ancient orders of chivalry where the inflexible rule had been to keep them exclusive to those of high social standing, rank or grade.

Accordingly, when the Great War was at its most critical period and there was no prospect of an early conclusion, King George the

Fifth decided to create a new order of chivalry. The first idea was that the order was to be given to those who rendered important service to the Empire directly connected with the war but mainly of a non-combatant nature. The greatest innovation of all was the inclusion of women in an order of chivalry. Up till then, apart from ladies of the Royal Family and a few Indian princesses,* recipients of certain Royal private orders and awards confined entirely to ladies (such as the Crown of India), the only lady who had received an appointment to one of the official orders to which men were appointed was Miss Florence Nightingale, who had been given the Order of Merit by King Edward the Seventh in 1907.

The new order was not intended primarily for members of the permanent Civil Service, but they were not to be excluded if they had performed especially onerous and valuable work connected with the war. It was decided that awards in the new order should be given on a particularly generous scale to foreigners who had been of assistance to the British war effort. At first the idea was that as long as the war lasted appointments in the order were to be given only to non-combatant 'war-workers' who were performing tasks which were helpful to the fighting services. None the less, King George the Fifth always intended that after the war the order should be utilised to reward services to the state, construed in a much wider sense than was possible in the case of the Orders of the Bath, Saint Michael and Saint George and the Indian orders. It was also intended that in peacetime the order should be used as a reward for distinguished service to the Arts, Literature and Science as well as for public services rendered by persons outside the senior ranks of the Civil Service. It was also to be given to members of such services as the Mercantile Marine and Special Constabulary, and to those employed with charitable and welfare organisations of all kinds, including nursing and hospital services. Members of the armed services who were engaged on administrative or experimental work of a hazardous or generally valuable nature were also to be eligible for appointment to the order.

There was great discussion as to the name to be given to this

*Queen Mary received the insignia of a Knight Grand Cross of the Order of the Star of India from King George the Fifth on the occasion of his visit to India. Earlier, H.H. the Begum of Bhopal had been appointed a G.C.S.I. in 1872, while another Begum of Bhopal was appointed a G.C.I.E. in 1904 and a G.C.S.I. in 1910.

new order. All kinds of titles were suggested. Amongst the most reasonable were the 'Order of George and Mary', the 'Patriotic Service Order', the 'Order of the United Empire', the 'Order of the Imperial Crown' and the 'War Service Order'. There were a number of other somewhat odd suggestions, such as the 'Order of Saint Martin', the 'Order of Saint Lewis', the 'Order of the Golden Rose', and even the 'Order of Mars'.

Eventually King George the Fifth decided that the title of the new order should be 'The Most Excellent Order of the British Empire'. He decided, too, that the order should consist of five classes. The decision to have five classes was influenced largely by the facts that a large number of appointments were to be given to foreigners who had assisted the British war effort and that many foreign orders at that time consisted of five classes. There was also to be a medal of the order and it was decided that among the first list of recipients a generous allotment was to be made to munition workers who had displayed courage and devotion to duty under hazardous circumstances.

It was originally intended by the King that the first two classes of the order would rank immediately after knights bachelor, and that knighthood should not be attached to these two senior classes. He thought that in that way the order would be more acceptable to many for whom a title was not an object of ambition.

The next suggestion was that in the first two classes knighthood should be optional, while for ladies appointed to these classes the title of 'Dame' similarly would be optional. It soon became clear, however, that 'optional knighthood' would be quite impracticable owing to difficulties over the precedence conferred by certain honours—a matter which was of far more importance in the year 1917 than it is now. Moreover, it was thought that those who accepted appointments in the two senior classes would sometimes be placed in an embarrassing position if they had to refuse knighthood in an order of chivalry when it had been offered to them by their Sovereign. It was eventually agreed that it was essential that appointment to the first two classes must automatically carry with it the honour of knighthood and in the case of ladies the appellation of 'Dame'.

In the same way as at that time a Commander of the Royal Victorian Order ranked senior to a Companion of the Order of the Bath and other orders of chivalry, it was at first intended that a Commander of the Order of the British Empire should also rank senior to companions of all orders. Very great objection was offered to this proposal both by the military and civil authorities on the ground that it would involve the degradation not only of the Order of the Bath, which was an ancient and highly coveted honour, but also of other senior orders—the Star of India, the Saint Michael and Saint George and the Indian Empire.

Objection had not been raised when a Commander of the Royal Victorian Order was given seniority over companions of the other orders, because the Victorian Order was the monarch's personal order and was given sparingly, but the proposal to extend this seniority to a commander of a new order which was to be given on a very liberal scale was a very different matter and caused great dissatisfaction.

After most careful consideration the King decided that it would be advisable that in future the three senior classes of the Royal Victorian Order should be placed below the corresponding classes of all other existing British Orders of Chivalry, and that the five classes of the new Order of the British Empire should be ranked next below the equivalent classes of the Royal Victorian Order.

The new order suffered from the same growing-pains as those which had affected the Order of the Bath when it was enlarged in 1815 from a small and very select order of one class to a much larger order of three classes. There is always the same feeling about a new order, particularly when it is given on so lavish a scale as was the case at the institution of the Order of the British Empire. Many of those who received appointments in the first three classes were disappointed at not having received an appointment in one of the more senior and more exclusive orders. One person who was connected with the Royal Household, when he was offered appointment as a Knight Commander of the new order (K.B.E.), instead of the K.C.V.O. for which he had hoped, refused it and only accepted it subsequently because he was told very plainly by the King to do so.

There is no doubt that appointments in the fourth and fifth classes (the O.B.E. and the M.B.E.) were given on far too lavish a scale, just as the C.B. had been awarded too lavishly in 1815, and there is no doubt that many of the recipients of appointments in the Order of the British Empire had not done anything sufficiently important to deserve an Order of any kind. To many senior officers in the armed services the C.B.E. was given as a sort of consolation prize because they had not been fortunate enough to obtain a C.B. or a C.M.G., while the O.B.E. and M.B.E. were given in many cases to those who, if they had been more fortunate, might have received some sort of gallantry award.

In the general estimation, to receive an O.B.E. was not at first regarded as anything of which the recipient could feel particularly proud. There were many jeering remarks and music-hall jokes about the new order. It was said, for instance, that the letters 'O.B.E.' stood for the 'Order of the Bad Egg' or the 'Order for Britain's Everybody'. The tragic mistake made was that no specific limits were placed on the number of awards to be allowed in the several classes, and as a result they became too 'cheap'.

In spite of this generous allotment of awards and the criticisms of the new order aroused thereby, a considerable number of personal applications for appointments therein were submitted by individuals to the heads of the departments under whom they had worked or to important members of the Government. In some of these applications the individual concerned wrote at great length to emphasise how greatly he or she deserved an award and how much more valuable work he or she had rendered than some other person who had already received recognition.

After a few years, however, when appointments began to be made on a very much smaller scale and in accordance with a strictly enforced maximum quota, the reputation and value of the order began to increase slowly but steadily. Nowadays appointment to the order is greatly sought after both in the Military and Civil Divisions and in the main it is only obtained after a long period of valuable and honourable service.

The colour of the riband selected originally was purple, and when in 1918 the order was divided into two divisions—Military and Civil—the riband of the Military Division was marked by a distinguishing scarlet stripe down the centre.

Later on, in 1937, at the wish of Queen Mary, who succeeded the Prince of Wales (now the Duke of Windsor) as Grand Master of the order, the colour of the riband was changed from purple to rose pink with edges of pearl grey, with the Military Division riband carrying a narrow grey stripe down the centre.

By the end of 1919 there were about twenty-two thousand members of the order, by 1938 there were about thirty thousand and now there are over eighty thousand, including many honorary members of foreign nationality. There are also about fourteen thousand holders of the British Empire Medal, as the medal of the order is now described.

Soon after the end of the war in 1918 the question of selecting a spiritual home for the order where regular services could be held began to receive consideration. As early as 1919 it was suggested that the chapel of the order should be in Saint Faith's Chapel in the Crypt of Saint Paul's Cathedral, but at that time the dean and chapter of the cathedral were not enthusiastic about the proposal. A few years later a proposal was made that the banners of the Knights Grand Cross of the order should be placed in Westminster Hall, while services would be held in Saint Margaret's Church, Westminster. No satisfactory conclusion was reached, and so the matter drifted on until 1937, when a new committee was set up and the project received reconsideration. It was decided that if services were to be held they must take place in a building large enough to accommodate representation of all the classes of the order. It was thought that, though some advantages would accompany the use of a large and well-known cathedral such as Canterbury, York, or Liverpool, the inconvenience of travel to these places would prevent many from attending services of the order and even from visiting the chapel. It was felt, therefore, that the chapel must be located in London and at some well-known place whose name meant something to members living overseas. In Saint Paul's there was already a chapel of the Order of Saint Michael and Saint George, while Westminster Abbey was used for services of the Order of the Bath. The placing of the chapel at Southwark Cathedral was considered, but the idea was ruled out because it was thought at that time that this cathedral was insufficiently known.

In 1938 the committee made a definite recommendation that Saint Margaret's Church, Westminster, should be the place selected. In 1939, after protracted correspondence and after elaborate plans had been prepared, just when it appeared that the problem had been settled to the satisfaction of all concerned, the scheme had to be abandoned owing to complications caused by the fact that Saint Margaret's was already the Church of the House of Commons.

Like many other projects, this one was shelved on the outbreak of war in 1939. In 1946, when the war was over, King George the Sixth directed that consideration of the project should be re-opened and a new committee was formed. Queen Mary, as Grand Master, took a great personal interest in this subject and favoured the choice of Southwark, particularly as there was at that time a strong move to develop the area on the south bank of the Thames for important national purposes. In 1949, however, after considerable planning and discussion, it was once more decided that Southwark Cathedral was not really suitable—partly because there was not sufficient seating accommodation there, partly because it was situated in a congested traffic area and partly because the name conveyed little or nothing to those residing overseas. Once more it was reluctantly decided that the attempt to select a suitable place for a permanent chapel for the order must be abandoned, at least for the time being.

In 1957 a new committee was formed and it decided that Saint Paul's was really the only suitable place, both by virtue of its being the cathedral of the capital city and the fact that it lent itself to services attended by very large congregations. Moreover, in the words of a distinguished member of the committee,* it was felt that 'Saint Paul's symbolised the victory of the British spirit during the war of 1939–45 in that, although badly damaged and shaken, it survived the ordeal by battle in an almost miraculous way'. With the approval of the Bishop of London (the Prelate of the Order) and the Dean and Chapter of Saint Paul's, a recommendation to this effect was submitted to the Queen by the chairman of the committee (then Sir Edward and later Lord Bridges), and Her Majesty was graciously pleased to approve the proposal.

In addition to the periodic large services of the order which would be held regularly in the cathedral, it was agreed that a chapel or shrine of the order should be constructed in the east end of the cathedral crypt. This chapel would be available for private prayer and would be furnished suitably so that a limited number of private services—marriages, christenings or memorial services—could be held there throughout the year.

*The Lady Freyberg, G.B.E. In addition to the officials of the order, the other members of the committee were the Dean of Saint Paul's, General Sir Brian Robertson, Sir Malcolm Trustram Eve, The Earl of Crawford and Balcarres, and Admiral Sir Cecil Harcourt.

To some minds the word 'crypt' suggests a damp, dark, cellar-like place below the floor of a church, but the crypt of Saint Paul's Cathedral is far from being that. It is a particularly dignified place in which the vaulting of the ceiling is quite beautiful and it was designed by the great Christopher Wren. In the ancient church which stood formerly on the site of the present cathedral were buried many of the early Saxon kings including Sebba, King of the East Saxons, in 677, and Ethelred, King of the Angles, in 1016. Later on, numerous prelates, poets and statesmen were interred there, but almost every monument and memorial was destroyed in the Great Fire of 1666.

Located there now are the tombs of Wellington and Nelson, together with tombs or memorials to many other distinguished soldiers and sailors such as Jellicoe, Beatty, Roberts, Wolseley, Gordon, Napier and Lawrence.

The tomb of Sir Christopher Wren is to be found there, and nearby lie Sir Joshua Reynolds, Sir Thomas Lawrence, Landseer, Leighton, Turner, and other great artists. There also are memorials for a number of famous musicians including Sir Arthur Sullivan.

The area dedicated to the uses of the chapel is demarcated by wrought ironwork, resembling the famous gates and screens by Tijou which adorn the main cathedral choir. This ironwork, which encloses the chapel and marks the entrances of the ambulatory on either side, consists of pilasters and overthrows to support decorative finials incorporating candle-type light fittings with the stars of the order surmounted by crowns.

Inset in the ironwork pilasters are glass panels, painted in grisaille. Portrait figures of the Royal Founder and his consort and their successors have been included in these panels. Intervening panels depict badges and symbols of the Commonwealth, emphasising the world-wide nature of the order. The floor of the chapel is laid with tiles and carpet to match the colours of the riband of the order. The altar frontal is embroidered with the star of a Knight Grand Cross. The altar, with its cross and candlesticks of wrought iron and gilt, is silhouetted against a dorsal curtain of gold and silver brocade above which are the east windows of the crypt. These are filled with stained and polished glass representing the insignia of the order. In the ambulatory are banners for the Sovereign of the order and other members of the Royal Family.

The shrine of the chapel was completed in April 1960, and it is a fine example of modern architecture which is blended most cleverly with the lovely ancient ceiling.

The architect of the chapel was the late Lord Mottistone, and the artist responsible for the design and production of the stained-glass windows and glass memorial panels was Mr. Brian Thomas.

Invitations to support the project financially were sent to all members of the order for whom addresses were available and the response was most generous. Well over twenty thousand members or relatives of deceased members have sent contributions and these have come from every part of the world and from persons of every creed and colour.

Before the first service was held a total of over £100,000 had either been received or promised under deed of covenant.

This first service, which included the formal dedication of the chapel, was held on 20th May 1960. It was attended by the Queen, the Sovereign of the order, and by the Duke of Edinburgh, the Grand Master of the order. Other members of the Royal Family who were also present were the Duchess of Gloucester G.B.E. and the Duchess of Kent G.B.E.

Amongst others attending were 55 Knights and Dames Grand Cross; 105 Knights and Dames Commanders; 2,700 Commanders, Officers and Members; and 225 holders of the British Empire Medal, making a total of over 3,000 members of the order.

The second Service of the order was held in 1963.

The Order of the British Empire is the order of chivalry of the British democracy. Valuable and useful service is the only test of admission, and in the opinion of many it is the most important order of the British Commonwealth. The order is now used to reward service in every conceivable useful activity.

The motto is *For God and the Empire.*

The original badge of the order had for its central design a figure of Britannia, holding a trident and seated beside a shield bearing the national flag. Later, under a statute dated 9th March 1937, this design was replaced by the effigies in gold of King George the Fifth, the founder of the order, and his consort Queen Mary.

Some sixteen years later, as a result of the retention in the centre of the insignia of the effigies of King George the Fifth and Queen Mary and the fact that the original purple riband had been replaced by one of rose-pink colour, a somewhat amusing complaint was made by the recipient of a badge of the Order of the British Empire in the year after the accession of Queen Elizabeth the Second. He complained that it was bad enough that stocks of insignia should have to be used up which were so many years out of date that they bore effigies of the Queen's grandparents instead of that of the present Sovereign, but when it came to using up riband so old that the original purple colour had faded to a watery pink, that was carrying economy too far!

There is now a medal of the order which is described in the statutes as 'The British Empire Medal'. It is of silver and on the obverse has a representation of Britannia with the motto of the order, and, upon the exergue, the words *For Meritorious Service*. On the reverse of the medal is the royal cypher of the Sovereign and the words *Instituted by King George V*. Services deemed worthy of recognition by the award of this medal but rendered by a person upon whom the medal has already been conferred may be rewarded by the award of a bar, or bars, to be attached to the medal.

The history of the Medal of the Order of the British Empire is as follows.

In 1917 a silver medal was instituted as a reward to those persons not eligible for appointment to the order itself but whose services warranted recognition.

From 1918 onwards there were Military and Civil Divisions of the medal.

In 1922 the award of this medal was discontinued and two new medals were instituted in its place. The first was 'The Medal of the Order of the British Empire for Gallantry', usually known as the 'Empire Gallantry Medal' or the 'E.G.M.'. The second medal was 'The Medal of the Order of the British Empire for Meritorious Service' and it was somewhat smaller than the medal for gallantry. Each of these new medals had a Military and Civil Division.

On the institution of the George Cross in September 1940 the Empire Gallantry Medal, which had been awarded very sparingly (only about a hundred being given), was abolished, and it was ordained that a holder of the Empire Gallantry Medal who was living on 24th September 1940 should return it to the Central Chancery and in its stead become eligible for the award of the George Cross, which he received at an investiture at Buckingham Palace.

In March 1941 instructions were given that the description 'Medal of the Order of the British Empire for Meritorious Service' should be changed to 'The British Empire Medal', and in June 1942 it was ordained that a holder of this medal was entitled to place the letters 'B.E.M.' after his name.

On 6th December 1957 a new statute of the Order of the British Empire was published for the purpose of differentiating between appointments to the order or awards of the medal which were made for the purpose of rewarding acts of gallantry and those which were made as rewards for meritorious service.

Since that date all appointments and awards made for gallantry have been distinguished by the wearing of a silver emblem of two oak leaves on the appropriate riband.

The insignia of the several classes now consist of the following.

For Knights and Dames Grand Cross there is a collar of silver-gilt, composed of six medallions of the royal arms and six medallions of the royal and imperial cypher of the late King George the Fifth alternately, linked together with cables bearing the imperial crown between two sea lions. From the collar hangs a badge which consists of a cross, enamelled pearl, surmounted by the imperial crown. On the reverse of the badge is engraved the royal and imperial cypher of the late King George the Fifth. The centre of the badge is similar to that of the star, described below. When the collar is not worn, the badge is worn suspended from a rose-pink riband edged with pearl grey, passing from the right shoulder to the left side. For Knights Grand Cross the width of the riband is four inches and for Military Knights Grand Cross there is in the centre of the riband a pearl-grey stripe of the width of a quarter of an inch. For Dames Grand Cross the width of the riband is two and a quarter inches, but it is of interest to note that for Military Dames Grand Cross the vertical pearl-grey stripe in the centre of the riband is not added. The reason for this is that Queen Mary, as Grand Master, did not wish any other Dame Grand Cross to wear a riband in any way different from that worn by her. The star is composed of chipped silver rays of eight points in the centre whereof there is a gold medallion bearing the crowned effigies of their late Majesties King George the Fifth and Queen Mary within a circle inscribed with the motto *For God and the Empire.*

The mantle for Knights and Dames Grand Cross is of rose-pink satin lined with pearl-grey silk, fastened with a cordon of pearl-grey silk having two rose-pink and silver tassels attached thereto. On the left side of the mantle is embroidered a representation of the star.

For Knights and Dames Commanders the insignia consists of a badge and star similar to those of the Knights and Dames Grand Cross but of smaller size. The knights wear the badge round the neck from a riband of a breadth of one and three-quarter inches. The dames, when wearing a coat of military pattern, wear the badge in a similar manner, but otherwise wear it on the left shoulder above the star, which both by knights and dames is worn on the left side.

The insignia of a Commander consists of a badge similar to that of the Knights and Dames Commanders and it is worn in the same manner.

The badge of an Officer is of the same form as that of a Commander except that it is of smaller size and is made of silver-gilt. The breadth of the riband is one and a half inches.

The badge of a Member is similar to that of an Officer except that it is made of silver.

The Queen is of course Sovereign of the order, and the Grand Master is His Royal Highness the Prince Philip, Duke of Edinburgh.

The officials of the order are as follows:

Prelate	The Bishop of London.
King of Arms	Air Marshal Sir Roderick Carr, K.B.E., C.B.
Registrar	The Secretary of the Central Chancery of the Orders of Knighthood.
Secretary	The Permanent Secretary to the Treasury.
Dean	The Dean of Saint Paul's.
Gentleman Usher of the Purple Rod	The Viscount Silsoe, G.C.B., G.B.E.
Prelate Emeritus	The Right Rev. and Right Hon. Bishop Wand, K.C.V.O., D.D.
Sub-Dean	The Archdeacon of London.

The number of appointments now permissible in the various classes of the order are as shown on the following pages. There is no statutory limit to the number of medals which may be given.

CLASS AND DIVISION	CLASSES, DIVISIONS, AND SUB-DIVISIONS	NUMBERS ALLOWED BY STATUTE
1st Class	KNIGHT AND DAMES GRAND CROSS	
Military Division	Admiralty (1 in 2 yrs.) War Office (1 in 2 yrs.) Air Ministry (1 in 2 yrs.) Commonwealth Relations Office (1 in 2 yrs.)	9 ⎫ 9 ⎪ 11 ⎬ 31 2 ⎭
Civil Division	United Kingdom (3 p.a.) Foreign Office (1 p.a.) Commonwealth Relations Office (1 p.a.) Colonial Office (1 p.a.)	49 ⎫ 15 ⎫ ⎪ ⎬ 36 ⎬ 85 13 ⎪ ⎪ 8 ⎭ ⎭
	TOTAL (8 p.a.)	116
2nd Class	KNIGHTS AND DAMES COMMANDERS	
Military Division	Admiralty (4 p.a.) War Office (7 in 2 years) Air Ministry (4 p.a.) Commonwealth Relations Office (3 p.a.)	65 ⎫ 69 ⎪ 65 ⎬ 229 30 ⎭
Civil Division	United Kingdom (16 p.a.) Foreign Office (4 p.a.) Commonwealth Relations Office (12 p.a.) Colonial Office (4 p.a.) Central African Office (1 p.a.)	274 ⎫ 60 ⎫ ⎪ ⎪ ⎪ 139 ⎬ 260 ⎬ 534 59 ⎪ ⎪ 2 ⎭ ⎭
	TOTAL (51 p.a.)	763

CLASS AND DIVISION	CLASSES, DIVISIONS, AND SUB-DIVISIONS	NUMBERS ALLOWED BY STATUTE		
3rd Class	COMMANDERS			
Military Division	Admiralty (14 p.a.)	206		
	War Office (30 p.a.)	459		
	Air Ministry (21 p.a.)	320		
	Commonwealth Relations Office (39 p.a.)	234		1248
	Colonial Office (1 p.a.)	27		
	Central African Office (1 p.a.)	2		
Civil Division	United Kingdom (210 p.a.)	3271		
	Foreign Office (18 p.a.)	272		
	Commonwealth Relations Office (72 p.a.)	763	1638	4909
	Colonial Office (32 p.a.)	583		
	Central African Office (8 p.a.)	20		
	TOTAL (448 p.a.)	6157		
4th Class	OFFICERS			
Military Division	Admiralty (30 p.a.)			
	War Office (68 p.a.)			
	Air Ministry (37 p.a.)	219 p.a.		
	Commonwealth Relations Office (80 p.a.)			
	Colonial Office (4 p.a.)			
Civil Division	United Kingdom (401 p.a.)			
	Foreign Office (34 p.a.)			
	Commonwealth Relations Office (170 p.a.)	725 p.a.		
	Colonial Office (120 p.a.)			
	TOTAL	944 p.a.		

CLASS AND DIVISION	CLASSES, DIVISIONS, AND SUB-DIVISIONS	NUMBERS ALLOWED BY STATUTE
5th Class	MEMBERS	
Military Division	Admiralty (27 p.a.) War Office (150 p.a.) Air Ministry (90 p.a.) Commonwealth Relations Office (120 p.a.) Colonial Office (6 p.a.)	393 p.a.
Civil Division	United Kingdom (730 p.a.) Foreign Office (50 p.a.) Commonwealth Relations Office (310 p.a.) Colonial Office (222 p.a.)	1312 p.a.
	TOTAL	1705 p.a.

CHAPTER IX

The Order of Merit and the Order of the Companions of Honour

THE ORDER OF MERIT

Though this order carries no title or rank, it is considered by many to be the most coveted distinction in the whole hierarchy of British honours. It was instituted by King Edward the Seventh on 23rd June 1902, and it has always been treated as a personal award from the Sovereign.

The persons eligible to receive it are those who have rendered particularly outstanding service in the armed services or exceptionally meritorious service towards the advancement of art, literature and science.

Since its foundation only one lady has been admitted to the order, Miss Florence Nightingale, who received her appointment on 29th November 1907 for her outstanding work as 'Organiser of the Nursing System during the Crimean War of 1854—1855'.

The badge of the order is a gold cross of red and blue enamel of eight points, having within a laurel wreath upon a centre of blue enamel the motto of the order, *For Merit*, in letters of gold. On the reverse, also within a laurel wreath, is the royal cypher in gold. The badge is surmounted by a Tudor crown. For those who are appointed for distinguished service with the armed services there is an addition to the badge of two silver swords with gold hilts, placed saltire-wise between the angles of the cross. By male holders the badge is worn round the neck suspended from a riband, half blue and half crimson, two inches in width. When worn with evening dress the riband should be fastened in such a way that the badge hangs immediately below the white tie.

When the order was first instituted its position in the order of precedence was not made clear. In 1910 the following ruling was given by King George the Fifth: 'A holder of the Order of Merit shall come directly after a "G.C.B." and as an order it has precedence immediately after the Bath.' Recipients are entitled to place the letters 'O.M.' after their names. The badge is worn on all occasions when insignia of orders are worn, but in accordance with a ruling given by King Edward the Seventh in 1903 it may not be worn in miniature, though it was decided later that it would be correct for the riband to be worn when ribands of other orders, decorations and medals were worn with undress uniform. The badge is not returnable on the death of the holder.

The statutory number of Ordinary Members (that is, citizens of any of the countries of the British Commonwealth of Nations) is twenty-four, and vacancies are seldom left unfilled for more than a few months. An unlimited number of Honorary Members may be appointed at the discretion of the Sovereign, but in fact the badge is only given on extremely rare occasions to a foreigner. At present there are three Honorary Members: General of the Army Dwight Eisenhower, United States Army, appointed on 12th June 1945, Dr. Albert Schweitzer, appointed on 25th February 1955, and Sir Sarvepalli Radhakrishnan, appointed on 12th June 1963.

The names of the Ordinary Members are at present:

John Masefield, Poet Laureate, (1935)
Admiral of the Fleet Lord Chatfield, formerly
    First Sea Lord, (1939)
Lord Adrian, scientist, (1942)
Sir Henry Dale, scientist, (1944)
The Right Hon. Sir Winston Spencer-Churchill, formerly Prime
    Minister, (1946)
Marshal of the Royal Air Force Viscount Portal of Hungerford,
    formerly Chief of Air Staff, (1946)
Thomas Stearns Eliot, author, (1948)
Sir Robert Robinson, scientist, (1949)
Earl Russell, philosopher and mathematician, (1949)
The Right Hon. Sir Alexander Cadogan, formerly of H.M. Foreign
    Service, (1951)
Earl Attlee, formerly Prime Minister, (1951)
Wilder Penfield, neurologist, (1953)

Lord Hailey, a great administrator in India, (1956)
Sir John Cockcroft, scientist, (1957)
Sir Frank Macfarlane Burnet, pathologist, (1958)
Field-Marshal Earl Alexander of Tunis, formerly Governor-
   General of Canada, (1959)
Sir Cyril Norman Hinshelwood, scientist, (1960)
Graham Sutherland, painter, (1960)
Sir Basil Spence, architect, (1962)
Sir Geoffrey de Havilland, aeroplane designer, (1962)
Sir Owen Dixon, Chief Justice of Australia, (1963)
George Peabody Gooch, historian, (1963)
Henry Moore, sculptor, (1963)

Though the order is only sixty years old, there have been many distinguished members who have rendered extremely meritorious service in the past. Amongst them are to be found the names of such famous scientists or medical men as Lord Lister (the discoverer of antiseptic treatment in surgery), Lord Rayleigh, Lord Rutherford, Sir William Crookes and Sir William Bragg. Among representatives of literature, music and painting are included Thomas Hardy, George Trevelyan and his son George Macaulay Trevelyan, James Barrie, John Galsworthy, Gilbert Murray, Edward Elgar, Ralph Vaughan Williams, Wilson Steer, Alma Tadema, Holman Hunt and Augustus John. Amongst politicians are Lord Haldane (the maker of the Territorial Army), David Lloyd-George, Arthur Balfour, Lord Samuel, Mr. Mackenzie-King and Field-Marshal Jan Smuts. Among representatives of the armed services are Admirals of the Fleet Fisher, Jellicoe, Beatty, Viscount Cunningham of Hyndhope, Field-Marshals Roberts, Kitchener, Wolseley, Haig, Alanbrooke, General Baden-Powell (the founder of the Boy Scout Movement), and Marshal of the Royal Air Force Lord Trenchard.

Amongst the comparatively few Honorary Members of the past are to be found the names of the great French Marshals Joffre and Foch and the famous Japanese Admiral Togo.

THE COMPANIONS OF HONOUR

This order might be described as being something in the nature of a junior class of the Order of Merit, and like that order it carries no title or rank. It was instituted by King George the Fifth on 4th June, 1917, at the same time as the Order of the British Empire was founded.

Those eligible for appointment to the order are such persons, male or female, as may have rendered conspicuous service of national importance. Appointments are made on the recommendation of the Prime Minister of the countries of the British Commonwealth in accordance with the following statutory quotas:

United Kingdom	45
Australia	7
New Zealand	2
Other countries of the Commonwealth	11
Total	65

In addition to these statutory quotas of Ordinary Members, Additional Members are made occasionally to commemorate some special event, while on very rare occasions a citizen of a foreign country is appointed an Honorary Member. At the present time there are only two Honorary Members, namely Monsieur René Massigli, formerly the French Ambassador at the Court of Saint James's and Monsieur Henry Spaak.

The badge of the order is a gold oval-shaped medallion bearing a representation of an oak-tree. Pendent from a branch of the tree is a shield bearing the royals arms, and on the right of it is a representation of a knight in armour mounted on a horse. The badge has a blue border with the motto *In action faithful and in honour clear* in gold letters. It is surmounted by the imperial crown. The riband is one and a half inches wide and is carmine in colour, with borders of gold thread. By men the badge is worn suspended from the riband round the neck, and by ladies on the left side of the dress suspended from the riband in the form of a bow. When worn by men in evening dress the badge should hang immediately below the white tie. Recipients are entitled to place the letters 'C.H.' after their name.

The statutes ordain that the badge shall be worn on all occasions when 'decorations' are worn, but when these statutes were published it was not anticipated that a holder of the C.H. would become also a holder of the O.M. In the event of a person holding both the O.M.

and the C.H. he should, when 'decorations' are being worn with formal civilian morning or evening dress, wear only the O.M. badge, as with such dress it is not in order to wear more than one 'neck decoration.' In the whole life of these orders there have been only a few persons who have held both awards. These include the late Field-Marshal Smuts and Walter de la Mare, Sir Winston Churchill and Lord Attlee, and, most recently, George Gooch and Henry Moore.

The C.H. badge is not worn in miniature, but it is correct for the riband to be worn when ribands of other orders, decorations and medals are worn with undress uniform.

In the order of precedence a 'C.H.' comes directly after a 'C.B.E.' and the order has precedence immediately after the Order of the British Empire.

The following are the present members of the order:

United Kingdom

Lord Layton, (1919)
Sir Winston Spencer-Churchill, (1922)
Viscount Davidson, (1923)
The Rev. Philip Clayton, (1933)
Mr. John Dover Wilson, (1936)
Mr. William George Stewart Adams, (1936)
Mr. George Gooch, (1939)
Mr. Arthur Mann, (1941)
Earl Alexander of Hillsborough, (1941)
Earl of Woolton, (1942)
Viscount Leathers, (1943)
Lord Hives, (1943)
Earl of Swinton, (1943)
Earl of Selborne, (1945)
Earl Attlee, (1945)
General Lord Ismay, (1945)
Professor Archibald Hill, (1946)
Lord David Cecil, (1949)
Lord Morrison of Lambeth, (1951)
Mr. Edward Morgan Forster, (1953)
Mr. Benjamin Britten, (1953)
Right Hon. James Chuter Ede, (1953)
Lord Fraser of Lonsdale, (1953)
Right Hon. Thomas Johnston, (1953)

Right Hon. Richard Austen Butler, (1954)
Mr. William Somerset Maugham, (1954)
The Rev. Hugh Martin, (1955)
Mr. Henry Moore,
Mr. Arthur David Waley, (1956)
Mr. Edward Gordon Craig, (1956)
Professor Arnold Toynbee, (1956)
Viscount Stuart of Findhorn, (1957)
Sir Osbert Sitwell, Bt. (1958)
Sir John Beazley, (1959)
Sir Kenneth Clark, (1959)
Viscount Boyd of Merton, (1960)
Earl of Limerick, (1960)
Rev. Charles Dodd, (1961)
The Very Rev. Walter Matthews, (1962)
Lord Hailes, (1962)
Right. Hon. Selwyn Lloyd, (1962)
Right Hon. John Scott Maclay, (1962)
Right. Hon. Harold Watkinson, (1962)

Australia

Viscount Bruce of Melbourne, (1927)
Lord Casey, (1944)
Right Hon. Sir Robert Menzies, (1951)

New Zealand

Right Hon. Walter Nash, (1959)
Right Hon. Keith Jacha Holyoake, (1963)

Other Commonwealth Countries

Viscount Malvern, (1944)
General Henry Crerar, (1945)
Right Hon. Vincent Massey, (1946)
General the Hon. Andrew McNaughton, (1946)
Right Hon. Sir John Kotelawala, (1956)
Yang Teramat Mulia Tunku, (1950)

CHAPTER X

Obsolescent Orders

THE MOST ILLUSTRIOUS ORDER OF SAINT PATRICK

The Order of Saint Patrick was instituted by King George the Third on 5th February 1783, on the advice of the Prime Minister, Lord Shelburne. It was founded as a gesture of good-will towards Ireland and in the intention of giving pleasure to a number of powerful Irish peers who had rendered distinguished service and for whom there were no vacancies in the Order of the Garter. The order was intended to be for the peers of Ireland what the Garter and Thistle were for those of England and Scotland respectively. The warrant for its institution, which was addressed to the General Governor of the Kingdom of Ireland, stated that:

> Whereas Our loving subjects of our Kingdom have proved them-
> selves steadily attached to Our Royal Person and Government
> and affectionately disposed to maintain and promote the welfare
> and prosperity of the whole Empire, and We, being willing to
> confer upon Our subjects of Our said Kingdom a testimony of
> Our sincere love and affectionate regard by creating an Order
> of Knighthood in Our said Kingdom, do hereby authorize you
> to cause Letters Patent to be passed under the Great Seal for
> creating a Society of Brotherhood to be called Knights of the
> Most Illustrious Order of Saint Patrick to consist of the Sovereign
> and fifteen Knights.

The order derived its title from the tutelar saint of Ireland and its emblems from the native badges of that country.

The statutes of the order were modelled largely on those of the Garter, and it was nominated as 'the third of the Great Orders'. In precedence it followed the Orders of the Garter and the Thistle and it ranked senior to the Order of the Bath. The Sovereign was the head of the order, while the Lord-Lieutenant of Ireland was *ex officio* the Grand Master.

As stated above, the order consisted originally of fifteen knights, but at the coronation of King George the Fourth, in 1821, six Extra Knights were appointed, while in 1831, at the coronation of King William the Fourth, another four Extra Knights were appointed. In 1833 the statutory maximum number of knights was fixed at twenty-two.

The motto of the order, *Quis Separabit*, was intended to symbolise the harmony and union which the Sovereign was desirous of establishing throughout his dominions—particularly between England and Ireland.

The chapters of the order were held in Dublin Castle, and the choir of Saint Patrick's Cathedral Church in Dublin became the chapel of the order and it was there that the installations of knights took place.

These installations were carried out with great ceremony. We read in an official document of that time issued by the Office of Arms, Dublin Castle, how on the day appointed for the installation of the Prince of Wales, namely 18th April 1868, all the streets from the castle to the Cathedral were 'lined with Military'.

The Grand Master of the order (the Marquess of Abercorn) and Their Royal Highnesses the Prince of Wales and the Duke of Cambridge drove in state to the cathedral. On reaching the chapter room in the cathedral the Prince of Wales

Stood at his seat while his Esquires deposited on the table His Royal Highness's Mantle and Sword and fixed his Banner in the appointed place. The Knights and Officers of the Order then proceeded to the Choir and, after the Prince had been girt with his sword by the two senior Knights and robed with his Mantle, The Grand Master invested him with the Collar of the Order and conducted him to his Stall. Thereupon the senior Esquire unfurled his Banner and, after a flourish of trumpets, Ulster King of Arms proclaimed his Titles.

In 1871, the date on which the disestablishment of the Irish Church took effect, the religious ceremonies were abolished. Thereafter investiture of new knights took place either in Saint Patrick's Hall in Dublin Castle or at Windsor Castle. While the banners of earlier knights were placed in Dublin Cathedral, in later years the knights' banners were erected in the Great Hall of Dublin Castle.

As recently as 1924 the order was maintained at full strength, but since that date the number of knights has dwindled steadily, and at the present time the only remaining knights are the Dukes of Gloucester and Windsor. There were during the period of the 1939–1945 war a number of very distinguished service leaders whose families were associated with Northern Ireland—Dill, Alexander, Alanbrooke and Montgomery and it was frequently suggested that the order should be kept alive by the appointment thereto of these and other distinguished Irishmen. Unfortunately, the separation of Northern from Southern Ireland made the revival of the order impracticable, particularly as it was made clear by the Government of Southern Ireland that such a revival would meet with their disapproval and, in fact, strong opposition.

The insignia of the order are particularly decorative and the mantle is of an extremely beautiful sky-blue colour. The insignia consist of a collar of gold composed of roses and harps, placed alternately and tied together with a knot of gold, the roses being enamelled. There is an imperial crown in the centre surmounting a harp of gold. Attached to the collar is an oval badge of gold, surrounded with a wreath of shamrock within which is a circle of sky-blue enamel containing the motto *Quis separabit*. When the collar is not worn, a second and smaller badge is worn from a light blue riband hanging from the right shoulder to the left hip on which the badge rests. The badges have varied from time to time in shape and size and in the colour of the enamelling. In recent years the collars and badges of deceased knights have always been handed back personally to the Sovereign by the nearest living male relative of the knight.

The star of the order consists of the Cross of Saint Patrick on a field argent, surmounted by a trefoil vert charged with three imperial crowns and surrounded by the motto. Prior to 1916 a knight was not given a star at the time of his investiture, but had to obtain this at his own expense. Thus the stars of those knights who were appointed before 1916 have never been handed back after their death.

In 1831 King William the Fourth gave orders for the Irish crown jewels to be used for making some particularly magnificent insignia for the Grand Master of the Order. In 1908, most regrettably, these

INSIGNIA OF ST. PATRICK, VICTORIAN ORDER, OF MERIT,
COMPANIONS OF HONOUR
Top left: Badge of Member of Companions of Honour.
Top right: Collar, riband and badge and star of a Knight Grand Cross of Royal
Victorian Order.
Bottom left: Collar, riband and badge and star of Order of Saint Patrick.
Bottom right: Badge of Member of the Order of Merit.

Victoria R. I.

Victoria by the Grace of God of the United Kingdom of Great Britain and Ireland Queen Defender of the Faith, Empress of India and Sovereign of the Most Exalted Order of the Star of India, To His Highness Raja Sir Shamsher Prakash, Bahadur, of Sirmur (Nahun) Greeting; Whereas We have been pleased to nominate and appoint you to be a Knight Grand Commander of Our said Most Exalted Order of the Star of India, And whereas in and by the Statutes of Our said Order, We have full power and authority to dispense with the regulations relative to Investiture, We therefore by virtue

Warrant dispensing with the personal Investiture of His Highness the Raja of Sirmur, as a Knight Grand Commander of Our Most Exalted Order of the Star of India

A DISPENSATION WARRANT
Signed by Queen Victoria in 1887, dispensing with the attendance at an Investiture of H.H. the Raja of Sirmur, G.C.S.I.

beautiful insignia disappeared mysteriously from Dublin Castle. The loss was investigated most thoroughly by an official commission which examined the evidence of Ulster King of Arms and others concerned with the safeguarding of these insignia. Nothing definite was ever proved, and the present whereabouts of these extremely valuable and historic jewels is unknown. In their report the commissioners stated that those concerned had showed

> A strange want of a sense of responsibility and in fact deliberate carelessness not only for failing to ensure that these priceless Crown Jewels were kept in a suitably-fitted strong-room, but also because after the gems had disappeared there was a strange delay in reporting their disappearance.

The Most Exalted Order of the Star of India

The order was instituted by Queen Victoria on 23rd February 1861, and consisted of three classes of members—Knights Grand Commanders, Knights Commanders and Companions (namely G.C.S.I., K.C.S.I. and C.S.I.).

The description of the first class of the Indian orders as Knights Grand Commanders instead of Knights Grand Cross was chosen so as to avoid any embarrassment to those recipients who were not members of the Christian faith.

The Governor-General of India was *ex officio* Grand Master of the order.

The first class consisted of ruling princes and chiefs of India and such British subjects as might merit this token of royal favour.

The insignia of this order are more beautiful and certainly more valuable than those of any other order, as they are ornamented with a considerable number of diamonds. The most recently purchased set of G.C.S.I. insignia, which was bought in 1947, cost £3,500.

Formerly all insignia of this order were returnable at death, but, while the collars must still be returned, from 1947, in which year appointments to the order were discontinued, and up to 1962 holders of insignia were permitted to purchase their badges and stars at specially reduced prices fixed by H.M. Treasury and which corresponded approximately to the 'break-up' value of these insignia.

It was also permissible, after the death of a holder for his executors, if they so desired, to purchase his insignia on behalf of his next of kin. The prices fixed for the purchase of the insignia were as follows:

G.C.S.I. badge and star £165, the cost price having been £820.
K.C.S.I. badge and star £35, the cost price having been £127.
C.S.I. badge £15, the cost price having been £70.

Under a ruling given in 1962 the Badges and Stars of living holders of G.C.S.I., K.C.S.I. and C.S.I. are no longer returnable at death, though the Collars must still be returned.

No appointments have been made since 1947, and the following Knights Grand Commanders are still living:

The Duke of Windsor
The Nizam of Hyderabad and Berar
Lord Hailey
The Nawab of Bahawalpur
Earl of Scarbrough
The Maharaja of Mysore
The Maharaja of Travancore
Earl Mountbatten of Burma
The Maharaja of Nawanagar
Sir Frederick Burrows
General Sir Archibald Nye
The Maharaja of Kolhapur
The Maharaja of Jaipur
General the Maharaja Padma Shumshere Jung Bahadur Rana, of Nepal

THE MOST EMINENT ORDER OF THE INDIAN EMPIRE

This order was instituted by Queen Victoria on 2nd August 1886.

As in the case of the Order of the Star of India, the Governor-General was *ex officio* Grand Master of the order, and the Governors of Madras, Bombay and Bengal were *ex officio* appointed Knights Grand Commanders of the order.

The order consisted of three classes: Knights Grand Commanders, Knights Commanders, and Companions (namely G.C.I.E., K.C.I.E. and C.I.E.). The first class was reserved for those persons who by their services to the Empire in India merited royal favour and for distinguished Eastern potentates.

The insignia of the first two classes were returnable on the death of the holder, but, as in the case of the Order of the Star of India, only the G.C.I.E. collars now have to be returned.

No appointments to the order have been made since 1947, and the following Knights Grand Commanders are still living:

The Duke of Windsor
The Sultan of Muscat and Oman
General Shumshere Jung
Lord Hailey
The Nawab of Bahawalpur
The Maharaja of Datia
The Ex-Maharaja of Indore
The Maharaja of Travancore
The Maharaja of Jaipur
Sir Herbert Emerson
Earl of Scarbrough
The Maharaja of Nawanagar
Field-Marshal Sir Claude Auchinleck
The Maharaja of Baroda
Sir Maurice Hallett
Sir Reginald Maxwell
The Nawab of Rampur
Sir Jeremy Raisman
Sir Frederick Burrows
The Maharaja of Patiala
The Maharaja of Mayurbhanji
The Prince of Berar
Sir John Woodhead
General Sir Archibald Nye
Earl Mountbatten of Burma
Sir Francis Wylie
Sir Evan Jenkins
Sir Hugh Dow
The Maharaja of Dungapur
Sir Eric Miéville

THE IMPERIAL ORDER OF THE CROWN OF INDIA

On 31st December 1877, to commemorate her assumption of the imperial title of Empress of India, Queen Victoria instituted the Order of the Crown of India. The order was 'to be enjoyed by the princesses of the Royal House who had attained the age of eighteen years and the wives and other female relatives of Indian princes and other selected persons'. Those eligible for inclusion amongst the latter persons were the Governor-General of India, the Governors of Madras, Bombay and Bengal, the Principal Secretary of State for India and the Commander-in-Chief in India.

Though obsolescent, the order still ranks immediately before the Royal Victorian Order.

The badge, which was made in accordance with a design approved by Queen Victoria, consisted of her royal and imperial cypher. It was composed of the letters *V*, *R* and *I* in diamonds, pearls and turquoises, encircled by a border set with pearls and ensigned with the imperial crown. The order is attached to a light blue watered riband, edged white, of an inch and a half in width, tied in a bow and worn on the left shoulder.

The badge is returnable on the death of a holder, but permission is sometimes given by the Sovereign for it to be retained by the holder's nearest relative as a family heirloom.

The most recent appointments to the order were those of the present Queen and Her Majesty's sister, the Princess Margaret, on 12th June 1947. Other living holders of the order are:

Queen Elizabeth the Queen Mother
The Princess Royal
The Duchess of Gloucester
Princess Marina, Duchess of Kent
The Maharani of Baroda
Lady Patricia Ramsay
The Marchioness of Crewe
The Dowager Countess of Halifax
The Dowager Countes of Lytton
The Maharani of Travancore
The Dowager Marchioness of Linlithgow
The Dowager Baroness Brabourne
The Dowager Countess Wavell

Mrs. Adeliza Florence Louise Amery
The Maharani of Jammu and Kashmir
The Dowager Baroness Clydesmuir

THE ORDER OF VICTORIA AND ALBERT

This Order for ladies was instituted on 10 February, 1862, to commemorate Queen Victoria's happy marriage. The Order was enlarged in 1864, 1865 and 1880, until eventually there were four Classes. The Badge of the first Class consists of a medallion of Queen Victoria and Prince Albert with a jewelled border, and sur mounted by a jewelled crown. The badge is worn from a bow of white moiré ribbon.

The only surviving members are:

Princess Alice, Countess of Athlone
The Princess Alfonso d'Orleans-Bourbon
Lady Victoria Patricia Ramsay

Part Two

CHAPTER XI

Investitures, Awards Which Qualify for Attendance Thereat, and Presentation of Other Insignia

INVESTITURES

Normally not less than thirteen investitures are held at Buckingham Palace each year. Of these, usually six are held during the period February–March, so that the Queen, or some other person appointed by Her Majesty for this purpose, may present awards announced in the New Year Honours List, which is published on the 1st January.

Two investitures are usually held in July and five in the autumn, so that awards announced in the Queen's Official Birthday List (which is published on a selected Saturday in June, the date of which varies each year) may be presented.

It is customary for the Queen to receive privately and invest with the appropriate insignia all those who are appointed Knights of the Garter or the Thistle, members of the Order of Merit and Companions of Honour. The Queen also receives privately some recipients of honours in other orders of chivalry, including particularly those who have rendered service to Her Majesty of a personal or private nature and who have received an appointment in the Royal Victorian order or a Royal Victorian medal.

In addition to those who are received privately, recipients of the following awards are eligible to attend an investiture at Buckingham Palace:

Victoria Cross
George Cross
All awards in the several orders of Chivalry (Bath, Saint Michael and Saint George, Royal Victorian and British Empire)

Distinguished Service Order
Imperial Service Order
Royal Red Cross
All decorations for gallantry (D.S.C., M.C., D.F.C.)
All medals for gallantry, except the B.E.M. (D.C.M., C.G.M.,
    D.S.M., M.M., D.F.M.)
Air Force Cross
Air Force Medal
Polar Medal
Royal Victorian Medal

In addition, knights bachelor attend an investiture so that they
may be dubbed. Those who have been granted peerages or baronetcies do not attend investitures.

If, through absence abroad, a person is unable to attend an investiture at Buckingham Palace within a year of the date of his
award, except in the case of the very senior awards, it is customary
for the insignia to be sent to the appropriate representative of the
Queen abroad so that they may be represented on Her Majesty's
behalf.

It is quite permissible for a person who, through illness, is unable
to attend an investiture, to defer his attendance for as long as he
desires. Similarly, if through permanent ill-health or for some other
reason beyond his control a recipient finds it is impracticable ever to
attend an investiture, it is quite in order for him to ask for his insignia
to be sent to him by post. In these circumstances it is customary
to send with the insignia a special letter from the Queen expressing
Her Majesty's regret at not being able to present the insignia
personally.

A person attending an investiture is normally entitled to bring
two guests to witness the ceremony. Unless the number of guests
already invited to attend is so large that the granting of extra tickets
is quite impracticable, one extra ticket may be obtained to enable
a second child of the recipient to attend. Under no circumstances
are more than three guest tickets ever allotted to a recipient and,
as explained above, the third guest ticket is only given when it is
to be used by a second son or daughter.

Recipients of awards who are attending an investiture, and also
two accompanying guests, are entitled to claim certain travelling

and other allowances, and applications for these allowances should be addressed to the Ministry or Department by which the recipient's name was submitted for an honour. Those in doubt as to the department to which they should address their applications for expenses should apply for advice on this point to the Central Chancery at 8, Buckingham Gate, London, S.W.1.

Those attending investitures, either as recipients or guests, may wear whatever suitable form of dress may be the more convenient to them. Normally, serving or retired members of the armed services wear uniform when receiving military awards, but, if for some reason uniform is not readily available, they may wear either civilian morning dress or a dark lounge suit. Members of civil organisations may, if they wish to do so, wear the uniform of the organisation to which they belong, but there is no obligation to do so and, if they so wish, they may, like other civilians, wear either morning dress or a dark lounge suit.

Those attending in uniform should not wear a sword, nor the insignia of orders, decorations and medals, but it is correct for them to include amongst the ribbons worn on the uniform jacket the ribbon of the award with which they are to be invested.

NEXT-OF-KIN CEREMONIES

When a gallantry award is gazetted posthumously, or when a person who has been awarded any order, decoration or medal for gallantry dies before that award has been presented to him, the next of kin, provided he or she is the person legally entitled to receive the insignia, is entitled to attend at Buckingham Palace to receive the insignia from the hand of the Queen, or from some person specially appointed to carry out this ceremony on behalf of Her Majesty. The next of kin may be accompanied on this occasion by a relative or friend and appropriate travelling expenses may be claimed. Next-of-kin ceremonies are held privately, and usually take place immediately prior to the first investiture in each series.

The next of kin of deceased recipients of the Air Force Cross, Air Force Medal and Polar Medal are also eligible to be invited to a next-of-kin ceremony at Buckingham Palace.

The Offices from Which the Summons to Attend an Investiture is Issued

(*a*) Invitations to attend a *private* ceremony to receive insignia from the Queen are sent direct to the recipient by Her Majesty's Private Secretary.

(*b*) A person who is due to be dubbed as a knight bachelor receives his summons to attend an investiture from the Secretary of State for Home Affairs, as the records in connection with the dubbing of knights bachelor are maintained at that office.

(*c*) A person who has received an appointment in the Order of Saint Michael and Saint George receives his summons to attend an investiture from the Permanent Under-Secretary of State at the Colonial Office. The reason for this is that the Chancery of that order is at the Colonial Office.

(*d*) Recipients of *all* other awards which qualify for attendance at an investiture at Buckingham Palace, including those for next-of-kin ceremonies, receive their formal summons to attend from the Central Chancery of the Orders of Knighthood, St. James's Palace.

(*e*) Tickets authorising guests to accompany recipients of awards to investitures are issued by the Central Chancery of the Orders of Knighthood, to whom all enquiries on this subject should be addressed.

Medals Which Do Not Qualify for Attendance at an Investiture at Buckingham Palace

It would obviously be quite impossible for the Queen herself to present personally every award which is published in the *London Gazette*. Consequently, those who are awarded the Medal of the Order of the British Empire (B.E.M.) or the Medal of the Imperial Service Order and who are domiciled in the United Kindgom have their medals presented to them in the following ways:

(*a*) *British Empire Medal (Military Division).* To those who are serving in the United Kingdom with the Royal Navy, Army or Royal Air Force this medal is presented at a ceremonial parade under arrangements made by the Admiralty, War Office or Air Ministry respectively.

(*b*) *British Empire Medal (Civil Division).* To those who are domiciled in the United Kingdom, this medal is presented either by one of Her Majesty's Lieutenants for a county, or by one of Her Majesty's Ministers, or by the Head of the appropriate government department. Arrangements for such presentations are made by the Ceremonial Officer at H.M. Treasury.

(c) *Imperial Service Medal.* When practicable, this medal is presented to the recipient, in the presence of his colleagues, by the head of the department or organization with which the recipient was serving at the time of the award of the medal. When such an arrangement is not practicable because the recipient is ill, or, having retired, finds it inconvenient to attend at his former place of employment, the medal is sent to the recipient by post.

(d) For recipients of the British Empire Medal and Imperial Service Medal who are domiciled or serving temporarily in places overseas the medals are transmitted through the proper channels for presentation by the appropriate Representative of the Queen.

CHAPTER XII

The Order in Which Insignia or Orders, Decorations and Medals Should be Worn

It must be noted that the order of precedence in which orders and decorations and medals are shown on the list below in no way affects the precedence conferred by the statutes of the several orders upon the members thereof.

This means, for example, that, although the holder of a Victoria Cross places the letters 'V.C.' immediately after his name and before all other post-nominal letters except 'Bt.', and although he wears the ribbon of the V.C. in front of all other ribbons, he is not ranked senior in the official order of precedence to those who hold an appointment in an order of chivalry.

It is also of interest to note that the exact place in which the letters 'V.C.' were to be placed after a holder's name with regard to other post-nominal letters and the exact place where the ribbon of the V.C. should be worn were not laid down clearly at the time of the institution of the Victoria Cross. In fact, at one time the position in which insignia of orders, decorations and medals were worn seemed often to depend on the whim of the individual concerned.

For example, in *Queen's Regulations* of 1898 it was stated that the V.C. was to be worn next after the C.I.E. badge (which was at that time worn as a breast decoration). In 1899 the Prince of Wales expressed his opinion that 'the V.C. should come immediately before the D.S.O.', but in 1902, after his accession to the throne, King Edward the Seventh ruled that the V.C. should 'precede all "Decorations" placed on the bar-brooch worn on the breast'. Such 'decorations' at that time included the badges of the C.B., C.S.I., C.M.G.

and C.I.E. as well as other orders (for example, the D.S.O. and I.S.O.) which were then worn on the breast.

After King George the Fifth had ascended the throne, as the Admiralty were still not satisfied that a clear decision had been given on this matter, it was requested that the king 'should be pleased to give a ruling thereon'. In 1912 he ruled that except for the abbreviation 'Bt.' the letters 'V.C.' should precede all other post-nominal letters including those indicating membership of the three 'great orders', namely the Garter, Thistle and Patrick.

Again when, at the coronation of the present sovereign, Garter King of Arms asked for a ruling on this point, the Queen commanded that the ruling previously given on this subject by her grandfather was to continue in force, namely that the letters 'V.C.' were to precede all post-nominal letters except 'Bt.'.

The order in which orders, decorations and medals should be worn, is as stated below, but *vide* Notes 1 and 2.*

In those cases in which it is permissible to place after the name of the holder of an honour certain letters to denote that he holds that particular honour, the appropriate letters are shown on this list in brackets after the name of the award.

SPECIAL AWARDS

Victoria Cross (V.C.).
George Cross (G.C.).

ORDERS OF KNIGHTHOOD AND OTHER ORDERS

Order of the Garter (K.G. for Men, no post-nominal letters for
  Ladies) (*vide* notes 4 and 5).
Order of the Thistle (K.T.) (*vide* notes 4 and 5).
Order of Saint Patrick (K.P.) (*vide* notes 4 and 5).
Order of the Bath (Classes I, II and III, viz. G.C.B., K.C.B., C.B.).
Order of Merit (O.M.) (ranks next after G.C.B.) (*vide* note 4).
Baronet's Badge (Bt.) (*vide* note 2).
Order of the Star of India (Classes I, II and III, viz. G.C.S.I.,
  K.C.S.I., C.S.I.) (*vide* note 8).
Order of Saint Michael and Saint George (Classes I, II and III,
  viz. G.C.M.G., K.C.M.G., C.M.G.).
Order of the Indian Empire (Classes I, II and III, viz. G.C.I.E.,
  K.C.I.E., C.I.E.) (*vide* note 8).

*See notes at end of this chapter on page 184.

Order of the Crown of India (C.I.) (*vide* notes 4 and 8).

Royal Victorian Order (Classes I, II and III, viz. G.C.V.O., K.C.V.O. and D.C.V.O., C.V.O.).

Order of the British Empire (Classes I, II and III, viz. G.B.E., K.B.E. and D.B.E., C.B.E.) (*vide* note 6).

Order of the Companions of Honour (C.H.) (ranks next after G.B.E.) (*vide* note 4).

The Distinguished Service Order (D.S.O.).

Royal Victorian Order (Class IV, viz. M.V.O.).

Order of the British Empire (Class IV, viz. O.B.E.) (*vide* note 6).

Imperial Service Order (I.S.O.).

Royal Victorian Order (Class V, viz. M.V.O.).

Order of the British Empire (Class V, viz. M.B.E.) (*vide* note 6).

Indian Order of Merit (Military) (I.O.M.) (*vide* notes 7 and 8).

DECORATIONS

Royal Red Cross, Class I (R.R.C.).

Distinguished Service Cross (D.S.C.).

Military Cross (M.C.).

Distinguished Flying Cross (D.F.C.).

Air Force Cross (A.F.C.).

Royal Red Cross, Class II (A.R.R.C.).

Order of British India (O.B.I.) (*vide* note 8).

Kaisar-I-Hind Medal (*vide* note 8).

Order of Saint John.

Albert Medal (A.M.) (vide note 9).

MEDALS FOR GALLANTRY AND DISTINGUISHED CONDUCT

Union of South Africa Queen's Medal for Bravery, in gold (*vide* note 8).

Distinguished Conduct Medal (D.C.M.).

Conspicuous Gallantry Medal (C.G.M.).

George Medal (G.M.).

Queen's Police Medal, for gallantry (*vide* note 9).

Queen's Fire Service Medal, for gallantry (*vide* note 9).

Edward Medal (E.M.) (*vide* note 9).

Royal West African Frontier Force Distinguished Conduct Medal (D.C.M.).

King's African Rifles Distinguished Conduct Medal (D.C.M.).

Indian Distinguished Service Medal (I.D.S.M.) (*vide* note 8).

Union of South Africa Queen's Medal for Bravery, in silver (*vide* note 8).

INSIGNIA OF A KNIGHT
GRAND COMMANDER OF
THE ORDER OF THE STAR
OF INDIA (G.C.S.I.)
Mantle with star embroidered
thereon and collar with badge
appendant.
A. C. K. Ware

INSIGNIA OF A KNIGHT
GRAND COMMANDER OF
THE ORDER OF THE INDIAN
EMPIRE (G.C.I.E.)
Mantle with star embroidered
thereon and collar with badge
appendant.
A. C. K. Ware

NEW FULL-DRESS UNIFORM OF AN ADMIRAL, ROYAL NAVY

This shows how the maximum of insignia should be worn, namely collar and badge appendant of senior order (in this case G.C.B.), riband and badge of next senior order (in this case G.C.M.G.), four stars (in this case G.C.B., G.C.M.G., G.C.I.E., G.B.E.), Royal Victorian Chain, two neck badges (in this case C.S.I. worn below collar of coat and C.V.O. on right side).

Grieves Copyright

Distinguished Service Medal (D.S.M.).
Military Medal (M.M.).
Distinguished Flying Medal (D.F.M.).
Air Force Medal (A.F.M.).
Constabulary Medal (Ireland).
Medal for Saving Life at Sea (S.G.M.) (*vide* note 10).
Indian Order of Merit (Civil) (I.O.M.) (*vide* note 8).
Indian Police Medal for Gallantry.
Ceylon Police Medal for Gallantry.
Colonial Police Medal for Gallantry.
British Empire Medal (B.E.M.) (*vide* note 6).
Canada Medal (C.M.).
Queen's Police Medal, for distinguished service.
Queen's Fire Service Medal, for distinguished service.
Queen's Medal for Chiefs.

WAR MEDALS

(in order date of campaign for which awarded) (*vide* note 11).

POLAR MEDALS (in order of date)

Royal Victorian Medal (gold, silver and bronze).
Imperial Service Medal.

POLICE MEDALS FOR VALUABLE SERVICES

Indian Police Medal for Meritorious Service.
Ceylon Police Medal for Merit.
Colonial Police Medal for Meritorious Service.
Badge of Honour.

JUBILEE, CORONATION AND DURBAR MEDALS

Queen Victoria's Jubilee Medal, 1887 (gold, silver and bronze).
Queen Victoria's Police Jubilee Medal, 1887.
Queen Victoria's Jubilee Medal, 1897 (gold, silver and bronze).
Queen Victoria's Police Jubilee Medal, 1897.
Queen Victoria's Commemoration Medal, 1900 (Ireland).
King Edward VII's Coronation Medal, 1902.
King Edward VII's Police Coronation Medal, 1902.
King Edward VII's Durbar Medal, 1903 (gold, silver and bronze).
King Edward VII's Police Medal, 1903 (Scotland).

King's Visit Commemoration Medal, 1903 (Ireland).
King George V's Coronation Medal, 1911.
King George V's Police Coronation Medal, 1911.
King's Visit Police Commemoration Medal, 1911 (Ireland).
King George V's Durbar Medal, 1911 (gold, silver and bronze).
King George V's Silver Jubilee Medal, 1935.
King George VI's Coronation Medal, 1937.
Queen Elizabeth II's Coronation Medal, 1953.
King George V's Long and Faithful Service Medal.
King George VI's Long and Faithful Service Medal.
Queen Elizabeth II's Long and Faithful Service Medal.

EFFICIENCY AND LONG SERVICE DECORATIONS AND MEDALS

Long Service and Good Conduct Medal.
Naval Long Service and Good Conduct Medal.
Medal for Meritorious Service (M.S.M.). The post-nominal letters are only permissible if the medal was awarded for service in the Royal Navy prior to 20th July 1928.
Indian Long Service and Good Conduct Medal (for Europeans of Indian Army) (*vide* note 8).
Indian Meritorious Service Medal (for Europeans of Indian Army) (*vide* note 8).
Royal Marine Meritorious Service Medal.
Royal Air Force Meritorious Service Medal.
Royal Air Force Long Service and Good Conduct Medal.
Indian Long Service and Good Conduct Medal (for Indian Army).
Royal West African Frontier Force Long Service and Good Conduct Medal.
King's African Rifles Long Service and Good Conduct Medal.
Indian Meritorious Service Medal (for Indian Army).
Police Long Service and Good Conduct Medal.
Fire Brigade Long Service and Good Conduct Medal.
African Police Medal for Meritorious Service.
Royal Canadian Mounted Police Long Service Medal.
Ceylon Police Long Service Medal.
Ceylon Fire Services Long Service Medal.
Colonial Police Long Service Medal.
Colonial Fire Brigades Long Service Medal.
Colonial Prison Service Medal.
Army Emergency Reserve Decoration (E.R.D.).
Volunteer Officers' Decoration (V.D.).
Volunteer Long Service Medal.

Volunteer Officers' Decoration (for India and the Colonies) (V.D.).
Volunteer Long Service Medal (for India and the Colonies).
Colonial Auxiliary Forces Officers' Decoration (E.D.).
Colonial Auxiliary Forces Long Service Medal.
Medal for Good Shooting (Naval).
Militia Long Service Medal.
Imperial Yeomanry Long Service Medal.
Territorial Decoration (T.D.).
Efficiency Decoration (E.D.).
Territorial Efficiency Medal.
Efficiency Medal.
Special Reserve Long Service and Good Conduct Medal.
Decoration for Officers of the Royal Naval Reserve (R.D.).
Decoration for Officers of the Royal Naval Volunteer Reserve (V.R.D.).
Royal Naval Reserve Long Service and Good Conduct Medal.
Royal Naval Volunteer Reserve Long Service and Good Conduct Medal.
Royal Naval Auxiliary Sick Berth Reserve Long Service and Good Conduct Medal.
Royal Fleet Reserve Long Service and Good Conduct Medal.
Royal Naval Wireless Auxiliary Reserve Long Service and Good Conduct Medal.
Air Efficiency Award.
Queen's Medal for Champion Shots of New Zealand Naval Forces.
Queen's Medal (for Champion Shots in the Military Forces).
Queen's Medal (for Champion Shots of the Air Forces).
Cadet Forces Medal.
Coast Life Saving Corps Long Service Medal (*vide* note 12).
Special Constabulary Long Service Medal.
Canadian Forces Decoration (C.D.).
Royal Observer Corps Medal.
Civil Defence Long Service Medal.
Union of South Africa Commemoration Medal.
Indian Independence Medal.
Pakistan Medal.
Nigerian Independence Medal.
Sierra Leone Independence Medal.
Ceylon Armed Services Inauguration Medal.
Ceylon Police Independence Medal.
Service Medal of the Order of St. John.
Badge of the Order of the League of Mercy.

Voluntary Medical Service Medal.
Women's Voluntary Service Medal.
South African Medal for War Services.
Colonial Special Constabulary Medal.
Other Commonwealth Members' Orders, Decorations and Mealsd
    instituted since 1949 otherwise than by the Sovereign, and
    awards by the States of the Federation of Malaya.
Foreign Orders (in order of date of award).   ⎫
Foreign Decorations (in order of date of award).   ⎬ (*vide* note 13.
Foreign Medals (in order of date of award).   ⎭

NOTE OF MENTIONS IN DESPATCHES, KING'S COMMENDATIONS AND QUEEN'S COMMENDATIONS

Mention in Despatches, 1914–1919.

The emblem of bronze oak leaves denoting a mention in despatches during the First World War, 1914–1919, is worn on the ribbon of the Victory Medal. The award of this emblem ceased as from 10th August 1920.

Mention in Despatches, 1920–1939.

The single bronze oak-leaf emblem, if granted for service in operations between the two World Wars, is worn on the ribbon of the appropriate General Service Medal. If a General Service Medal has not been granted, the emblem is worn directly on the coat after any medal ribbons (*vide* note 14).

Mention in Despatches, 1939–1945.

The single bronze oak-leaf emblem signifying in the armed forces and the Merchant Navy, either a mention in despatches, a king's commendation for brave conduct, or a king's commendation for valuable service in the air, if granted for service in the Second World War, 1939–1945, is worn on the ribbon of the War Medal, 1939–1945. If the war medal has not been granted, the emblem is worn directly on the coat, after any medal ribbons (*vide* note 14).

Mention in Despatches, 1945, and subsequently.

The single bronze oak-leaf emblem, if granted for service in operations after the cessation of hostilities in the Second World War, is worn on the ribbon of the appropriate General Service or Campaign

Medal. If such medal has not been granted, the emblem is worn directly on the coat after any medal ribbons (*vide* note 14).

The single bronze oak-leaf emblem is also used in the forces to denote a king's or queen's commendation for brave conduct or a king's or queen's commendation for valuable service in the air granted since the cessation of hostilities in the Second World War.

King's Commendation for Brave Conduct, 1939–1945, and subsequently;
Queen's Commendation for Brave Conduct, 1952, and subsequently.

The emblem of silver laurel leaves granted to civilians, other than those in the Merchant Navy, to denote a king's commendation for brave conduct during the Second World War, 1939–1945, is worn on the ribbon of the Defence Medal. When the Defence Medal has not been granted or the award is for services subsequent to the war, the emblem of silver laurel leaves is worn directly on the coat after any medal ribbons (*vide* note 14).

King's Commendation for Valuable Service in the Air, 1939–1945, and
subsequently; Queen's Commendation for Valuable Service in the Air,
1952, and subsequently.

The oval silver badge granted to denote a civil king's commendation or queen's commendation for valuable service in the air is worn on the coat immediately below any medals or medal ribbons, or in civil air line uniform, on the panel of the left breast pocket (*vide* note 14).

Notes

1. The instructions given above apply to those orders of similar grades. When the miniature or ribbon of a higher class of a junior order is worn with that of a lower class of a senior order, the higher-class miniature or ribbon should come first, e.g. the miniature or ribbon of a K.B.E. will come before those of a C.B., while those of a G.C.M.G. will come before those of a K.C.B.

When no insignia are being worn the ribbons of orders of more than one class should be of the width of the ribbons of the membership, or fifth class of the order. If there is no membership, or fifth class, the ribbon should be of the width of the ribbon of the companionship or third class of the order.

2. The letters 'Bt.' should be shown immediately after the surname and *before all other post-nominal letters,* even the V.C.

The baronet's badge is worn suspended round the neck from the ribbon described on page 48, in the same manner as the neck-badge of an order is worn. The badge takes precedence immediately after that of the Order of Merit. It is not worn in miniature and the ribbon should not be worn on the breast in non-ceremonial dress uniform. Authority to purchase the badge can be obtained by application to the Home Office.

3. The badge of a knight bachelor is worn on the left breast, next after the star of a Knight Commander of the Order of the British Empire. There is no ribbon which can be worn to denote that a person is a knight bachelor, nor is there any miniature for this badge. Authority to purchase the badge can be obtained by application to the Home Office.

4. Not worn in miniature.

5. No ribbon of this order is worn on the breast in non-ceremonial dress uniform.

6. Appointments to or promotions in the Order of the British Empire and awards of the British Empire Medal which have been granted on or after 14th January 1958 for 'Gallantry' are so described when published in the *London Gazette*, and a silver oak-leaf emblem is worn on the ribbon from which the insignia is suspended.When only a ribbon of the order is worn the emblem is worn in miniature. A person appointed to the order after 14th January 1958 'For Gallantry', and subsequently promoted in the order, retains and wears the emblem whether promoted for gallantry or otherwise. A holder of the British Empire Medal awarded for gallantry since 14th January 1958, if subsequently appointed to the order, continues to wear the emblem on the ribbon of the medal but only wears the emblem on the ribbon of the order also if appointed to the order for gallantry.

7. The Indian Order of Merit (Military and Civil) is quite distinct from the Order of Merit.

8. This award is now obsolescent.

9. Now only awarded posthumously.

10. The official medal awarded previously on the recommendation of the Board of Trade, Minister of Shipping, Minister of War Transport or Minister of Transport, and now awarded on the recommendation of the Minister of Transport and Civil Aviation.

11. Campaign stars and medals awarded for service during the First World War (1914–19) should be worn in the following order:

1914 Star; 1914–15 Star; British War Medal; Mercantile Marine War Medal; Victory Medal; Territorial Force War Medal; India General Service Medal (1908) (for operations in Afghanistan in 1919).

Campaign stars and medals awarded for service in the Second World War (1939–45) should be worn in the following order:

1939–45 Star; Atlantic Star; Air-Crew Europe Star; Africa Star; Pacific Star; Burma Star; Italy Star; France and Germany Star; Defence Medal; Volunteer Service Medal of Canada; War Medal (1939–45); Individual service medals of the countries of the Commonwealth in order of institution.

12. Formerly known as The Rocket Apparatus Volunteer Long Service Medal and awarded on the recommendation of the Board of Trade, the Minister of Shipping, Minister of War Transport or Minister of Transport, and now awarded on the recommendation of the Minister of Transport and Civil Aviation.

13. Foreign awards may be worn only when permission to do so has been given by the sovereign. For further details for order and method of wear see Chapter XV.

14. If there are no medal ribbons the emblem is worn in the position in which a single ribbon would be worn.

CHAPTER XIII

Wearing of Insignia on Formal Occasions

Prior to the 1914–1918 war the number of persons who were holders of insignia of official orders, decorations and even medals was extremely small compared with that of the present day. In those days, in the armed services, the wearing of 'Full-Dress Uniform' was compulsory while many members of the Government, diplomats and others holding official appointments wore civil uniforms on ceremonial occasions. In addition, civilians of non-official status attending state functions usually wore court or levée dress or some other formal attire. It was thus possible to lay down fixed rules as to how insignia should be worn on all kinds of uniform on ceremonial occasions. Nevertheless, it would seem from the portraits, records and correspondence of that period that up till about the year 1900 most of those who held insignia of orders often wore all the stars and badges they possessed, while the position in which these were worn also depended largely on the whim of the wearer.

Some portraits of male members of the Royal Family painted about the beginning of the twentieth century show them wearing a great quantity of insignia. For instance, in one well-known official portrait of King Edward the Seventh he is shown wearing five stars, in addition to the collar and badge of the Garter, the broad riband and badge of a Knight Grand Cross of the Royal Victorian Order, the Royal Victorian Chain, with the Sovereign's badge of the Order of the Bath round his neck and the Sovereign's badges of all the other British orders of chivalry mounted on a bar-brooch, together with several commemorative medals, on his breast.

Numerous portraits of distinguished service leaders of those times also show them wearing many British or Foreign stars and badges. It must be remembered that until the Order of the British Empire was instituted in 1917 there were comparatively few British badges which were worn round the neck. The only insignia worn up till then as neck-badges were the badge of the Order of Merit, badges of Knights Commanders of orders of chivalry and the badge of the third class, namely Commander of the Royal Victorian Order.

The badges of the third class of the other orders, namely Companions of the Bath, Star of India, Saint Michael and Saint George, and the Indian Empire, were not worn as neck-badges, but were worn, together with lesser orders, decorations and medals, on the breast.

The institution, in 1917, of the Order of the Companions of Honour and the Order of the British Empire and the subsequent changes in the several statutes, whereby the badges of Companions of the orders of chivalry were thenceforth worn as neck-badges, completely changed the situation.

Prior to the institution of the Order of the British Empire, as a result of which awards were given to many ladies, it was very rare for ladies, except for those connected with nursing services or certain charitable organisations, to be entitled to wear any insignia other than those of decorations confined entirely to women. After 1917, when great numbers of women not only began to be admitted to the Order of the British Empire, but also to receive war and other medals, the situation as far as women were concerned altered completely. The subsequent admittance of ladies to the Royal Victorian Order and the Order of Saint John also increased considerably the number of ladies entitled to wear insignia. Further information in connection with the wearing of insignia by ladies is to be found in Chapter XIV.

When the 1914–1918 war ended, though full-dress uniform was no longer compulsory except for certain Household troops, the rules fixing the maxima of insignia of the various grades and classes which should be worn were not altered. It was not until the occasion of a levée at Buckingham Palace in 1924, when a number of very senior army officers happened to be attending, that King George the Fifth expressed strong disapproval of the wearing of what he considered an excessive amount of insignia with khaki service-dress uniform. On this occasion two members of the Army Council each wore eight stars, the majority of which belonged to foreign orders.

Immediately after this levée the King gave a ruling that in future not more than four stars of orders, including foreign awards, were ever to be worn with uniform or, in fact, with any other form of day or evening dress. Thereupon all concerned—both the armed and civil services—altered their dress regulations to conform with this rule. At the same time King George the Fifth ruled that not more than three neck-badges were to be worn at any one time with uniform, while not more than one such badge was to be worn with civilian evening-dress.

The situation became confused again after the end of the 1939–1945 war because no service department seemed able either to reach a final decision on the form of ceremonial dress to be worn by those under its administration or to decide whether or not the wearing of this dress was to be made compulsory. Various interim arrangements were introduced, with each service department making its own rules and apparently changing them whenever it felt inclined to do so.

The reaching of agreement on this subject by the armed services was made particularly difficult owing to the fact that on ceremonial occasions officers in the Army wore high-collared jackets, the collar being fastened at the neck with hooks and eyes, while officers below the rank of Rear-Admiral in the Royal Navy and officers in the Royal Air Force wore ordinary jackets with linen collars and ties. There were, too, the added complications caused by the fact that numerous types of uniform existed for each of the services for wear in those countries where the temperature made tropical or semi-tropical dress essential.

However, by about 1956 it had been universally agreed that the former maxima of four stars (including foreign awards) and three neck-badges should never be exceeded by any service with any kind of uniform. In fact the Royal Navy and the Royal Air Force limited the number of neck-badges to be worn to two. None the less, even now the armed services constantly appear to have new forms of ceremonial or mess dress under consideration and it is wiser for those members of these services who are in doubt as to what uniform and insignia they should wear on some special ceremonial occasion to seek a ruling from the service department under whose administration they are serving or served formerly.

It may be assumed, however, that, unless special instructions are issued by the Earl Marshal or the Lord Chamberlain in connection with some particular state occasion, the present rule is that on those occasions when collars of orders are not being worn the maxima of insignia to be worn on ceremonial occasions are as follows:

One broad riband and badge (*vide* note 1 below), four stars (including Foreign orders), three neck-badges and breast-decorations (*vide* note 2).

Those who are holders of the Royal Victorian Chain should also wear this in ceremonial dress on all occasions on which British orders are being worn, even though a collar of an order is being worn.

The Rules governing the wearing of collars of orders are to be found on page 205 of this Chapter.

Notes

1. e.g. either K.G., K.T., K.P., G.C.B., G.C.S.I., G.C.M.G., G.C.I.E.,G.C.V.O. G.B.E. or, if more appropriate, the riband of a foreign order of the first class. The senior riband is worn unless, for some special occasion instructions to the contrary are given.

2. viz V.C., G.C., D.S.O., M.V.O., O.B.E., I.S.O., M.B.E. and decorations and medals.

How Insignia Should be Worn With Ceremonial Dress Uniform when a Collar of an Order is Not Being Worn
(*Vide* diagrams on page 205)

Knights of the Garter and Knights of the Thistle.

The insignia of the Orders of the Garter and the Thistle should be worn in the following manner:

The broad riband should be worn over the left shoulder and in such a position that the bow from which the gold badge, i.e. the Lesser George, is suspended rests on the right hip immediately below the belt or uniform-sash, whichever is worn.

The star should be affixed to the left breast of the coat.

Knights of Saint Patrick, Knights Grand Commanders (G.C.S.I. and G.C.I.E.) and Knights Grand Cross (G.C.B., G.C.M.G., G.C.V.O., G.B.E.) and Bailiffs Grand Cross of the Order of Saint John.

They should wear their insignia in the following manner. The broad riband should be worn over the right shoulder in such a position that the bow from which the badge is suspended rests on the left hip immediately below the belt or uniform-sash, whichever is worn.

The star should be affixed to the left breast of the coat.

When wearing ceremonial uniform Ladies of the Garter or the Thistle and Dames Grand Cross of the Royal Victorian Order and of the Order of the British Empire should wear their Badges and Stars in exactly the same way as men holding equivalent ranks of those orders wear these insignia.

Knights and Dames Commanders (K.C.B., K.C.S.I., K.C.M.G., K.C.I.E., K.C.V.O. and D.C.V.O., K.B.E. and D.B.E.) and Knights and Dames of the Order of Saint John.

They should wear their insignia in the following manner. The riband with appendant badge should be worn round the neck, inside and under the collar of the coat in the manner described in the dress regulations of the service to which the holder belongs or belonged formerly and as described on pages 204 and 205 and as shown in the diagrams on page 205 and illustration opposite page 193.

The star should be affixed to the left breast of the coat, below the bar-brooch to which breast orders (e.g. D.S.O., O.B.E., I.S.O.), decorations and medals are attached.

Members of the Order of Merit or Companions of Honour and Companions and Commanders of the Orders of Chivalry and of the Order of Saint John.

They should wear the respective badges in the following manner. The riband with appendant badge should be worn round the neck, inside and under the collar of the coat in the manner described in the dress regulations of the service to which the holder belongs or belonged formerly and as described on pages 204 and 205.

Holders of orders which are "breast-decorations" (D.S.O., M.V.O., O.B.E., I.S.O. and M.B.E.).

They should wear these mounted on a bar-brooch, together with decorations and medals, on the left side of the coat.

Rules for Wearing Stars with Ceremonial Dress Uniform

(*a*) Not more than four stars should ever be worn at one time.

(*b*) If only one star is being worn, it should be worn on the left side, over the heart.

(*c*) If two stars are being worn, *either* the senior star may be worn directly above the junior *or* the two stars may be worn in line with one another and with the senior star nearer to the centre of the body.

(*d*) If three stars are being worn, the senior star should be worn above the two junior stars, in a triangular pattern.

(*e*) If four stars are being worn, the three senior stars should be worn in the manner described in (*d*) above and the fourth star should be worn beneath (*vide* diagrams on page 205 and in illustration opposite page 193).

Rules for Wearing More than One Neck-Badge With Ceremonial Dress Uniform

Not more than three neck-badges should ever be worn at one time. Normally these would be the neck-badges of the three senior British orders held, but it may be appropriate on some occasions to wear the badge of a foreign order in the senior position, namely, above British badges. In this connection reference should be made to Chapter XV, which deals with foreign orders.

With the high-necked ceremonial-dress uniform coat of the Army, a coat with which a linen collar and tie are *not* worn, the senior badge, suspended from its riband, should be worn inside the collar of the uniform coat in such a way that the badge, with about three and a quarter inches of riband showing, hangs outside the coat, so that the riband emerges between the opening to the collar, while the badge hangs immediately below the top button of the coat. The second and third badges should be worn in a similar manner but so that the ribands emerge from the second and third buttons of the coat respectively.

Small 'eyes' should be stitched inside the uniform coat to which the ribands can be fastened by 'hooks'. It is advisable to have these fittings made by a naval or military tailor. With the 'monkey-jacket' uniform coat of the Royal Navy and with the ceremonial dress uniform coat of the Royal Air Force, with both of which a linen collar and a tie are worn, it is not permissible to wear more than two neck-badges (*vide* diagram for the Royal Air Force below).

With the new ceremonial-dress uniform coat of the senior ranks of the Royal Navy also only two neck-badges are worn. The first

ARMY FULL DRESS

Showing maximum which may be worn:
One Grand Cross riband and bagde (Collar in addition on Collar Days).
Four Stars (in order of seniority).
Three neck decorations (in order of seniority).
Reproduced by courtesy of Messrs. Harrison and Sons. Limited.

For Naval Dress see illustration facing page 193

ROYAL AIR FORCE

Number 1 (Home Dress)

Showing method of wearing:
One Grand Cross riband and badge.
Two Stars (the senior above the junior).
Two neck decorations (the senior above the junior).
Medal bar—maximum length with full-size medals.

or senior badge is worn in the manner described above for the Army uniform, but the second badge is worn in such a manner that the riband emerges from the first button-hole on the right-hand side of the coat (*vide* Plate facing page 193).

WEARING OF COLLARS OF ORDERS OF KNIGHTHOOD

At ceremonies for which insignia of orders, decorations and medals are being worn, collars of orders of knighthood should also be worn if the ceremonies take place on any of the following days:

Collar Days

1st January	New Year's Day.
6th January	The Epiphany.
6th February	The Queen's Accession.
1st March	St. David.
17th March	St. Patrick.
25th March	Lady Day.
21st April	The Queen's Birthday.
23rd April	St. George.
1st May	St. Philip and St. James.
29th May	Restoration of the Royal Family.
2nd June	The Queen's Coronation.
10th June	The Duke of Edinburgh's Birthday.
24th June	St. John the Baptist.
29th June	St. Peter.
4th August	Queen Elizabeth the Queen Mother's Birthday.
29th September	St. Michael and All Angels.
1st November	All Saints.
30th November	St. Andrew.
25th December	Christmas Day.

Also Easter Sunday, Ascension Day, Whit Sunday and Trinity Sunday.

Collars are worn when the Queen opens or prorogues Parliament, and by those taking part in the ceremony of an introduction of a peer in the House of Lords. They are also worn when so ordered by the Queen in connection with religious services of the Orders of the Garter, Thistle, Bath, Saint Michael and Saint George, and the British Empire.

Under present rules it is not customary to wear collars and mantles at services of the Royal Victorian Order.

METHOD OF WEARING

With uniform, when neither mantles nor other robes are being worn, collars should be worn under the shoulder straps or epaulettes of the coat and over aiguillettes, and they should be fastened by white satin bows, one and a half inches wide, the collar hanging at an equal distance back and front (*vide* Plate facing page 193).

When worn with mantles of orders of chivalry or with peers' robes, collars should be worn outside these mantles and robes.

Collars are not worn with morning dress unless ordered for a special occasion, such as a service of an order of chivalry when mantles are not being worn. When so ordered they should be fastened to the shoulders of the coat by white satin bows as described above.

Collars should *not* be worn after sunset nor by those who are mounted on ceremonial parades such as Trooping the Colour, unless directions to that effect are specially given by the Sovereign.

Not more than one collar should ever be worn at one time, but in the case of those who are holders of two or more collars, when the collar and badge appendant of the senior order is being worn, as the broad riband of that order cannot be worn at the same time, it is permissible to wear the riband and badge of the next senior order.

WEARING OF INSIGNIA WITH MESS DRESS

Here again no clear and permanent rules have been issued by the various services stating whether or not mess dress is compulsory, but in those cases where mess dress is authorised the rules for wearing insignia are as follows:

(*a*) One broad riband and badge, viz. that of a knight of one of the "great orders", namely, Garter, Thistle or Patrick, or of a Knight Grand Cross or of a Knight Grand Commander.
(*b*) A maximum of four stars (including foreign orders).
(*c*) One neck-badge.
(*d*) Miniatures of all orders, decorations and medals, except for those orders which by regulation are not worn in miniature.

WEARING OF INSIGNIA WITH FULL EVENING DRESS (CIVILIAN)

In full evening dress Knights and Ladies of the Orders of the Garter and Thistle and Knights Grand Commanders and Knights and Dames Grand Cross of the other orders of chivalry should wear across the body the broad riband with badge attached thereto. The riband of the senior British order held should be worn unless for some special occasion it is more appropriate to wear that of a junior British order or that of a foreign order.

By men the riband should be worn under the evening dress coat but over the waist coat. The riband should not pass over the shoulder and down the back of the body, as is the case when the ordinary full-size riband is worn with ceremonial dress military uniform. For wear with evening dress a shortened riband (*vide* diagram

EVENING DRESS

(Waistcoat)

Method of fastening the riband of a Knight Grand Cross or Knight Grand Commander with evening dress, also method of wearing a neck badge with evening dress.

EVENING DRESS

(Jacket)

Showing arrangement of three stars in order of seniority. If a fourth star is worn, it should be mid-way below stars 2 and 3.

Reproduced by courtessy of Messrs. Harrison and Sons, Limited.

above) should be obtained from either the makers of the insignia (as shown on the lining of the insignia case) or from a tailor. One end of this riband should be fastened with two buttons at the front of the arm-hole of the waistcoat, while the other end is fastened to the bottom of the waistcoat by a button-holed pointed flap in such a way that the bow from which the badge is suspended rests on the left hip, except for the Orders of the Garter and the Thistle when the badge should rest on the right hip.

Up to four stars may be worn by Knights and Dames Grand Cross. Stars should be worn on the left side of the coat or dress. Similarly, Knights and Dames Commanders may wear such stars as they possess—up to a maximum of four.

Knights Commanders should wear round the neck one badge only. Normally this will be the badge of their senior British order. But if it is more appropriate for some special occasion to wear the badge of a junior British order or a foreign order, this should be done. This badge should be suspended from a riband of miniature width, and this riband should be worn under the white tie and in such a way that the badge hangs about one inch below the tie. As ladies cannot wear a badge round the neck with evening dress, their badge or badges should be worn on the left side of the dress, from the alternative 'fitting with a bow' which is provided for this purpose in the case containing the insignia. The badge or badges should be worn below miniatures and above stars, which should be placed about six inches above the waist.

If a baronet does not possess a more senior neck-badge—for example the O.M.—he should wear his baronet's badge round the neck in the same manner as the neck-badge of an order is worn.

If worn alone, the badge of a knight bachelor should be worn in the position in which the star of an order is worn. If worn together with a star of one of the orders of chivalry it should be worn below that star, but it should be worn above the star of the Order of Saint John and above the star of a foreign order, except on those occasions when it may be appropriate to give 'pride of place' to the foreign order.

Except for those orders which are never worn in miniature (the Garter, Thistle, Order of Merit, Crown of India and Companions of Honour and the badge of a baronet) miniatures of all orders, decorations and medals held should be worn by gentlemen and ladies. It is advisable to have the miniatures mounted on a bar in brooch form. Gentlemen should attach this bar-brooch to the left lapel of the coat, while ladies should wear this bar-brooch on the left side of the dress and above any badges and stars of orders which they may be wearing. Other information in connection with the wearing of miniatures is to be found on page 211.

The following are the occasions upon which full-size orders and miniatures of orders, decorations and medals should be worn with full evening dress:

(*a*) At all parties and dinners when any of the following members of the Royal Family are present:
> *Their Majesties*

The Queen

Queen Elizabeth the Queen Mother
> *Their Royal Highnesses*

The Duke of Edinburgh

The Princess Margaret, Countess of Snowdon

The Duke and Duchess of Gloucester

The Princess Royal

The Duke of Windsor

Princess Marina, Duchess of Kent

The Duke and Duchess of Kent

Princess Alexandra of Kent

Princess Alice, Countess of Athlone

(*Note*. The host should notify his guests if any of these members of the Royal Family will be present.)

(*b*) At all parties and dinners given in honour of ambassadors and ministers accredited to the Court, unless notified to the contrary by the ambassador or minister concerned.

(*Note*. An order of the country concerned should be worn in preference to a British order, and if both are worn the former should take precedence over the latter.)

(*c*) At all official dinners and receptions, including naval, military and Air Force dinners, dinners, of city Livery Companies and public dinners.

(*Note*. The word *Decorations* on the invitation card is the intimation that the entertainment is an official occasion.)

(*d*) On official occasions when entertained by the following:
H.M. Lieutenant of a county, within his county.
The High Sheriff of a county, within his county.
Cabinet Ministers.
Ex-cabinet ministers.
Knights of the Orders of the Garter or Thistle.
Great Officers of State and of the Queen's Household.
Lord Mayors and Mayors.
Lord Provosts and Provosts.

(*Note.* The word *Decorations* on the invitation card is an intimation that the entertainment is an official occasion.)

With Dinner Jackets

In 1946, when clothing coupon regulations were in force, thus preventing many men from obtaining full evening dress, King George the Sixth ruled that on all occasions when orders, decorations and medals were being worn with full evening dress, miniatures of these might be worn with dinner jackets by those not possessing full evening dress. This rule is still in force.

Neither stars of orders nor full-size neck-badges should be worn with dinner jackets.

Wearing of Miniatures of Orders, Etc.

In 1923 King George the Fifth observed that miniatures of orders and decorations varied considerably in size and design. The cause of this was that a number of firms were making these miniatures according to what they considered to be suitable sizes. To clear up misunderstandings on this point the King made the following rulings:

(*a*) The miniature badges for the Orders of the Bath, Star of India, Saint Michael and Saint George, Indian Empire, Distinguished Service Order and Imperial Service Order were to be half the size of the Companion's badge.

(*b*) The miniature badge for the first four classes of the Royal Victorian Order was to be half the size of the M.V.O. fourth-class badge and for the fifth class half the size of the M.V.O. fifth-class badge.

(*c*) For the Order of the British Empire the miniature of the first three classes was to be a replica in enamel of the badge of the first three classes, but half the size of the fourth class (the O.B.E.) badge, while the miniatures of the fourth and fifth classes of the orders were to be respectively half the size of the badges of those classes.

(*d*) The miniatures of decorations such as Royal Red Cross, Distinguished Service Cross, Military Cross, Distinguished Flying Cross and Air Force Cross were to be half the size of these crosses. It was subsequently decided that the miniatures of medals were also to be half the size of the full-size medals.

The king also ruled that ribbons from which miniatures were suspended need not all be of the same length, and all that mattered was that the top and bottom ends of each miniature and its ribbon should be in line with those of the other miniatures.

All these rules still hold good.

In the same way as miniatures may be worn with dinner jackets on formal occasions, on those *evening* occasions such as formal gatherings of Regimental Old Comrades Associations, when those attending are asked to wear 'decorations' with lounge suits, some holders prefer to wear miniatures rather than full-size 'decorations'. and there is no objection to this.

WEARING OF ORDERS, DECORATIONS AND MEDALS WITH FORMAL CIVILIAN MORNING DRESS

All members of the various orders of knighthood and all holders of other orders, decorations and medals may, *if they wish to do so*, wear these insignia with formal morning dress on *official* occasions and at *public functions*.

The correct method of wearing these insignia is as follows:

Knights and Ladies of the Orders of the Garter and Thistle, Knights and Dames Grand Cross, Knights Grand Commanders, Knights and Dames Commanders	Should wear the *stars* of orders *only*. By men stars should be worn on the left side of the coat, *as for evening dress*, and by ladies on the left side of the dress, about six inches above the waist.
Men who are Members of the Order of Merit Order of the Companions of Honour Companions or Commanders of the various orders of chivalry	Should wear the riband to which the badge is suspended under the tie which should be a *bow*, worn with a winged collar, so that the badge hangs about an inch below the bow.
Ladies who are Commanders, Officers or Members of any of	Should wear the insignia, *if worn separately*, suspended from the

the British orders or holders of any British decorations or medals

riband in the form of a bow on the left side of the dress. Those orders, decorations and medals which, with uniform, both by men and ladies, would be worn mounted on a bar in brooch-form should be worn in the same manner with civilian dress.

Men who are officers or members of any of the orders of chivalry (i.e. the fourth and fifth classes, viz. M.V.O., O.B.E., M.B.E.) or holders of any other orders (e.g. D.S.O., I.S.O.) and decorations or medals

Should wear the insignia mounted on a bar in brooch-form on the left side in the same manner as they would wear them in uniform.

WEARING OF INSIGNIA WITH LOUNGE SUITS

There are some occasions in the day-time such as Armistice Day services, regimental gatherings, etc., at which those attending are requested to wear medals with lounge suits. It is not customary to wear either stars, broad ribands with badges or neck-badges with lounge suits on such day-time occasions, and the only insignia which should be worn are those which with uniform would be worn mounted on a bar in the form of a brooch on the left side, e.g. V.C., G.C., D.S.O., O.B.E., M.B.E. and all decorations and medals.

When so desired, the ribbons of orders, decorations and medals may be worn with all forms of civilian dress, *at the discretion of the holder, on all occasions*. If worn, they should be sewn on the left side of the coat or dress.

CHAPTER XIV

Wearing of Insignia by Ladies

As a result of the two great wars of this century, and the fact that ladies are now admitted to certain orders of chivalry, many ladies now hold orders and decorations and they sometimes possess as many medals as men of equivalent social position and age.

It should be made clear immediately, therefore, that the rule now is that, when wearing service uniforms, or 'coats of military pattern' connected with the various charitable, welfare and other uniformed organisations, ladies should wear their insignia in *exactly the same* manner as insignia of a similar grade are worn by men in uniform.

There are, however, some differences between the wearing of insignia by men and ladies with civilian morning or evening dress. Ladies of the Garter, for instance, wear on the left arm above the elbow a 'garter' exactly similar to that worn by knights of the order below the left knee.

While Dames Grand Cross of the Royal Victorian Order and the Order of the British Empire *with all forms of dress* wear their insignia in a manner exactly similar to that laid down for Knights Grand Cross of those orders (*vide* Chapter XIII), there is a difference between the manner of wearing the *badges* of Knights Commanders and Dames Commanders and the badges of men and women Commanders, when the women are not wearing uniform or 'coats of military pattern', as described above.

Women who are holders of insignia equivalent to what for men would be neck-badges (e.g. D.C.V.O., D.B.E., C.V.O., C.B.E.) should only wear these badges round the neck with uniform or with coats of military pattern. With other forms of dress they should wear these badges on the left side of the body, above stars of orders and immediately below the bar-brooch on which either full-size or miniature decorations and medals are mounted.

To enable ladies who are either Dames or Commanders of orders to wear their insignia in an appropriate manner, with either uniform or civilian dress, when their insignia are presented to them the case containing these is provided with two alternative riband 'fittings'. One of these fittings enables the lady holder to wear the badge round the neck, when uniform or a coat of military pattern is being worn, in the same way as a badge of equivalent grade is worn round the neck by a man in uniform. The other fitting enables the lady holder, when wearing civilian morning and evening dress, to wear the badge on the left side of the body, below the medal-brooch or miniatures-brooch and above a star if the lady possesses one.

On those official occasions—either in the daytime or the evening—on which men wear full-size 'breast-decorations' and medals, because they are wearing either ceremonial dress uniform or court dress, ladies should also wear full-size decorations and medals.

Otherwise, when men in evening dress wear their decorations and medals in miniature, ladies should also wear their decorations and medals in miniature.

Ladies who possess a star should wear this on the left side, about six inches above the waist.

A lady who possesses more than one star should wear these stars in the same manner as a similar number of stars would be worn by a man, as explained in Chapters XII and XIII.

CHAPTER XV

Foreign Orders, Decorations and Medals

British subjects are not permitted to accept or wear the insignia of an order or decoration of a foreign power unless permission to do so has been granted by the Queen. This permission is granted on the advice of the Secretary of State for Foreign Affairs, to whom the foreign government concerned will have submitted previously the appropriate recommendation through the correct diplomatic channels.

Permission to wear foreign insignia is of two kinds, namely *unrestricted* and *restricted*. If *'unrestricted permission'* to wear a certain foreign order has been given, that means that the insignia of the order can be worn on all occasions when British insignia are worn. In that event the Secretary of State for Foreign Affairs makes the necessary arrangements for a warrant of approval to be prepared and signed by the Queen and for a notice of such approval to be published in the *London Gazette*.

The Department of the Foreign Office which deals with these matters is the Protocol Department and the wording of the notice in the *London Gazette* is on the following lines:

> The Queen has been pleased to give and grant unto ....
> Her Majesty's Royal License and Authority to wear the insignia of the Order of .... which award has been conferred upon him by His Majesty the King (or the President) of .... in recognition of valuable service rendered by him.

If only *'restricted permission'* to wear certain foreign insignia has been given, then the person concerned receives from the Private Secretary to the Queen instructions to that effect and these insignia may then be worn only on the occasions stated below:

(*a*) In the presence of the Sovereign, reigning prince or head of the state to which the decoration belongs.

(*b*) In the presence of any member of the Royal Family of the country concerned.

(*c*) At the residence of any ambassador, minister or consular officer of that country, either in England or abroad, but not if meeting them elsewhere.

(*d*) When attached to or when meeting officially any officers of the Army, Navy or Air Force or any official deputation of that country.

(*e*) At any official or semi-official ceremony held exclusively in connection with that country, such as a memorial service, the unveiling of a monument or the opening of an official institution.

(*f*) On all official occasions whilst in that country.

Enquiries are often made as to the position in which insignia of foreign orders, decorations and medals should be worn with regard to British insignia. In the United Kingdom or other countries of the British Commonwealth for normal occasions (those not connected with the foreign country concerned as described above) the rule is that foreign insignia should *all* be worn after British orders, decorations and medals. When a person possesses several foreign orders, decorations and medals these should be worn *respectively* in the order of the dates on which they were awarded. When, however, insignia are being worn on any of the occasions mentioned above, i.e. (*a*) to (*f*), 'pride of place' should be given to the foreign insignia of the country concerned.

Thus, on such occasions, if a person is the holder of the highest class of a foreign order he should wear the riband and badge of this in preference to those of his highest British order and he should wear the star of that foreign order in a position senior to that in which the highest-ranking British star is worn. Similarly, on such occasions, holders of foreign insignia of other less highly graded orders, decorations and medals should wear these in positions senior to those of equivalent British insignia.

To sum up, the main point to note is that on the occasions mentioned above foreign insignia should be worn in such a way that due honour is paid to the country concerned.

CHAPTER XVI

Insignia Which Must be Returned at Death and Replacement of Lost Insignia

SECTION I

The following insignia are normally handed back privately and *personally* to the Sovereign, by the nearest male relative of the deceased holder, under arrangements made direct with that person by the Private Secretary to the Queen:

(*a*) The badge and star of the Order of the Garter.

(*b*) The badge and star of the Order of the Thistle.

(*c*) The badge only of the Order of St. Patrick, the star having been paid for by the knight.

(*Note.* The collars, with badges appendant, of the orders mentioned above, and, in the case of the Order of the Garter, the actual garter, should be returned direct to the Central Chancery of the Orders of Knighthood at 8, Buckingham Gate, S.W.1.)

SECTION II

On the death of the holders, the following insignia should be returned by the executors concerned, direct to the Central Chancery of the Orders of Knighthood:

(*a*) The collars, and badges appendant, of the Orders of the Garter, Thistle and Saint Patrick, as described above in the Note to Section I.

(*b*) The collar of the Order of the Star of India (namely G.C.S.I.)

(*c*) The collar of the Order of the Indian Empire (namely G.C.I.E.)

(*d*) The collars of Knights Grand Cross of the Order of the Bath (G.C.B.), of the Order of Saint Michael and Saint George

(G.C.M.G.), unless received prior to 14th December 1948, of the Royal Victorian Order (G.C.V.O.) and the Order of the British Empire (G.B.E.).

(*e*) The Royal Victorian Chain.

(*f*) The badge of the Order of the Crown of India.

(*g*) *All* official insignia and robes held by officers of the various orders (e.g. Prelates, Chancellors, Deans, Kings-of-Arms, Registrars, Secretaries, Gentlemen-Ushers of Orders of Chivalry).

(*h*) *All* insignia and tabards held by officers of the College of Heralds (namely Kings-of-Arms, Heralds and Pursuivants).

(*i*) Collars of 'S's' held by Serjeants-at-Arms.

SECTION III: LOST INSIGNIA

Application for replacement of lost insignia of the orders of chivalry and of the Distinguished Service Order, the Imperial Service Order, and Medals of the Royal Victorian Order and Order of the British Empire should be addressed to the Secretary, Central Chancery of the Orders of Knighthood at 8, Buckingham Gate, S.W.1.

Applications for replacement of lost George Crosses, George Medals, and the King's Medals for Courage and/or Service in the Cause of Freedom (awarded to foreign nationals for service during the 1939–1945 war) should also be addressed to the Central Chancery.

Applications for replacement of lost gallantry decorations or gallantry medals of the armed services (e.g. Distinguished Service Cross, Military Cross and Distinguished Flying Cross, Air Force Cross, Conspicuous Gallantry Medal, Distinguished Conduct Medal, Distinguished Flying Medal, Military Medal, etc.) and for Campaign Medals and Long Service and Good Conduct Medals should be addressed to the Under-Secretary of State at the Ministry of the service with which the applicant is serving, or served formerly.

Applications for replacement of lost Coronation or Jubilee medals should be addressed to the Treasurer to the Queen at Buckingham Palace.

Replacement of all insignia lost as a result of enemy action can be obtained *free of charge*. Replacements of insignia lost through fire, theft or some other cause can be obtained on payment of the actual cost price of the insignia at the date of application for replacement. Replacement of lost insignia of those no longer living is not permissible.

Applications for replacement should be accompanied by a full statement of the circumstances of the loss and the efforts made to recover the lost insignia.

Duplicates of lost Warrants of Appointment to the several orders cannot be obtained, as in many cases those who signed the original warrants are no longer living, but certified copies of these warrants can be obtained free of charge on application to the Central Chancery, 8 Buckingham Gate, S.W.1.

Index to Part One

William IV, 81, 94, 97, 123, 175, 176
Williams, Dr. Ralph Vaughan, 170
Willis, Adm. of Fleet Sir Algernon, 131
Wills, Sir Charles, 109
Wilmington, Earl of, 110
Wilson, John Dover, 172
Wimberley, Major-Gen., D. 137
Winchester, Bishop of, 90
Winchester, Marquess of, 57
Windsor, Dean of, 90
Windsor, Duke of, 51, 87, 89, 104, 146, 150, 157, 176, 178, 179
Wolseley, F. M. Viscount, 112, 128, 160, 170
Wolsey, Cardinal, 63, 93
Wood, F. M. Sir Evelyn, 112

Woodhead, Sir John, 179
Woolton, Earl of, 172
Worcester, Earl of, 93
Wren, Sir Christopher, 160
Wrottesley, Sir Hugh, 58
Wylie, Sir Francis, 179
Wynn, Rt. Hon. William, M. P., 114

Yang Teramat Mulia Tunku, 173
Yonge, Sir William, 110
York, Duke of, 110, 117, 118, 122
York, Edward, Duke of, 38
Young, Adm. Sir William, 119

Zaharoff, Basil, 40
Zanzibar, Sultan of, 143
Zetland, Earl of, 96